D1351151

A guide to the Southern Upland Way

ARRAN

GLASGOW

■ KILMARNOCK

■ AYR

S T R A T H C L Y D E   R E G I O N

• Ailsa Craig

Girvan •

Loch Doon

The Merrick

GALLOWAY
FOREST
PARK

Loch Trool

Bargrennan

LOWTH

Wanlockhead

SANQUHAR •

HILLS

Daer Wa
Res

KENDOON
YOUTH HOSTEL

Craigarie Fell

STRANRAER

New Luce

Knowe

Clatteringshaws
Loch

St John's Town
of Dalry

Loch Ken

GALLO

Portpatrick

Castle Kennedy
Glenluce

Newton Stewart

D U M F R I E S   A N D

DUMFRIES

Luce Bay

David Williams

A guide to the Southern Upland Way

Constable   London

First published in Great Britain 1989
by Constable and Company Limited
10 Orange Street London WC2H 7EG
Copyright © 1989 by David Williams
Set in Linotron Times 9pt by
Rowland Phototypesetting Limited
Bury St Edmunds, Suffolk
Printed in Great Britain by
The Bath Press Limited, Bath

British Library CIP data
Williams, David, *1948–*
A guide to the Southern Upland Way
1. Scotland. Southern Uplands. Long
distance footpaths: Southern Upland Way
Recreations: Walking. – Visitors' guides.
I. Title.
796.5'1'094137

ISBN 0 09 467910 X

By the same author

Iceland: the visitor's guide (Stacey International, London, 1986)
Myvatn: a paradise for nature lovers (Orn og Orlyglur, Reykjavik, Iceland, 1988)

Contents

Part 3 The Guide

Contents

Illustrations

Maps

The photographs were taken by the author. **The maps** were prepared by John Mitchell.

Acknowledgements

Many people have helped me in the preparation of this book: employees of the regional councils' planning departments, employees of the tourist boards, librarians, farmers and numerous individuals who work or live near the Way and who gladly gave me information. In particular, I would like to thank the following people for reading the text and making valuable suggestions: Margaret Kirk, Maurice Hall, Richard Mearns and Donald Urquhart of Dumfries and Galloway Planning Department, Quentin McLaren of Borders Planning Department, Andrew Llanwarne of the Dumfries and Galloway Tourist Board, Michael Ambrose of the Scottish Borders Tourist Board and Dr Allan MacQuarrie of the Scottish History Department, University of Glasgow. I would also like to thank John Bartholomew and Son Ltd. for the use of their maps.

I am very grateful to Margaret Kirk and Jenny Kirk who walked the Way with me and to Margaret for all the encouragement and help she gave me during the work on this book.

Introduction

The Southern Upland Way is Scotland's third long-distance path and the first one that runs across the country from coast to coast. The route goes from Portpatrick on the west coast to Cockburnspath near the east coast and it follows paths, tracks and country roads across some of Scotland's loveliest countryside. Most of the route is through quiet country areas and there are small towns and villages in which to stay at the end of a good day's walk. The walk is 326 km (202 miles) long.

As the route crosses the hills and valleys of southern Scotland it meets many scenic spots, such as Castle Kennedy, the picturesque St Mary's Loch and the town of Melrose, which boasts a fine medieval abbey. These places have many stories to tell, and the Way meets numerous historic sites associated with the Iron Age people, the Romans, the medieval kings, the Covenanters and the cattle drovers. The strategic position of many of the southern towns and villages meant that they were often caught up in hostilities during the centuries of warfare between Scotland and England, and the Way meets many places associated with tales of those tragic days.

Although the Southern Uplands are generally not as rugged and wild as the Scottish Highlands, the Way crosses many high moors and climbs many hills of over 450 m (about 1,500 ft). Indeed, near its mid-point the Way reaches a height of 710 m at Lowther Hill, and it climbs three ranges of hills that are higher than the highest point on Scotland's best-known long-distance path, the West Highland Way. The Way must therefore be considered as a tough challenge to any walker – but it has great rewards. It can be tackled as one long walk (probably taking about two weeks to complete) or it can be considered as a series of shorter walks that can be attempted at a more leisurely pace.

Scotland is fortunate in having much fine scenery and the Scots take great pleasure in wandering over the hills; indeed, as city life becomes more hectic, more people take to the hills for the peace and quiet they offer. This is certainly not a new phenomenon; in 1809 Sydney Smith remarked that:

There is moral as well as bodily wholesomeness in a mountain walk, if the walker has the understanding heart, and eschews picnics. It is good for any man to be alone with nature and himself, or with a friend who knows when silence is more sociable than talk . . . As the body, harassed with the noxious air of cities, seeks relief in the freedom and the purity of the fields and hills, so the mind, wearied by commerce with men, resumes its vigour in solitude, and repairs its dignity.

While many walkers prefer to ignore 'official' paths and signs, others like to have their route arranged for them and to have a good guidebook that will help them enjoy their leisure hours. It is the hope of the author that this book will help those who walk the Southern Upland Way and who seek to learn more about the history, scenery and culture of our country.

The book is divided into three parts. Part 1 gives a brief outline of the area covered by the Southern Uplands, with a general description of the geography of the area and a very brief introduction to some of the important historical developments that have shaped the lives of the people. Part 2 contains practical information and advice that walkers can use both in preparation for the walk and during it. Part 3 is the Guide. This is divided into fifteen sections and gives the route taken by the Way. It also describes the scenery and the most interesting places that are met *en route*.

Part 1 The Southern Uplands

The land

The Southern Uplands is the large tract of hilly country that extends across southern Scotland, from south of Scotland's industrial belt down to the English border. The area has a number of important ranges of hills such as (from west to east) the Galloway Hills, the Lowther Hills and the Lammermuir Hills. To the south of these, the volcanic Cheviot Hills mark the boundary between Scotland and England. Many of these ranges are in the form of undulating moorlands but there are many significant summits that dominate the surrounding countryside; the major hills on or near the Southern Upland Way are The Merrick (843 m), Benbrack (580 m), Lowther Hill (725 m) and Ettrick Pen (692 m).

The hilly areas are sparsely populated and the main centres of population in southern Scotland are in the more important valleys and on the coasts; large towns are few and far between.

Scotland can be divided into three distinct geological (and geographical) areas: the Highlands, the Central Lowlands and the Southern Uplands. These areas are separated by two important geological faults: the Highland Boundary Fault and the Southern Upland Fault. The Highland Boundary Fault runs from Dumbarton to Stonehaven and is marked by a distinct change in scenery as the higher land on the northern side of the fault is formed from rocks that are more resistant to erosion than those on the southern side. The Southern Upland Fault runs from Ballantrae to Dunbar but there is rather less of a sharp change in scenery across the fault as the rocks on either side generally have a similar resistance to erosion.

Most of the rocks found in the Southern Uplands were formed during the periods known to geologists as the Ordovician (500 to 430 million years ago) and the Silurian (430 to 395 million years ago). During the Ordovician, the land that we now know of as Scotland was south of the equator and moving northwards. The European landmass (which included England) was farther south and following Scotland into the northern hemisphere. Between them was the narrowing sea known as Iapetus and a vast quantity of sediment was deposited from both landmasses into Iapetus. The most important sediments eventually became greywacke (which often looks similar to a dark-coloured sandstone) and shale (a very dark fine-grained rock that is usually very crumbly); fossils may be found in both of these rocks. The later collision of the landmasses joined Scotland and England and raised what is now southern Scotland into the Southern Uplands mountain range. This has since undergone a long period of erosion.

The valley of Nithsdale (which the Way crosses at Sanquhar) marks an important boundary between two types of scenery. To the west of Nithsdale, the existence of three important masses of granite (at Criffel, Cairnsmore of Fleet and Loch Doon) has given the areas around them a rugged topography. This western side of the Southern Uplands is generally wetter than the eastern side but the lowest-lying land is suitable for dairy farming using breeds that are tolerant of the damp climate. In Galloway the tracts of poorly drained land have much peat, together with plants which can tolerate wet soils; heather becomes more common at higher altitudes.

To the east of Nithsdale the hills are more generally rounded, smooth and covered in grass (or sometimes heather). These hills are usually formed entirely from sedimentary rocks (mainly greywacke and shale) and the important ranges are separated by valleys such as those that carry the Moffat Water, the Ettrick Water and the River Tweed. The Borders' moors are much drier than those of the west due to a lower rainfall on better-drained soils and the hills are dominated by grasses suitable for raising sheep. Towards the coast the heights of the hills decrease and the land-use generally changes from hill farming (specialising in sheep) to arable farming, with the most productive farms found near Berwick-upon-Tweed in the area called the Merse.

The final glacial period of the last Ice Age was from about 70,000 years ago to about 10,000 years ago. At the greatest extent of the ice, the whole of mainland Scotland was buried under a great complex of ice-sheets and the two main centres of ice accumulation in the Southern Uplands were Loch Doon and the Moffat Hills. The great domes of ice covering these areas sent important streams of ice to the north and the south. The northern stream coalesced with ice coming southwards from the Highlands, resulting in combined flows towards the east and west coasts. The southern stream moved across the Cheviot Hills into northern England.

During the Ice Age the enormous weight of the ice depressed the land by hundreds of metres. The sea-level dropped even farther, as so much sea water had been removed to build the ice-sheets, and thus the Scottish landmass was much bigger in area than it is today. After the ice melted, both the land and the sea-level rose, though not at the same rate. The Way will pass many examples of the glaciated landscape; erosional features such as glacial valleys are noticeable at higher altitudes while depositional features such as moraines are common at lower levels.

Most of the types of rocks that make up the Southern Uplands are easily eroded by the ice and during the glacial and post-glacial periods the great torrents of water that flowed down the rivers carried away an enormous mass of boulders, gravel and sand. Much of this detritus was dumped in the valleys, thus flattening the valley bottoms, and today these level sandy 'haughs' are used for settlements, arable farming and (very important in the Borders) rugby pitches. In many cases the sediments were eroded by later (and narrower) rivers leaving definite 'terraces' above the present-day rivers.

Few lochs are found in the Southern Uplands but of the natural lochs, the most important are Loch Trool and St Mary's Loch. Lochs such as Clatteringshaws Loch and Daer Reservoir are entirely man-made.

In the western half of the Southern Uplands the rivers tend to flow towards the Clyde coast or southwards towards the Solway Firth, while in the eastern half they generally flow towards the east, many of them joining up with the River Tweed which flows into the North Sea at the English town of Berwick-upon-Tweed. It is believed that southern Scotland's drainage pattern was formed many millions of years before the Ice Age and that the glaciers tended to follow the pre-existing valleys.

When Scotland was inhabited after the Ice Age, much of the land was covered by forest, with oak very common in the Southern Uplands, but the development of sheep farming and the need for charcoal for iron making were important factors in the destruction of these forests. Very few significant natural forests exist today though some small, long-established woods containing birch, oak and Scots pine will be seen near the Way. Forestry is becoming increasingly important in many areas in the Southern Uplands, notably around Loch Trool, where the Galloway Forest Park has been established. The expansion of these forests and their encroachment on hill pastures previously used by sheep is a much-debated topic and walkers may feel that too much of the Way goes through conifer plantations.

Although towns, villages and forestry operations have encroached on the hills and moorlands, many of the upland areas still support interesting wildlife. Curlews, wheatears, meadow pipits and skylarks are common in the summer months, while in the winter months some of the exposed hilltops have flocks of snow buntings. Birds of prey including hen harriers, merlins, kestrels and peregrines may be seen from the Way. The hoarse croak of the raven and the song of the ring ouzel are occasionally heard in the uplands. The forests have large flocks of crossbills – which are red (males) or yellow-green (females) – and (yellow and black) siskins. The younger plantations provide hunting areas for short-eared owls, which may be quite common if it is a good year for voles.

Red deer can be found in some areas of the Southern Uplands and there is an important herd in the Galloway Forest Park. The park also has a herd of wild goats which is a popular tourist attraction. Many of the forests have large numbers of the small roe deer, so many that there is a lot of grazing pressure on newly planted broad-leaved trees – hence the plastic tree guards that are often seen in new plantations.

The people

At the end of the Ice Age the margin of the ice-sheets moved northwards and Nature started the long task of reclaiming the land. Tundra plantlife colonised the thin soil and 9,700 years ago birch and hazel were established at Din Moss near Kelso; it took another thousand years for mixed forests to develop and the dominant trees were oak, elm and hazel. Animals such as red deer, great elk, great ox, beaver and brown bear then moved into Scotland, away from the rather warmer climate farther south.

Around 8,000 to 6,000 years ago, people followed the animals northwards; the first settlements were around the coast but the rivers would have provided natural routes for these hunter-gatherers when they ventured inland in search of food. The land had not yet been drained and a number of the large swampy areas would have been navigable by dugout canoe. Many settlements were in crannogs – man-made islands in lakes that were built as a defence against enemies and wild animals.

The earliest inhabitants would have found it easier to cross the sea than travel over land and it was not until after the arrival in AD 80 of the Roman armies that significant attempts were made to establish proper routes across the country. The Romans finally retreated from Scotland in the second half of the fourth century and they left behind their roads (some of which the Way will meet) and important defensive boundaries on either side of the Southern Uplands: Antonine's Wall (between the Firth of Clyde and the Firth of Forth) and Hadrian's Wall (between the Solway Firth and the River Tyne).

After the Romans' withdrawal, the tribes that had established themselves in Scotland continued to fight for domination. In the north were the Picts, and Ptolemy mentions that there were four British tribes in southern Scotland: the Novantae (in Galloway), the Selgovae (in the Solway basin and Southern Uplands), the Damnonii (in Strathclyde) and the Votadini (in Lothian and the Merse). Centuries of civil strife, together with numerous invasions, made the land a very unsettled place. However, the nation we now know as Scotland was slowly forged – largely as a result of the ambitions, intrigues and infighting of the most powerful landed families.

In medieval times, the influence of foreign ideas and customs increased with the arrival of English (and Norman) landowners like the family of Robert the Bruce; these people were gradually assimilated and often played an important part in the history of the country. Religious influences were also important in medieval Scotland and many religious houses were started in the reign of David I (*c.*1084–1153), including Melrose Abbey. Some of these communities were forward-looking centres of learning and agriculture and the early development of sheep farming in the Borders owes much to the efforts of practical men from the abbeys.

Rural life was far from peaceful in southern Scotland due to the depredations of local robber barons and the centuries of war between Scotland and England, especially during the Wars of Independence in the thirteenth and fourteenth centuries when Galloway was a stronghold from which uprisings came. This meant that theft, the destruction of property and violent deaths were all too common. The Borders area has suffered from having more than its 'fair' share of Scotland's history. For many centuries during the Middle Ages the land around the Scotland–England border was a lawless tract, with the dominant families based in fortified houses ('peel towers'), a number of which can still be seen today. Cattle raising in this rich agricultural area was a risky business in those days as 'Border reivers' (or cattle thieves, to use a less romantic name) were wont to swoop on a farm and drive the herd away.

No matter how ambitious the Scots were, in territorial matters they could not push the southern border far into England and the border question had to be settled for the sake of peace in both countries. The Union of the Crowns took place in 1603 when James (VI of Scotland and I of Great Britain) became king, and the Union of the Parliaments was in 1707.

Galloway's position to the west of the main north–south routes between Scotland and England meant that it was relatively isolated during some of the most turbulent periods of Scottish history and even today it is one of the less-visited areas of Scotland. However, the area was not immune from civil strife and saw much bloodshed during the tragic period in the late seventeenth century known as the 'Killing Times'. This was a reaction against those who sought to revive the National Covenant (1638) after the Restoration. The Solemn League and Covenant of 1643 (a separate document) had been abandoned. There was more to the Covenant than an attack on episcopacy (which in any case had a very long history in Scotland); it was a statement of political grievances as well. The Covenanters were dealt with in a very brutal manner and many memorials to this time will be met near the Way.

Prior to the industrial age, many of the people of the Southern Uplands lived in small communities in the valleys and near where a river could be used to power a corn-mill. Water power was put to even greater use when woollen mills were built in the Borders in the seventeenth and eighteenth centuries. Towns like Galashiels grew up beside the important rivers and many of the mills that were established at that time still remain as part of the Borders' most important manufacturing industry. However, many of the mills have to look far afield for the wool most suited to their needs.

The eighteenth and nineteenth centuries saw immense changes on the land. The great wealth that was generated by the Industrial Revolution meant that rich industrialists, merchants and others who profited from the new factories in the squalid towns and cities had huge sums of money available to purchase country estates. These improving landowners had the fields cleared and boulders were used to build unmortared 'drystane dykes' to enclose the fields. Great parklands were laid out and a wide variety of trees planted in order to protect and grace the improved land. The Way will pass a number of these estates, one of the best known being Sir Walter Scott's Abbotsford which is near Galashiels.

Great changes have taken place in southern Scotland since the middle of the nineteenth century and the population has become more concentrated into the towns and larger villages. This has meant the running down or abandonment of many old-established small settlements, for example Knowe, near Bargrennan. The railways have come and gone as the most important form of long-distance transport and the local people now rely on cars for getting around. Walkers will soon discover how infrequent the bus services are in the sparsely populated parts of the Southern Uplands. The handiness of the car has meant that many people can live in the countryside and commute to their work in the main towns (notably Dumfries, Hawick, Galashiels and Berwick-upon-Tweed) and a large proportion of the inhabitants of the country villages no longer live off the land.

Economic change continues to alter the face of the Southern Uplands and agriculture, textiles and clothes manufacturing have all gone through major changes in recent decades. Afforestation of large areas is the most obvious change in many districts. Newer manufacturing industries, such as electronics, have been introduced to diversify the local economies and tourism is becoming increasingly important, though this industry is largely seasonal.

The history of much of southern Scotland has been greatly romanticised by many writers (notably by Sir Walter Scott, one of the most frequently met characters on the Way) but the walker will find that the true story of the area is just as fascinating as the old tales. The area is steeped in history, literature and tradition and it has been said that 'Lowland Scotland as a distinct nationality came in with two warriors and went out with two bards. It came in with William Wallace and Robert Bruce and went out with Robert Burns and Walter Scott. The first two made the history, the last two told the story and sung the song.'

Part 2 General Information

Organisation

Planning the walk

The Southern Upland Way is the first of Scotland's official long-distance paths to follow a route across the entire breadth of the country. On its journey across southern Scotland the Way follows roads, tracks and paths as it passes through farmland, moorland and forest.

Beattock should be considered the half-way point of the 326 km (202 mile) walk; not only is the village about half-way along the whole route, it is also conveniently situated beside the A74, the road that connects Glasgow with north-west England. The Way is divided into fifteen sections, with seven sections in the western half and eight in the eastern half. The western half is the more difficult of the two as it is higher and hillier and the route is more exposed. The western sections are usually longer and the low population density in that part of the country means that there are more problems with transport and accommodation. Generally speaking, the sections start and finish at places where accommodation can be found; however, although the Way passes through many towns and villages, these are not necessarily at the ends of the sections.

Weather conditions, transport, accommodation and shopping for food are four of the most important concerns when planning the whole undertaking and careful preparation is essential. Many walkers will start their planning on the basis of one section per day, but tiredness or bad weather may force a change in plan so the Guide (i.e. Part 3) mentions places on the route (referred to as 'breaks') where the Way can be left in order to seek shelter and/or accommodation.

Walkers are strongly advised to walk from west to east as this should put the wind, rain and sun behind them; it also means that the harder half will be tackled while the walker is still fresh.

The Way can be tackled in a number of different manners: some walkers will be walking the whole route (or half of it) in one attempt while others will be doing one or more sections over a few days; others may be walking just at weekends. This book therefore has to cater for the different needs of many classes of walkers. Part 2 deliberately focuses on the problems that walkers will face – the need to plan transport, accommodation and shopping, to take three examples – as successful planning will lead to a more enjoyable walk. Walkers should therefore take from the text the information that will be most relevant to them. Experienced walkers will find some of the information and advice directed towards more inexperienced walkers rather obvious. Scots should remember that the book will be used by many non-Scots and that some of the information is directed specifically towards this latter group.

The following table is provided to bring together much of the generalised information that walkers will want to consider when making overall plans. More details on how the Guide is to be used are given in 'How to use the Guide' (p. 28) and each of the Guide's fifteen sections considers the information mentioned below much more fully. Note that the length of each section given below is generally by the shortest route mentioned in the Guide; see 'Diversions, alternative routes and spurs' on p. 30.

Section	Length	Places with most facilities	Main points to be considered
1 Portpatrick – Castle Kennedy	21·5 km	Portpatrick, Stranraer	No major problems
2 Castle Kennedy – New Luce	9·5 km	New Luce, Glenluce (off the Way)	No major problems
3 New Luce – Bargrennan	28 km	Newton Stewart (off the Way)	Long; exposed moorland; no shops until after the end
4 Bargrennan – St John's Town of Dalry	36 km	St John's Town of Dalry	Long; not much accommodation (and no shops) until the end

Section	Length	Places with most facilities	Main points to be considered
5 St John's Town of Dalry – Sanquhar	41·5 km	Sanquhar	Very long; exposed moorland; not much accommodation (and no shops) until the end
6 Sanquhar – Wanlockhead	12·5 km	Wanlockhead	No major problems
7 Wanlockhead – Beattock	31·5 km	Beattock, Moffat (off the Way)	Long; exposed moorland; hilly; no accommodation (except a bothy) or shops until the end
8 Beattock – St Mary's Loch	32 km	No settlements	Long; exposed moorland; not much accommodation until the end; no shops at all
9 St Mary's Loch – Traquair	19 km	Innerleithen (off the Way)	Exposed moorland; no accommodation or shops until after the end
10 Traquair – Yair Bridge	15 km	Selkirk (off the Way)	Exposed moorland; no accommodation or shops until well after the end
11 Yair Bridge – Melrose	12 km	Galashiels, Melrose	No major problems
12 Melrose – Lauder	15·5 km	Lauder	No accommodation or shops until the end
13 Lauder – Longformacus	24·5 km	Duns (off the Way)	Exposed moorland; hardly any accommodation; no shops at all
14 Longformacus – Abbey St Bathans	11 km	Duns (off the Way)	Hardly any accommodation; no shops at all
15 Abbey St Bathans – Cockburnspath	16·5 km	Cockburnspath	No major problems

Summary of distances:

Western half (Portpatrick – Beattock)		180·5 km	(112 miles)
Eastern half (Beattock – Cockburnspath)		145·5 km	(90 miles)
Total	(Portpatrick – Cockburnspath)	326 km	(202 miles)

How to use the Guide

The Guide has the following information at the start of each of the
fifteen sections.

Start of section: A six-figure map reference is given; this position can
be located on the appropriate Ordnance Survey 1:50,000 map.
End of section: As above.
Diversion: Information is given on any official diversions,
alternative routes or spurs. See p. 30.
Distance: The total map distance of the section.
Stages: Each section is divided into a number of stages; each of
these is further divided. Some of the stages describe important
towns off the Way where accommodation can be found.
Breaks in route: These are places where a walker can end a day's
walk to meet a car, find accommodation or get to low ground if the
weather is bad. Many of the breaks are at road junctions or where
the Way meets a distinct track.
Conditions: This describes the type of terrain that is crossed and the
exposure of the route.
Points of interest: These are interesting places to visit or good
viewpoints where walkers may want to spend some time.
Maps: This lists the Ordnance Survey and Bartholomew maps
required for the section. See p. 45.
Transport: This mentions the bus and train services that might be of
use; no distinction is made between frequent and infrequent
services. See p. 53.
Car parking: This is a brief (and very incomplete) list of places
where walkers may arrange to get picked up or set down by a car.
Some of these places may only have space for a couple of cars and
many of the country roads are very narrow. Some places can only be
reached via a track so it is best to consult the relevant Ordnance
Survey map.
Accommodation: This mentions places where accommodation is
available. The word 'various' is used where a number of
establishments exist; see the accommodation brochures for further
details (p. 47).

Notes: Any other important miscellaneous information, especially on shopping facilities.

The Way is defined by a series of waymarkers – wooden posts about 1–2 m tall. These incorporate a thistle in the design as this is the logo of Scotland's long-distance paths. At important changes of direction, for example where the Way joins or leaves a road, tall waymarkers are used; these are over 2 m in height and have arms pointing in the direction taken by the Way. The Guide mentions many of these tall waymarkers, and also some of the ordinary waymarkers where route finding may be a bit tricky, especially in poor visibility. Many of these references are given in order to help east-to-west walkers follow the route.

The moorland paths followed by the Way may be more obvious late in the summer when many feet have trampled down the grass, though a strong growth of grass or bracken can obscure the route in some places. Bracken may be tall enough to hide some waymarkers. In a number of places, cows may knock waymarkers over and on some moorlands this can be a serious problem, especially in poor visibility, so walkers should re-position any displaced waymarkers.

Only approximate compass directions have been given in the Guide, e.g. north, north-east, north of east; if a compass is essential at any time then an accurate bearing should be taken. If you lose the Way and cannot find your position on a map then it may be necessary to walk back to the last waymarker that was passed or to the last significant feature mentioned in the Guide or shown on a map.

In good weather, the route taken by the Way will generally be quite obvious so the walker need only look out for waymarkers and stiles, many of which are mentioned in the Guide. However, the route might not be so clear in bad visibility, or on a piece of rough ground; this is why the Guide often gives detailed information. The detail will be unnecessary on a fine day but may be essential in bad weather conditions.

There may be some alterations to the route over the years. It is the waymarkers, not the Guide, that define the Way, so walkers intending to keep on the Way should follow the waymarkers when

these take a route different from that described in the Guide. As
more walkers use the Way and as the route becomes more obvious,
some of the waymarkers may be considered superfluous and so
might be removed by the Rangers.

When to walk the Way

Most walkers will walk the Way between Easter and October,
especially between May and September when there are more hours
of daylight and the weather should be good – hopefully! Walkers
who are on the Way outside the Easter–October period should be
aware of the following points:

1. Daylight hours will be fewer and the weather may be much
    worse (see 'Weather' on p. 38), consequently less distance can be
    covered in a day.
2. Less accommodation will be available; this particularly applies to
    campsites, youth hostels and houses offering bed and breakfast
    accommodation.
3. Some of the bus services may have a winter timetable that differs
    from the summer one; school buses will be running during term
    time.
4. More equipment will be needed.

Diversions, alternative routes and spurs

A number of sections have official diversions or alternative routes
that take the Way away from its original route; these changes may
only operate while a bridge is unusable or during the lambing or
grouse-shooting seasons. A spur is used to lead the walker to some
particular place, e.g. a youth hostel.

   Full details of the current changes in the route are in the Guide,
but a summary is given below:

Section	Details
2 Castle Kennedy – New Luce	Diversion at the end of the section
3 New Luce – Bargrennan	Diversion at the start of the section
5 St John's Town of Dalry – Sanquhar	Spur to Kendoon Youth Hostel
6 Sanquhar – Wanlockhead	Alternative route during the lambing, grouse-breeding and grouse-shooting seasons
8 Beattock – St Mary's Loch	Alternative route during the lambing season

These changes may be altered or cancelled and other changes may come into being for various reasons. Current details should be given on notices at the start and end of each particular diversion or alternative route.

The Guide suggests some (unofficial) alternative routes or detours that may be taken. These are included so that high ground can be avoided in bad weather or where a more interesting route can be taken.

Distances and times

It may be tricky to estimate the time to be allowed for each section, but many walkers will average around 4 km per hour (2½ m.p.h.), allowing for short stops. Strong walkers may go more quickly but few walkers can or want to keep up a fast pace for long. The terrain, the weather and the weight of the rucksack are important factors in determining speed.

The distances referred to in the Guide are map distances; actual distances (i.e. taking the slope of the hills into account) will be rather more, and the extra effort of ascending hills will also add to the time taken. It should be remembered that walkers habitually underestimate the time needed for a section. This is particularly important on long walks or where definite arrangements have been made to meet other people at the end.

Safety

Safety is paramount when walking the Way, especially on the lonely and exposed moors. The major factors to be considered are:

1. Weather: Since the weather will generally be worse at altitude, in poor conditions it is worth considering taking low-level routes to avoid the high exposed moors. See 'Weather' on p. 38.

2. Fitness: It is a mistake to attempt too much in a day so it is important to make a realistic estimate of what you can manage in the time available. Always plan to arrive at your destination well before it gets dark. Many fit walkers can happily manage 40 km (25 miles) in a day; others will be more than happy to do half that distance.

3. Equipment: Any walker venturing on to the open moors must be properly equipped; see p. 41 for a list of equipment. Know how to use a compass and how to take a bearing if the weather and visibility are deteriorating. Keep your whistle round your neck, not at the bottom of the rucksack.

4. Food: Make sure that you have enough food and drink. See 'Food' on p. 44.

5. Emergencies: It is good practice to leave a note with someone (e.g. at the place where you spent the previous night) with information on your route and estimated time of arrival. Telephone the person when you have safely arrived at your destination.

If someone has been seriously hurt during a walk then the first things to do are to make a realistic assessment of the injury, decide how help is to be obtained and how the injured person is to be cared for before and after the rescue. If there are at least three people in the group, one person should be left with the injured walker and someone should go for assistance; this person must know exactly where the injured person was left. If the injury is bad or if the rescue is going to be tricky then the emergency services should be contacted. See 'Emergency services' on p. 37.

A lone walker in difficulties is in a very different position as far as rescues are concerned – which is why a lone walker must pay special attention to any deterioration in the weather.

   The internationally recognised distress signal is six blasts on a
whistle repeated at one minute intervals. However, an 'SOS' signal
(three short blasts, three long blasts, three short blasts) is probably
more widely recognised by hillwalkers. A torch can be used to send
these distress signals.

6. *First aid*: A suggested list of items for a first-aid kit is given on
p. 41. In a group of walkers, the first-aid kit should not be carried
by a person who is at the front and who might be far ahead if
someone needs help.

7. *Groups*: Groups should ensure that there are experienced
walkers at the front and rear. It is vitally important that slow
walkers are not left trailing behind, especially if the weather is
deteriorating. Groups should not straggle in difficult conditions –
keep together. It is advisable for everyone to carry their own food
so that walker and sustenance do not get separated.

8. *Miscellaneous*: Spectacle wearers should consider taking a spare
pair of spectacles with them; one stumble resulting in a smashed
pair of spectacles could mean a very frightening experience when
trying to get off a hill.

   There is always a fire danger in forests during a period of hot, dry
weather, especially where there is a lot of white grass i.e. last year's
grass that has not yet rotted.

   When walking on the road, walk on the right-hand side (facing
oncoming traffic) if there is no pavement. Use a torch when walking
along a road at dusk or at night.

Information

Tourist information

The Way passes through three local government regions: Dumfries
and Galloway, Strathclyde and Borders; the Guide mentions when
the Way crosses the regional boundaries. The three tourist boards
that operate in these regions are, respectively, the Dumfries and
Galloway Tourist Board, the Clyde Valley Tourist Board and the

Scottish Borders Tourist Board. The addresses of the tourist
boards' head offices are given on p. 40. The Way goes through only
a small part of the area covered by the Clyde Valley Tourist Board
(from Lowther Hill to just after Daer Reservoir, about 15 km of the
Way); accommodation at Leadhills is covered by this board.

The following Tourist Information Centres (TICs) near the Way
operate during the summer months (from April to mid-October):

Section	Location	Tourist board
1 Portpatrick – Castle Kennedy	Stranraer	Dumfries and Galloway
3 New Luce – Bargrennan	Newton Stewart	Dumfries and Galloway
7 Wanlockhead – Beattock	Abington Moffat	Clyde Valley Dumfries and Galloway
10 Traquair – Yair Bridge	Selkirk	Scottish Borders
11 Yair Bridge – Melrose	Galashiels, Melrose	Scottish Borders

The TIC in Dumfries is open throughout the year and can deal with
telephone enquiries (24 hour service). All the TICs can arrange
accommodation locally and can give information about local
transport and things to see in the area; they should not be depended
on for accurate weather forecasts. In addition to these offices,
information boards have been erected in some villages which give
details of local accommodation and transport. The Countryside
Commission for Scotland (see p. 40) has started to erect
'Information Shelters' at various places along the Way. As well as
giving general information about the locality, these shelters will give
details of nearby shops and accommodation.

Useful publications

The most important publications to get from the tourist boards are
their accommodation guides; these give much useful information
and they are free. When writing to the tourist boards ask them for
general information as well. In particular, mention that you are

walking the Way and that you would like a copy of each of the free items mentioned below (if the boards have a stock of them).

The following publications are published annually and they give up-to-date information that is invaluable to the walker; the first five items on the list are free.

Publication	Published by	Available from	Notes
1. Accommodation guide	Dumfries and Galloway Tourist Board	Dumfries and Galloway Tourist Board	A list of hotels, bed and breakfast accommodation and campsites
2. Accommodation guide	Clyde and Forth Valleys Tourist Boards	Clyde Valley Tourist Board	A list of hotels, bed and breakfast accommodation and campsites
3. Accommodation guide	Scottish Borders Tourist Board	Scottish Borders Tourist Board	A list of hotels, bed and breakfast accommodation and campsites
4. The Southern Upland Way: general information and accommodation	Countryside Commission for Scotland	Countryside Commission, youth hostels, accommodation leaflet boxes, tourist boards' offices and TICs	Includes a small map, a short article on the Way and a long list of all kinds of accommodation along the route
5. Southern Upland Wayfarer	Famedram	Famedram, tourist boards' offices	Includes a small map, a short article on the Way and many adverts for accommodation along the route
6. SYHA handbook	SYHA	SYHA, most youth hostels	See the item entitled 'Youth hostels' on p. 49

The addresses of the organisations mentioned above are given on p. 40.

Information for foreign visitors

Visitors from abroad can get general information about Scotland
from the British Tourist Authority, which has offices in a number of
countries. Further general information on Scotland can be obtained
from the Scottish Tourist Board (see p. 40 for address). These
bodies can give information on accommodation, transport to and in
Scotland, touring in other parts of Scotland etc. Specific questions
relating to the Southern Uplands are best sent to the appropriate
local tourist boards.

Shopping facilities and other services

The Way goes through a number of towns and villages but some
sections of the Way do not pass any shops at all. Shopping for food
thus requires some planning and the Guide mentions places where
shops may be found. The following points should be noted:

1. Most shops will be closed on Sundays, although there may be
   some shops open primarily for the sale of Sunday newspapers.
2. Some campsites have shops but their range of supplies is usually
   limited. They may be open for only a few hours each day but this
   may be when other shops are closed (e.g. on Sundays).
3. The youth hostels have small shops, with the exception of Abbey
   St Bathans.
4. Melrose Youth Hostel is the only hostel that provides meals, but
   only during part of the year.
5. Most hotels (and many public houses) provide bar meals,
   generally served until 8.30 p.m. or 9 p.m.
6. Hotels and bed and breakfast establishments can usually provide
   packed lunches.
7. The towns and some of the villages have banks but it may be
   more convenient to use post offices as these are more numerous
   and have longer opening hours. The Guide mentions where a
   number of post offices are found. In general, it is better to carry
   cash from the start of the walk, backed up by cheques where
   necessary.

8. Check with your own bank for the locations of cash-dispenser machines. Walkers from outside Scotland should find out which of the Scottish banks' cash-dispenser machines will accept their cards.

9. The Countryside Commission for Scotland has recently introduced a 'Walkers Welcome Scheme' whereby walkers are encouraged to patronise establishments (including shops and places to stay) that display the scheme's stickers.

Emergency services

Foreign visitors should be aware that in an emergency the police can be contacted by telephone by dialling 999 (no coins are necessary in a public telephone box). The ambulance service, the fire brigade and the coastguard service can also be contacted through this number.

If a rescue is to be mounted then the police may contact a local mountain-rescue team; the police can also alert a local doctor to an emergency. Some police stations may not be manned outside office hours. The locations of the police stations, mountain-rescue teams and hospitals with accident units near the Way are listed below:

Section	Police stations	Mountain-rescue teams	Hospitals with accident units
1 Portpatrick – Castle Kennedy	Portpatrick, Stranraer		Stranraer
3 New Luce – Bargrennan	Newton Stewart	Newton Stewart	Newton Stewart
4 Bargrennan – St John's Town of Dalry	St John's Town of Dalry		Dumfries
5 St John's Town of Dalry – Sanquhar	Sanquhar		
6 Sanquhar – Wanlockhead	Leadhills		
7 Wanlockhead – Beattock	Moffat	Moffat	Moffat
9 St Mary's Loch – Traquair	Innerleithen		Peebles
10 Traquair – Yair Bridge	Selkirk	Selkirk	

Section	Police stations	Mountain-rescue teams	Hospitals with accident units
11 Yair Bridge – Melrose	Galashiels, Melrose		Melrose
12 Melrose – Lauder	Lauder		
13 Lauder – Longformacus	Duns		Duns
15 Abbey St Bathans – Cockburnspath	Cockburnspath		Berwick-upon-Tweed

Weather

Weather is a very important factor to consider when walking the Way. Much of the route crosses open moorlands which can be most enjoyable in good weather, or downright miserable in wet weather. Walkers should expect a mixture of weather and this means that the clothes they carry must be suitable for the conditions they are likely to encounter (see 'Clothing' on p. 43).

Rain is perhaps the most important element in the weather and the table below gives the average rainfall in millimetres over the year for some places near the Way. These figures can be used as a rough guide to the likely weather in these different districts. The Glasgow and Edinburgh figures are given for comparison. The five places near the Way are:

West Freuch	(15 m altitude)	5 km south of Castle Kennedy (Section 1)
Loch Dee	(244 m altitude)	on the Way (Section 4)
Eskdalemuir	(242 m altitude)	8 km south-west of Craigmichan Scar (Section 8)
Kelso	(59 m altitude)	18 km east of Melrose (Section 11)
Dunbar	(23 m altitude)	12 km north-west of Cockburnspath (Section 15)

	Jan	Feb	Mar	Apr	May	Jun	Jul	Aug	Sept	Oct	Nov	Dec	Year
West Freuch	97	61	63	56	57	62	73	86	102	99	101	105	962
Loch Dee	235	162	148	143	136	121	147	181	227	234	233	265	2,232
Eskdalemuir	155	106	100	100	99	102	114	133	151	144	147	155	1,506
Kelso	64	48	38	41	56	51	65	87	62	59	71	56	698
Dunbar	46	34	33	34	48	38	55	74	50	49	62	48	571
Glasgow Airport	94	71	61	61	68	61	74	91	101	103	93	104	982
Edinburgh	52	42	37	39	57	47	75	78	65	56	60	53	661

(Source: Meteorological Office, 1979)

In general, the wetter weather is found in the west (due to the influence of the moist winds from the south-west) and on the high ground. It must be remembered that although low ground may be dry when the walker sets off in the morning, the nearby higher ground may be quite wet.

Hot days are welcomed by most people in the summer, but walkers must be aware of the necessity of increasing liquid intake and the need for rest periods in order to combat fatigue. The air temperature falls by about 0.5°C to 0.7°C for every 100 m increase in altitude. This does not take into account the higher wind speeds on the hills. Warm and damp conditions may bring out lots of midges, especially in still conditions.

Weather forecasts can be obtained from newspapers, television and radio. Radio Scotland carries a useful weather forecast especially for walkers and climbers on Fridays around 5.30–5.45 p.m.

General weather forecasts can be obtained by telephoning the Weatherline service, details of which can be found in the front of telephone directories. For more detailed information (which is frequently updated) the Weathercall service can be used. This service is expensive so lots of coins may be needed if you are phoning from a call box! The Weathercall numbers for the Southern Uplands are: South-west Scotland: 0898 500 420; Lothian and the Borders: 0898 500 422.

The telephone number of the local Meteorological Office is listed in the telephone directory.

Walking holidays

Recently, some companies specialising in outdoor pursuits have arranged guided walks along all (or part) of the Way. This may involve using a minibus to carry all the equipment and clothes not needed by walkers while out for the day. Accommodation may be at youth hostels. There may only be a small number of such trips each year, but details can probably be obtained from the tourist boards.

Useful addresses

Borders Regional Council Planning Department: Department of Planning and Development, Borders Regional Council, Regional Headquarters, Newtown St Boswells, Roxburghshire TD6 0SA.
Borders Regional Council Transport: Department of Roads and Transportation, Borders Regional Council, Regional Headquarters, Newtown St Boswells, Roxburghshire TD6 0SA.
British Rail, ScotRail House, 58 Port Dundas Road, Glasgow G4 0HG.
Clyde Valley Tourist Board, Horse Market, Ladyacre Road, Lanark ML11 7LQ.
Countryside Commission for Scotland, Battleby, Redgorton, Perth PH1 3EW.
Dumfries and Galloway Regional Council Planning Department: Department of Physical Planning, Dumfries and Galloway Regional Council, Council Offices, Dumfries DG1 2DD.
Dumfries and Galloway Regional Council Transport: Department of Roads and Transportation, Dumfries and Galloway Regional Council, Council Offices, Dumfries DG1 2DD.
Dumfries and Galloway Tourist Board, Dumfries Tourist Information Centre, Whitesands, Dumfries DG1 2SB.
Famedram Publishers, Gartocharn, Alexandria, Glasgow G83.
P. & O. Ferries, Ferry Terminal, Cairnryan, Stranraer DG9 8BR.
Scottish Borders Tourist Board, Municipal Buildings, High Street, Selkirk TD7 4JX.
Scottish Tourist Board, 23 Ravelston Terrace, Edinburgh EH4 3EU.
Scottish Youth Hostels Association, 7 Glebe Crescent, Stirling FK8 2JA.
Sealink British Ferries, Sea Terminal, Stranraer DG9 8EJ.

Equipment

Equipment list

The type and amount of equipment that is needed depends on such factors as the weather, the type of terrain, the length of the walk and the arrangements made for accommodation. A general checklist is given below. Few walkers will want to take all the items mentioned, but this should help people draw up their own personal equipment lists.

1. Rucksack: rucksack, polythene bags to go into rucksack. See 'Rucksack' on p. 42.
2. Clothing: walking boots, socks, underwear, shirt, jersey(s), jacket, waterproof cagoule, waterproof trousers, gaiters, woollen hat, cotton hat, woollen gloves, light shoes, nightwear, midge net, spare clothes. See 'Clothing' on p. 43 and 'Boots' on p. 44.
3. Food: sandwiches/rolls, butter/margarine, fillings for sandwiches/rolls, cake, biscuits, tea/coffee, sugar, sweets, chocolate, fruit, food for main meals, cereals, dried milk, salt, emergency food, water bottle, vacuum flask. See 'Food' on p. 44.
4. Information: details of accommodation, details of transport, maps, useful telephone numbers, guidebook. See 'Useful publications' on p. 34, 'Timetables' on p. 54 and 'Maps' on p. 45.
5. First aid: sticking plaster, scissors, antihistamine cream, antiseptic cream, insect repellent, zinc oxide tape, aspirin/paracetamol, toilet paper, suntan cream, bandages, powder for feet, lip salve.
6. Winter walking: warm jacket, winter-weight boots, thermal underwear, balaclava, mitts, bivvy bag, reflective blanket, ice-axe, crampons, soup.
7. Camping: tent, flysheet, poles, pegs, guys, stove, billies.
8. Miscellaneous: torch, knife, compass, waterproof map case, pen, paper, binoculars, whistle, watch, sleeping bag, sheet sleeping bag, sleeping mat, toiletries, reading spectacles, spare spectacles, sunglasses, photographic equipment, matches, money, change for

the telephone, cheque book, cheque card, credit card, bank pass book, youth hostel membership card, tea-towel, cutlery, waterproofing for boots. See 'Binoculars' on p. 46 and 'Photography' on p. 46.

Rucksack

Walkers who are on a single day's walk will need only a daysack; this should be big enough to carry waterproofs, food, water and other items of equipment that are needed. Those who are camping or who have to carry a few days' clothes and food will need a rather larger rucksack. The large rucksacks often have a large external frame or a more compact internal frame. Walkers thinking of buying a large rucksack should seek specialist help in a good outdoor sports shop. The rucksack should be tried out before starting on the Way. The following points should be borne in mind when buying or using a rucksack:

1. Rucksacks made of canvas soak up a lot of water when wet and become heavier, so it is better to use one made of the synthetic materials that do not absorb much water.
2. A padded hipbelt is a useful device as it enables much of the rucksack's weight to be borne on the hips rather than on the shoulders. It thus improves the rucksack's stability when the walker is moving over rough ground.
3. Heavy-duty polythene bags should be used to protect items inside the rucksack from getting wet.
4. Put soft items such as clothes where they will be nearest your back, to prevent harder items digging into you.
5. Try to keep the weight fairly high up in the rucksack and close to your back in order to improve stability.
6. Rucksacks that are fairly old may be improved by reproofing.

Clothing

The main weather-related problems during the summer months will probably be rain and wind; overheating on hot summer days may cause early fatigue. The essentials to consider when choosing clothing are to have clothes that are waterproof, windproof, comfortable and reliable. Most walkers will already have all the walking clothing that is needed and it is best to wear clothing that is well 'broken in'. It is not advisable to rely on brand-new outer clothing without first testing its performance.

A good jacket should be taken; a heavy jacket will be too warm for the summer so it may be best to have woollen jerseys for warmth under a good waterproof jacket. Some clothing materials that are both waterproof and windproof may also make the wearer sweat a lot; the effect of this is rather unpleasant and may lead to overheating and fatigue. Modern semi-permeable materials such as Goretex get over this problem by allowing sweat to pass through the fabric without letting the rain in. Unfortunately, clothes made of these materials can be expensive. Jackets with front openings are preferable to the 'pull over' type as they allow better ventilation. Some materials used for jackets may require occasional reproofing.

Trousers should be strong and hardwearing; cotton and tweed are suitable materials. Denim should be avoided as it absorbs a great deal of water and can take a long time to dry – this can lead to rapid chilling of the body in wet and windy conditions. Waterproof overtrousers should be of the type that can be put on and taken off whilst wearing boots. Gaiters are very useful when crossing wet moorlands, especially in late summer when the grass can be rather high.

The head may also need protection from sun, wind and rain – and perhaps all three in the same day! Midges may be a real problem in some places (Caldons Campsite has a reputation for them) but walkers can protect their faces by buying a midge net. However, these are rather difficult to find, even in good outdoor sports shops.

Boots

Summer-weight walking boots should be suitable for the walk
during most of the year. Heavy winter-weight boots should only be
necessary in the winter months and their extra weight may tire the
legs more quickly – especially when walking 30 km or more a day.
However, in very wet conditions, a pair of winter-weight boots
(which are generally thicker and more waterproof than summer
ones) will keep the feet drier. New boots must be thoroughly
broken in before starting on the Way; in addition, resoled boots
should be tried before setting out.

Walking shoes (i.e. stout footwear without a sewn-in tongue or a
padded ankle support) may be sufficient for tracks and well-worn
paths, but they do not offer protection or support to the ankles
when crossing boggy moorland or going over rough ground.

Good socks should be worn; socks made of nylon and those that
have been darned should be avoided.

Food

This should be filling and nutritious and should provide enough
energy for a full day's walking. Extra food should always be carried
in case of emergencies – if you come off the hills with no food left
then you didn't take enough to begin with!

While it is better to take mostly high-fibre, low-fat foods, e.g.
wholemeal bread sandwiches and fruit, their sheer bulk makes it
impractical to carry sufficient of them to provide adequate energy
for a full day's walking. Chocolate, sweets and cake provide energy
in a more concentrated form but should only be regarded as extras
and not the mainstay since they provide a rapid but shortlived
energy boost.

Water (or some other drink) should be carried, especially on a
hot day; water on its own is more thirst-quenching than any other
drink. The high moors are often very peaty and many of the streams
may not be suitable for drinking so it is best to carry a full day's
water supply. Milk should not be carried for long distances in hot

weather as it can curdle. Alcohol should not be consumed while out walking.

Walkers wanting to reduce the weight of the food they carry may consider taking packets of dehydrated meals and these can be bought at outdoor sports shops. However, it is best to try them before starting on the walk – opinions differ on their tastiness! Many shops sell tins of ready-cooked meals, e.g. curry, lasagne and stew, that only need heating; these are heavy to carry but are worthwhile considering because of their handiness. Rice and dehydrated potato are less bulky alternatives to potatoes.

Maps

The maps that will be of most use to the walker are:

1. Ordnance Survey Landranger Series (scale: 1:50,000).
   The maps that cover the Way are (from west to east): numbers 82, 76, 77, 78, 79, 73 and 67. These are the most useful maps for the walker to have. The most up-to-date maps show the Southern Upland Way and mark it with the legend 'Southern Upland Way' or 'LDP' (long-distance path). The maps do not show all the other paths and tracks that will be encountered. The maps in this series give most of the names of the farms, streams and other physical features that are referred to in the Guide. The spelling of place names mentioned in the Guide is generally taken from these maps; the spelling of some names may differ on other maps.
2. Bartholomew (scale: 1:100,000).
   These maps are used as illustrations in this book. The four maps that cover the route are:
   National Series no. 37 (now called 'Stranraer and Galloway')
   National Series no. 40 (now discontinued)
   National Series no. 41 (now called 'The Borders')
   National Series no. 46 (now called 'Edinburgh and the Forth')
   The most up-to-date maps show the Way.

3. Estate Publications (scale: 1:200,000).
   Numbers 17 ('Burns Country') and 16 ('Borders of England and
   Scotland') cover southern Scotland and are useful for route
   planning. They both show the Way.
4. Ordnance Survey Routemaster Series (scale: 1:250,000).
   Number 4 ('Central Scotland and Northumberland') shows the
   area covered by the whole of the Way, except for a few
   kilometres at the start. It is useful for route planning.

Walkers using maps that do not show the Way may find it useful to
mark the route on the maps before they start walking. Long-sighted
walkers should remember to take their reading spectacles with them
so that they can read the maps!

Binoculars

Many walkers carry binoculars with them as they add to the
pleasure of exploring the countryside. A small folding pair (e.g.
8×21) are light and compact and can be kept in a pocket when not
in use. Not only are binoculars handy for studying buildings and
birds and looking at distant objects, they are exceptionally useful
when trying to spot waymarkers on open moorland.

Photography

Many walkers will want to take a camera with them and the
following points are intended to help them get the best out of the
camera they use.

1. If a new camera has been bought for the walk, ensure that you
   know how to use it. Film is relatively cheap, so it is best to run
   at least one film through the camera before relying on it for the
   whole walk.
2. Walkers who have a 35 mm single lens reflex camera may find
   that a 35 mm or a 50 mm lens will be all they need for the
   majority of pictures.

3. If the camera uses a battery then a spare one should be carried, especially in cold weather. Batteries don't like low temperatures so in winter the spare battery should be kept in an inside pocket.

4. If a filter can be fitted on to the lens, a 'skylight' filter should be kept on the lens all the time. This will cut haziness in long-distance shots as well as giving some protection to the lens.

5. A lens hood will cut down on unwanted light getting into the lens when shooting towards the brightest part of the sky.

6. The lens should be covered at all times when not taking pictures.

7. The camera should be protected from the rain by keeping it in a waterproof bag in the rucksack when it is not in use.

8. Use lens tissues, not a handkerchief, to clean a lens or filter. A handkerchief can be used to clean the camera body; this is of particular importance near the sea, where the salty air is very corrosive.

9. Film may be relatively expensive to buy in some of the villages that the Way goes through. For this reason, and since there will be few places to buy film anyway, it is best to take sufficient film with you.

10. Since most photographs will probably be landscapes or pictorial shots, medium speed film (ASA 50 to 100) will probably be sufficient for most occasions.

Accommodation

Types and availability of accommodation

Finding suitable accommodation is one of the tricky tasks facing the walker – especially if plans have to be altered because of a change in the weather. While some sections start and end near villages or towns, other sections have very little accommodation. Many different types of accommodation are available on or near the Way, including hotels, farmhouses, private houses and youth hostels; campsites and bothies are found in handy locations. The introduction to each section of the Guide gives an indication of the places where accommodation may be found and there is special mention of some small establishments that might otherwise be overlooked.

In a number of out-of-the-way places on the Way, there are 'accommodation leaflet boxes' which contain the CCS accommodation leaflet (see p. 34). These boxes are mentioned in the Guide, but it is unwise to rely on them for a leaflet – get one before you start.

Arranging accommodation

It is best to make enquiries about accommodation well before starting on the Way and the publications mentioned on p. 34 will be of great use. The establishments listed in the tourist boards' brochures are only those that pay a subscription to the local board. The following points are worth noting:

1. Some caravan sites (and some farms) may have caravans for hire for single nights; this is more common outside the July/August peak of the tourist season.
2. Some of the hotels and bed and breakfast establishments may not be open outside the summer period.
3. Most places, including bothies and youth hostels, may be very busy at the height of the tourist season and on holiday weekends.
4. All of the TICs can arrange local accommodation, but only at establishments listed in the board's accommodation brochure.
5. The Guide mentions many public telephones boxes near the Way so that walkers can use them to arrange or confirm accommodation.

Hotels and bed and breakfast accommodation

Many of the hotels near the Way are mentioned in the Guide, except those in towns or large villages, where there are a number of establishments to choose from. The tourist boards' brochures give the necessary information about these.

Many walkers will want to minimise costs by staying at private houses offering bed and breakfast accommodation. The houses vary from small cottages with only one room to let, to larger houses with facilities more usually found in a small hotel. A number of farms also offer bed and breakfast accommodation. Many of the bed and breakfast establishments are far from other facilities, but are conveniently placed near the Way – this makes them particularly useful to walkers.

Some of the establishments near the Way are quite small so groups of walkers may have a problem in getting everyone accommodated in one place; groups should book ahead where possible.

Youth hostels

Many walkers will be members of the Scottish Youth Hostels Association (SYHA) or a similar body (e.g. the YHA in England and Wales) that is affiliated to the International Youth Hostel Federation (IYHF). The current SYHA handbook (see p. 35) gives full details of all the hostels (exact location, dates and times of opening, number of beds, telephone number (if the hostel has a telephone) etc.).

SYHA membership cards are available to Scottish residents from the National Office (see p. 40 for address) or the hostels (Abbey St Bathans excepted). Walkers from outside Scotland should have a membership card from their own hostels association; this should have a passport-size photograph on it. Non-Scottish residents who do not belong to a hostels association can get an IYHF card from the National Office or the hostels (Abbey St Bathans excepted); a passport-size photograph is required.

The following points should be noted:

1. Sleeping bags can be used in grade 3 hostels.
2. Sheet sleeping bags (which can be hired at hostels) should be used.
3. Walkers should take their own cutlery and tea-towels.
4. The hostels will rarely be fully booked under normal circumstances, but large parties at holiday weekends may leave little room for other hostellers. It is probably not realistic for walkers to book ahead by letter, but it is often possible to phone a hostel the previous night to find out what accommodation may be available. Large groups of walkers should book ahead if possible.
5. Abbey St Bathans is very small (twelve beds) and as there is little alternative accommodation near it, it is strongly advised that walkers (even when on their own) book ahead at that hostel.
6. Credit cards cannot be used for advance bookings or for payment of hostel fees.

The hostels near the Way are listed below.

Section	Hostel	Grade	Notes
3 New Luce – Bargrennan	Minnigaff	3	Near Newton Stewart; 14 km off the Way
5 St John's Town of Dalry – Sanquhar	Kendoon	3	Small; reached by 2·5 km waymarked spur from the Way
6 Sanquhar – Wanlockhead	Wanlockhead	3	On the Way; very handy
10 Traquair – Yair Bridge	Broadmeadows	3	At Yarrowford; just 1·5 km off the Way as it crosses the hills
11 Yair Bridge – Melrose	Melrose	2	Only 1 km off the Way; very handy
14 Longformacus – Abbey St Bathans	Abbey St Bathans	1	On the Way; very handy, but very small
15 Abbey St Bathans – Cockburnspath	Coldingham	2	14 km off the Way

Camping

Those walkers who intend to backpack should seriously consider
the nature of the problems they will be letting themselves in for and
then plan accordingly. The Way is a demanding challenge for those
carrying an ordinary daysack, but for those carrying a full kit the
going could be very tough. A group sharing the weight of the tent
and other common equipment should fare better than a lone walker
carrying everything himself or herself.

As recompense for the labour of carrying everything, the
backpacker has fewer worries about where to spend the night.
There are campsites and bothies *en route* and many out-of-the-way
places where campers can put up tents – this could be very
important if the weather deteriorates quickly.

Many backpackers will be tempted to take a lot of equipment
with them but the length of the walk and the hilly nature of the
terrain must be considered when choosing what to take; it is too
easy to overload the rucksack. Those who have not done much
backpacking before should try some shorter walks before
attempting the Way as this should help in deciding what equipment
is essential. A suggested list of camping equipment is given on p. 41.

The following list gives details of a number of places near the
Way that have campsites; the Guide mentions all of these and gives
directions to most of them. Fuller details can be obtained from the
tourist boards' accommodation brochures. Note that the youth
hostels do not allow camping in their grounds.

Section	Location
1 Portpatrick – Castle Kennedy	Portpatrick (three sites), Stranraer
2 Castle Kennedy – New Luce	Glenluce (two sites)
3 New Luce – Bargrennan	Derry, Knowe, Bargrennan, Newton Stewart
4 Bargrennan – St John's Town of Dalry	Caldons
5 St John's Town of Dalry – Sanquhar	Sanquhar (two sites)
7 Wanlockhead – Beattock	Beattock (three sites), Moffat

Section	Location
8 Beattock – St Mary's Loch	Cossarshill, Ettrick Valley (three sites), Tibbie Shiels Inn
9 St Mary's Loch – Traquair	Innerleithen
10 Traquair – Yair Bridge	Selkirk
11 Yair Bridge – Melrose	Galashiels, Melrose
12 Melrose – Lauder	Lauder
15 Abbey St Bathans – Cockburnspath	Cockburnspath, Coldingham

Bothies

In many parts of Scotland, old buildings on the hills have been taken over for use as bothies (basic shelters). These buildings may have been dilapidated cottages previously used by shepherds. Many are still owned by the local landowner but are cared for by the Mountain Bothies Association (MBA).

Four bothies are situated near the Way. They have very simple facilities – a roof over your head plus a fireplace (any wood used should be replaced). In those bothies that are under the care of the MBA their members have first call on their use. The bothies near the Way are listed below (full details of their locations are given in the Guide).

Section	Name of bothy	Location	Notes
4 Bargrennan – St John's Town of Dalry	White Laggan	On the south side of Loch Dee	Under the care of the MBA
5 St John's Town of Dalry – Sanquhar	Polskeoch	5 km north of Benbrack	Very new building, owned Dumfries and Galloway Region
7 Wanlockhead – Beattock	Brattleburn	On the east side of Daer Reservoir	Under the care of the MBA
8 Beattock – St Mary's Loch	Over Phawhope	Near the head of Ettrick Valley	Under the care of the MBA

Transport

The transport system

A glance at a map of southern Scotland will show that the Southern Upland Way has a general trend in a north-easterly direction; unfortunately, the main rivers (and hence the communication routes that follow them) generally lie in altogether different directions. Thus the Way seldom runs parallel to the main transport routes – it generally cuts across them. This provides a number of difficulties for walkers who want to use public transport near the Way.

Railways

Some walkers may find that trains provide a useful service from their homes to near either end (or to near the middle) of the Way. Four railway lines cross the Way and details of these are given below.

Section	Route	Railway stations near the Way
1 Portpatrick – Castle Kennedy	Glasgow – Stranraer	Stranraer
2 Castle Kennedy – New Luce	Glasgow – Stranraer	Barrhill
5 St John's Town of Dalry – Sanquhar	Glasgow – Carlisle via Dumfries	Kirkconnel
7 Wanlockhead – Beattock	Glasgow – London via Carlisle	Lockerbie
15 Abbey St Bathans – Cockburnspath	Edinburgh – London	Dunbar, Berwick-upon-Tweed

Buses

It is hardly surprising that the Way crosses a great number of bus routes, but unfortunately not very many of the services are of real use to the walker. References to bus services are given under the heading 'Transport' in each section's introduction in the Guide, but it is essential to obtain up-to-date bus timetables before starting the walk.

The individual bus services may be run by a large or a small local operator. In the case of very local services, some of these may be 'school buses' that run only during the school term. In some districts the post office runs a 'post-bus'; this may be an ordinary car, so space in it will be limited. Post-bus services may be very slow as their first duty is to ensure delivery of the mail.

Ferries

Two ferry services operate between Ireland and Scotland. They are run by Sealink (Larne–Stranraer) and P. & O. (Larne–Cairnryan). See p. 40 for addresses.

Timetables

The timetables that are most useful are as follows:

1. Leaflets giving details of bus services in Dumfries and Galloway Region are available free from the region's Department of Roads and Transportation (see p. 40 for address).
2. The most comprehensive listing of services in the Borders Region is the 'Borders Travel Guide', available (not free) from the region's Department of Roads and Transportation (see p. 40 for address). It gives details of bus and train services and also has information on school holidays, public holidays and early-closing days for shops. It is also available from the Scottish Borders Tourist Board and its TICs.

3. Rather more useful (and much smaller) than the item above is the department's free leaflet which details bus services in the Borders Region that operate near the Way. This exceptionally useful leaflet has been designed for the use of walkers on the Way and it is essential reading for those needing public transport. It is available from the Department of Roads and Transportation and the Scottish Borders Tourist Board.
4. Railway timetables are available (free) from ScotRail (see p. 40 for address) and major railway stations in Scotland.
5. Ferry timetables are available from the operators' terminals or from travel agents.

How to get to either end (and the middle) of the Way

1. To Portpatrick: by bus from Stranraer (via Lochans).
   To Stranraer:
   1) By train from Glasgow via Ayr.
   2) By bus from Girvan (connections with Ayr and Glasgow).
   3) By bus from Dumfries via Castle Douglas, Kirkcudbright, Newton Stewart, Glenluce and Castle Kennedy. Dumfries is connected to Carlisle by bus and train.
   4) By bus from London (Victoria) via Birmingham, Preston and Carlisle.
   5) By ferry from Larne.
2. To Moffat:
   1) By bus, using the Glasgow–Dumfries or Dumfries–Moffat services.
   2) By bus from Edinburgh via Broughton.
   3) To Lockerbie by train (Glasgow–Carlisle line) and then by bus.
3. To Cockburnspath:
   1) By bus from Edinburgh, Dunbar or Berwick-upon-Tweed. All of these towns are on the east-coast railway line.

Cars

Groups of walkers may be attracted to the idea of using cars to help them walk the Way over a series of weekends. This needs careful planning of how to position cars at either end of a day's walk and how to recover them at the end of the day. However, in a number of sections, the route followed by the Way is much shorter than the road distance between the start and the end of the section. In these cases a disproportionate amount of time may be spent in positioning cars where they are needed and recovering them at the end of the day. In such cases, public transport may be more useful.

Bicycles

Cyclists will note that many stretches of the Way follow quiet country roads and forest tracks and these provide safe and pleasant cycling. However, the stretches in between these roads and tracks can be rough and may be rather boggy, especially after a lot of rain. Each section of the Way should be taken on its own merit. Maps and the text of the Guide should be studied carefully in order to decide if a bicycle could be of use.

Miscellaneous

Who is responsible for the Way?

The Countryside Commission for Scotland (CCS) is the body responsible for the establishment of Scotland's long-distance paths. Maintenance of the route, however, rests with the appropriate regional councils and they look after the many stiles, waymarkers, bridges and notices. Some major engineering structures on the route such as bridges have been built by teams of army engineers.

The day-to-day work of maintaining the Way is the responsibility of Countryside Rangers employed by the planning departments of Dumfries and Galloway and Borders Regional Councils; the small part of the Way that is in Strathclyde Region is looked after by Dumfries and Galloway Regional Council. Should you encounter any difficulties on the Way you should report these to the regional council's Ranger Service (see p. 40 for addresses).

HMSO has published an official guide to the Way (see p. 34) and the CCS publishes an annual accommodation list (see p. 35).

The Southern Upland Way is Scotland's third long-distance path promoted by the CCS. The first two were the West Highland Way (Milngavie–Fort William) and the Speyside Way (which follows the River Spey).

Metric/imperial conversions

The Guide generally uses metric measurements, with some of the important distances also quoted in imperial units. The following (approximate) conversion factors may be of use:

1 centimetre = 0.39 inches
1 metre = 3 feet 3 inches
1 kilometre = 0.62 miles (8 km is approximately 5 miles)
1 litre = 0.22 gallons
1 kilogram = 2.20 pounds
1 tonne (i.e. 1,000 kg) = 0.98 tons

Glossary of topographical names

Many topographical names found in southern Scotland use local words that may be unfamiliar to many walkers – including many Scots. The following list gives some words that occur in place names with an indication of their meaning, though it should be noted that the same word may have a slightly different meaning in different districts. A number of the words are so expressive that it is difficult to give an exact 'translation'.

Bing, a pile of waste material beside a coal mine
Brae, a stretch of ground rising fairly steeply
Burn, a stream
Cleuch or *cleugh*, a gorge or ravine
Craig, a crag or cliff
Dean or *dene*, a narrow valley, especially one with trees
Dod or *dodd*, a bare, round hill
Dyke, a wall
Drystane dyke, a wall made of unmortared boulders
Fell, a tract of hill moor
Gill, a ravine or gully
Haugh or *holm*, a piece of level ground beside a river
Hope, a hollow among the hills or a small enclosed upland valley
Kirk, a church
Know or *knowe*, a knoll
Lane, a slow-moving winding stream
Law, a rounded hill; frequently an isolated or conspicuous hill
Linn, a waterfall
Loch, a lake
Lochan, a little loch
Loup, a cascade of water
Mains, the home farm of an estate
Moss, a stretch of boggy ground
Mote or *motte*, a mound or hillock
Muir, a moor or an area of unenclosed uncultivated land
Mull, a promontory or headland
Rig, a ridge of high ground or a long narrow hill
Shaw, a small wood, especially a natural one
Shiel, a summer-pasture hut
Shieling, a high or remote summer pasture
Sike or *syke*, a small stream or a marshy hollow
Water, a small river

The Country Code

The Way crosses farmland that provides a living for local people
and the Country Code, as issued by the Countryside Commission
for Scotland, should be followed.

1. Guard against all risk of fire.
2. Fasten all gates.
3. Keep your dogs under close control.
4. Keep to public paths across farmland.
5. Use gates and stiles to cross fences, hedges and walls.
6. Leave livestock, crops and machinery alone.
7. Take your litter home.
8. Help to keep all water clean.
9. Protect wildlife, plants and trees.
10. Take special care on country roads.
11. Make no unnecessary noise.

Dogs

Many parts of the Way cross open farmland where sheep and cattle
are grazing and at some farms there are quite straightforward signs
like 'No dogs allowed'. Dogs can be a danger to livestock and
farmers whose animals are worried by walkers' dogs may,
understandably, withdraw their support for the Way.

Youth hostels don't allow dogs; some hotels and some houses
offering bed and breakfast accommodation will not take dogs
either.

The advice is clear – don't take dogs.

Bulls

Walkers may occasionally come across bulls beside the Way and as
long as they are accompanied by cows there should be no danger.

However, they are best avoided if they are very near the path or are moving towards you.

Grouse shooting

Some of the moors that the Way crosses are used for grouse shooting. The young grouse feed on fresh heather shoots so the moors are regularly burned to get rid of the older heather. This burning (called 'muirburn') is done in a planned manner early in the year, so some patches of the moor have new shoots while nearby patches have the older and bigger plants that give the birds the shelter they need when breeding.

The grouse-shooting season starts on 12 August (the so-called 'glorious twelfth') and from then until 10 December there may be shooting parties on the hills. Walkers should therefore be careful not to walk across the line of fire of the guns when shooting is in progress. The Guide mentions the moors where shooting may be taking place.

Adders

Adders may be seen on the moorlands and they should not be approached. These are Britain's only poisonous snakes but they will be more intent on getting away from your feet than attacking them. They are brown in colour and have a dark zigzag line down their backs (this is more pronounced on the male); they are about 60 cm or less in length. It is very rare for anyone to be bitten by an adder but if this should occur then the wound should be thoroughly cleaned as soon as possible; no tourniquet should be applied. Prompt medical attention should then be sought.

Part 3 The Guide

Section 1 Portpatrick to Castle Kennedy

Information

Start of section: At the north end of Portpatrick harbour
(NW997542).
End of section: On the A75 at the entrance to Castle Kennedy
Gardens (NX108598).
Distance: 21·5 km (13½ miles).
Stages:
1. Portpatrick.
2. Portpatrick to Killantringan lighthouse (3·5 km).
3. Killantringan lighthouse to Mulloch Hill (5·5 km).
4. Mulloch Hill to Ochtrelure (4 km).
5. Stranraer (off the Way).
6. Ochtrelure to Castle Kennedy (8·5 km).
7. Castle Kennedy.
Breaks in route:
1. At the A764 after Killantringan farm (to Portpatrick).
2. At the T-junction before Ochtrelure (to Stranraer).
3. At the A77 after Whiteleys farm (to Stranraer or Lochans).
Conditions: The section starts with a coastal walk along the cliffs to
Killantringan lighthouse. Special care should be taken on this
pleasant start to the Way as the path goes above the sea-cliffs
and these can be very dangerous if visibility is poor because of sea
mist.

Minor roads and tracks take the Way up through farmland on the
Rhins of Galloway. Then there is a short walk over open moorland
between Mulloch Hill and Knockquhassen farm; this may be boggy
and the route may be difficult to follow in poor visibility.

Minor roads and tracks take the Way to the village of Castle
Kennedy.
Points of interest: Portpatrick, Killantringan lighthouse, the view
from Mulloch Hill, Stranraer.

Maps:
1. Ordnance Survey no. 82.
2. Bartholomew no. 37.

Transport: See p. 55 for services to Portpatrick and Stranraer. Castle Kennedy is on the Dumfries–Stranraer bus route (see p. 55).

Car parking: At Portpatrick: around the harbour. On route: near Killantringan lighthouse, near Knockquhassen, on the track after the A77. At Castle Kennedy: beside the petrol station.

Accommodation: Portpatrick (various), Stranraer (off the Way; various), Lochans (off the Way), Meadowsweet (at Soulseat Loch, off the Way), Castle Kennedy (various).

Notes: This first section has a wide variety of interesting things to look at and it is a pleasant and (in good weather) straightforward start to the Way. There are no shops until Castle Kennedy.

Portpatrick

Portpatrick is a picturesque seaside village that is very popular with daytrippers during the summer. Its history goes back many centuries and it owes its importance to its connections with Ireland which is only 34 km across the North Channel. Indeed this distance is short enough, so the story goes, for St Patrick (after whom the village is named) to have crossed it in a single stride. On landing, he left a deep footprint in a rock.

Portpatrick's important position has meant that its prosperity has been intimately tied to the sea-borne traffic between the two countries. England's military involvement in Ireland led to the army's use of the crossing as far back as the time of Elizabeth I (1533–1603) and the names Barrack Street and Colonel Street are reminders of the village's military history. In 1662 a weekly mail

Portpatrick. Portpatrick Hotel stands above the harbour and the old lighthouse can be seen in the foreground. The Way starts behind the harbour, climbs some steps and then goes along the top of the cliffs seen on the left.

service was started and the harbour's first pier was built by the Post Office in 1774; a lighthouse was added in 1790. Trade developed in horses, linen, lime, coal and cotton. Passenger traffic also increased and for a time the village fulfilled the same role for the Irish as Gretna Green did for the English, as young Irish couples were able to get married in the village at very short notice. This facility wasn't cheap and in the late eighteenth century the local minister charged £10 for his duties.

The first substantial harbour was built south of the present north harbour and was enlarged in 1820. The rocky promontory between the north harbour and the old lighthouse is called McCook's Craig and it provided valuable shelter for the boats. There was meant to be a long pier to the north of this promontory, but this was never finished and its remains can be seen running seawards from the north harbour.

The introduction of the steam-powered ships that operated out of the larger west-coast ports hit Portpatrick's trade, but a new lease of life was given by the construction in 1862 of a railway line which ran from Stranraer; this was eventually closed in 1950. The railway service was linked with a ferry running between Portpatrick and the Irish port of Donaghadee which is near the mouth of Belfast Lough. The railway line's approach to Portpatrick can be seen in a cutting south of the village and a spur ran down to the north harbour.

The lighthouse at Portpatrick was built in the 1880s and replaced one which was dismantled and re-erected in Colombo in Sri Lanka. The lighthouse has been unused since 1900 when it was replaced by the one at Killantringan, which is north-west of Portpatrick (see later).

Many ships have foundered on the rocks along the coast and in June 1850 the *Orion* ran aground during a clear night and sank just a short distance from the harbour; a number of people survived, but about sixty perished. The lifeboat service in Portpatrick was inaugurated in 1877 and the old lifeboat house at the harbour is now a museum, open during the summer months. The present lifeboat is stationed in the harbour.

Many of the buildings in the village date back to the nineteenth century and many of these have some association with fishing or the sea trade. The cliff above the harbour is dominated by the Portpatrick Hotel, a rather fine building built in 1902–3 and enlarged only a few years later.

The ruins of Portpatrick Old Parish Kirk stand behind the sea-front houses and to the west of Main Street. It was cruciform in shape and a gable-end has the date 1629 inscribed on it. Its most noticeable feature is a four-storey circular tower which may have been both a belfry and a beacon for the harbour. The tower, which has walls about 1 m thick, was probably built later than the rest of the church and it has a steeply sloping slate roof topped by a slender spire. The graveyard has the remains of many who died at sea, including those who lost their lives when the *Orion* sank.

The most historic building in the district is the sixteenth-century Dunskey Castle. It is reached by walking southwards along the coastal road and then climbing a steep flight of steps on the left; the castle is about 1 km from there. It stands on a rocky promontory and was built about 1510 on the site of a previous fortification; it was ruinous in 1684. It is in a very strong position and was protected by steep sea-cliffs on three sides, while on the fourth was a deep ravine about 15 m wide.

Portpatrick has many hotels, houses offering bed and breakfast accommodation, eating establishments and shops. There are public toilets at the northern end of the harbour, near the start of the Way. A public telephone box is situated behind the harbour, near the putting green. There are three campsites at Portpatrick and they are on the road that goes south-east from the A77 at The Old Mill House Restaurant.

Portpatrick to Killantringan lighthouse (3·5 km)

Portpatrick to Port Mora (1·5 km)
The Way starts its long journey to Cockburnspath from the Way notice-board behind the north harbour. Walk through a children's play area, past a tall waymarker and up the flight of concrete steps at the side of the cliff. There is now a wide view over Portpatrick

and down the coast towards the cliffs on the Mull of Galloway. In good visibility the 195 m high chimney at Kilroot Power Station near Carrickfergus in Ireland can be seen 50 km to the south-west. The Mull of Kintyre, the southern tip of the long peninsula of Kintyre, is about 65 km to the north-west.

The path turns away from the Portpatrick Hotel and runs above the steep greywacke sea-cliffs which are home to numerous sea-birds including fulmars and gannets. Pass to the left of the British Telecom radio station; this dates back to 1905 and was originally manned by the Royal Navy. The station keeps a continuous watch on the international radio distress frequencies for SOS and Mayday calls. Should a distress call be received, the station will transmit a message to all shipping in the area so that they may give assistance. The station's day-to-day work is sending and receiving telegrams and making telephone calls, with ships at sea. Weather forecasts and other shipping information is broadcast at frequent intervals. The station has four aerials nearly 40 m high.

A flight of steps takes the Way on to the road behind the radio station; turn left and walk to the left of Dunskey Golf Course. On the seaward side of the road is a building that belongs to the Royal Aircraft Establishment and which is used in the testing of sonar equipment. The road ends here, so continue on the well-used path that skirts the golf course. About 3 km to the east is a tall metal gantry with a large number of dish aerials. This is Enoch Hill Radio Station and it is associated with a microwave communications link with Northern Ireland. This gantry is a useful landmark to note as it helps in route finding later on. Pass to the left of the British Telecom aerials that are on Cove Hill.

The stretch between Cove Hill and Killantringan lighthouse can be good for butterflies, particularly on fine days in mid- and late summer. Grayling is a local speciality in some of the rockier places.

After passing Cove Hill, Dunskey House can be seen in the woods to the north-east. The building was started in the seventeenth century and was finished in 1706, though there have been extensive alterations since then. The path now descends to the little bay of Port Mora ('Moran's landing place'), known locally as Sandeel Bay. Just before the beach is reached, the Way passes two caves and a waterfall can be seen falling over the entrance to the second cave (the Cave of Uchtriemacken). The stream that falls over the cliff was once believed to have healing powers and up until 1791 people would bring the ill to be bathed in the water on the first night in May. In those days it was thought that children suffering from rickets had been bewitched so they were brought to the stream for a cure.

Port Mora to Killantringan lighthouse (2 km)

Cross the beach and follow a path for a few metres before turning sharp left. Climb some stone steps up the side of Islay Knoll in order to gain some height above the sea. The next bay is Port Kale, known locally as Dunskey Bay or Laird's Bay. This has a shingle beach behind which there is a tall post marking where a telephone cable leaves the shore and goes over to Northern Ireland. The cable is no longer used and the modern cables come ashore at Port Mora. The first cable was laid in 1854 and the Victorian cable house is nearby. This unusual little structure is made up of two small hexagonal buildings joined together.

Cross the wooden bridge over Dunskey Burn and turn left at the foot of the cliffs. Keep to the top of the storm beach and go through a gap behind the enormous chunks of rock that have broken off the main cliff, then follow the narrow path that leads over a jumble of boulders. There is now a very steep climb up the cliff on the right and this needs care, especially in wet conditions; chains have been provided in two places to hold on to. Cross a fence at a stile and pass a notice requesting walkers to keep to the marked path. This is not just for the sake of the livestock but also to keep walkers away from the sea-cliffs which can be very dangerous, especially in poor visibility.

Killantringan lighthouse is the next important landmark to be seen ahead. The path descends to a stile and a narrow sandy path then runs to the left of a dyke; follow the dyke as it heads towards the sea and then towards the lighthouse. The bay of Portmaggie lies below the lighthouse and in it is the wreck of the *Craigantlet*. This container ship, which was owned by a German-based company, ran aground on 26 February 1982 after following the wrong course on its

night-time journey from Belfast Lough to Liverpool. The ship broke its back and was stranded on the rocks but her crew of eleven were all lifted out of danger by helicopter. However, the cargo of containers began to break up and a toxic chemical, methyl sulphate, escaped into the sea. Because of the danger, the area around the wreck was cordoned off by the police and the families living in the lighthouse were evacuated for a few weeks. Many of those who worked on the difficult salvage operation had to undergo a decontamination process at the hospital in Stranraer.

Continue following the dyke and pass to the left of a knoll. The path then meets a tall waymarker at the road to the lighthouse. Turn right at the road.

The 60 m high lighthouse was opened in 1900 and replaced the one at Portpatrick. Its light emits two flashes every fifteen seconds and this signal can be seen about 34 km away.

Killantringan lighthouse to Mulloch Hill (5·5 km)

The road heads northwards towards the very fine line of cliffs at the back of Killantringan Bay and Knock Bay. The headlands are made of hard rocks such as greywacke, while the softer rocks have been cut back by the sea. The House of Knock is the prominent building above the cliffs. Continue on the road as it heads inland and through pleasant pastures; Killantringan farm is passed on the left. The A764 is met at a tall waymarker and a signpost with 'Killantringan lighthouse 1½ miles' on it.

Turn left (a right turn leads to Portpatrick) and follow the road for about 400 m before turning right at a minor road. A standing stone can be seen in the field on the left. The road soon gains height and there are good views over to Ireland and the Mull of Kintyre. The local landscape is one of rolling hills that were smoothed by the passage of ice over them. Keep on the road as it bends to the right and passes to the left of the farm of Knock and Maize.

Turn right at a track (signposted to High Auchenree and Knock)

Looking towards Killantringan lighthouse.

about 500 m after the farm. Walk to the left of some abandoned farm buildings and pass an accommodation leaflet box. Continue uphill on a track that soon peters out, then bear left to reach the summit of Mulloch Hill (164 m) where there is a cairn that was specially built for the Way.

The view from Mulloch Hill

The hill gives a superb view in all directions, especially to the north and north-east, and many important landmarks can be picked out.

To the north-east are the Galloway hills; the highest of these is The Merrick which is about 45 km away. These hills will be reached during Section 4 when the Way goes through Glen Trool.

To the north is Loch Ryan, and the pier at what was a ship-breaker's yard at the village of Cairnryan can be seen. Loch Ryan has been an important base for shipping from at least the time of the Romans, who called it Rerigonius Sinus. For centuries, sailors dropped anchor near the quiet little village, but the district was transformed during the Second World War when a large harbour was built for landing supplies from America. Convoys of ships gathered in the shelter of the loch and many of them were protected on their Atlantic crossings by two squadrons of flying boats based at Stranraer. The loch was also one of the sites where sections of the Mulberry Harbour were built; this was the transportable harbour used during the Normandy landings in France in June 1944. After the war, Cairnryan was the point of departure of warships that were taken out into deep waters to be scuttled. About 1 km south of Cairnryan's long pier is a ferry terminal from which ferries sail to Larne.

The loch has provided good fishing for whitefish and oysters. Oyster-fishing rights were mentioned in a 1701 charter and their exploitation goes back at least 6,000 years – a mesolithic 'oyster midden' has been found beneath the streets of Stranraer.

Loch Ryan and Luce Bay (which is to the south-east of Loch Ryan) were joined at the end of the Ice Age, making the land to the west of them a narrow island; this is now known as the Rhins (headland). The land slowly rose once the great burden of ice was lifted and 'raised beaches' were formed in the area between Loch

Ryan and Luce Bay. The eastern shore of the loch also has raised beaches and there are many old sea caves well above the present sea-level.

The island of Ailsa Craig is due north of Mulloch Hill and from this direction it has a distinct pointed shape. Ailsa Craig is one of Scotland's best-known landmarks because of its prominent position in the middle of the west-coast shipping lane and many Scots refer to it as Paddy's Milestone as it lies half-way between Ireland and Clydeside. The Irish give it the name of Brian's Stone, after the Irish King Brian Boru (926–1014), and there is also the tale that the island owes its existence to having fallen through a hole in the apron of Cailleach Bheur, the Irish goddess who was carrying the rocks with which she was building the new land of Caledonia.

The island, which is the remnant of the base of a volcanic 'vent', is composed of a very fine-grained microgranite and this rock has been quarried for making curling stones. The rock contains the unusual mineral riebeckite, which is a speckled bluish-grey colour, and geologists have been able to make great use of its rarity in tracing the movement of Ice Age glaciers. A powerful flow of ice followed the course of the present-day Firth of Clyde and travelled southwards into the Irish Sea. The ice pulverised the rocks over which it moved and carried sand, gravel and boulders over huge distances. This material was dumped when the ice melted and from the location of boulders (called 'erratics') containing riebeckite in various places along the shores of the Irish Sea, it has been possible to trace the route taken by the glacier.

Tens of thousands of gannets nest on Ailsa Craig. They are often seen at sea off Killantringan and Portpatrick.

About 6 km to the north of Mulloch Hill is the hill known as the Tor of Craigoch (125 m), on top of which is a monument erected in 1850 to Sir Andrew Agnew (1793–1849). In 1830 he was unanimously (!) elected Member of Parliament for the county of Wigtownshire after his opponent withdrew at the last moment. At the time of the election, Wigtownshire had a population of 35,000 but only seventy people had the vote and the *Dumfries Courier* reported that 'thirty-five [of the seventy electors] have neither property nor residence in the county'. In 1832 he promoted a Bill that would have prohibited all work on Sundays, except in cases of necessity and mercy. His Bill was introduced on four occasions, the last time successfully, but it failed to become law due to the dissolution of Parliament caused by the death of King William IV in 1837.

Behind the monument are the hills of the island of Arran; the highest peak is Goatfell (874 m).

Mulloch Hill to Ochtrelure (4 km)

Mulloch Hill to Knockquhassen (1 km)
Knockquhassen farm is at the eastern end of Knockquhassen Reservoir. The Way will be passing well to the right of the farm and the route near the reservoir crosses boggy moorland on a path that may be indistinct.

Turn right at the cairn on Mulloch Hill, head towards the microwave aerials on Enoch Hill and cross a fence at a stile. Turn left, cross another fence and bear right; the Way now heads eastwards over boggy ground to a little knoll. It may be preferable to gain the higher ground on the right in order to avoid the wettest places. The path becomes more distinct and rather drier after the knoll and the Way heads north of east in order to meet the reservoir's perimeter fence which should now be followed.

The path gets close to the reservoir and then bears right to a stile over another fence. Bear to the left, taking care to use a little bridge to cross a deep ditch. Pass to the left of a small quarry and turn right at a waymarker at the track that goes to the reservoir and Knockquhassen farm; the farm is seen on the left.

Loch Ryan and the Princess Victoria
There is now a good view over Loch Ryan and to the ferry terminal near Cairnryan. The loch can be very busy and ferries and other ships will be seen sailing up and down it. The loch's sheltered position and its nearness to Ireland are its two major advantages as a base for the ferries that operate out of Stranraer and Cairnryan. With the late eighteenth century's development of the railway

network and the use of large ships on the Scotland–Ireland sea crossing, Stranraer became the major port in the area. The Stranraer–Larne service was established and in 1891 the *Princess Victoria* made her first mail packet crossing. The sea was so bad on her first trip that all the other boats were forced to remain in port.

Sixty-two years later a new *Princess Victoria* was engaged on the crossing that was then operated by British Railways. On 31 January 1953 the ship set out in stormy conditions and all seemed to be well until the shelter of Loch Ryan was left behind. Then the ship became unmanageable and distress signals were sent out. She slowly drifted towards the Irish coast and listed badly before sinking 10 km from Donaghadee. Although lifeboats, a naval destroyer and numerous other boats came to the aid of the passengers and crew, 133 people were lost, twenty-three of them from Stranraer. The Irish Sea was not the only part of the British Isles to be affected that dreadful night as the weather caused havoc in places as far apart as Banff (where the gasworks was swept into the sea), Loch Broom (where twenty-seven ships were driven ashore) and the south-east of England (where 125 people lost their lives in various incidents).

Knockquhassen to Ochtrelure (2 km)

The road generally heads in an easterly direction and there is soon a view over to Luce Bay which is to the south-east. The low-lying land between Loch Ryan and Luce Bay is only 20–30 m above sea-level and on it are many small round hills. These 'drumlins' are made of boulder clay, not solid rock, and were formed when glaciers moved over the land; they are generally highest and steepest at the end that faced the advancing ice. A landscape in which there are many drumlins is described as having a 'basket of eggs topography'.

To the south-east can be seen the hangars of the Royal Aircraft Establishment's airfield at West Freuch. The airfield was opened during the First World War as a base for the airships that patrolled shipping lanes on the look-out for enemy submarines.

Turn to the right at the T-junction at Hillside Piggeries and turn left 300 m later on to the old military road that connected Stranraer and Portpatrick. Portpatrick was once an important embarkation point for soldiers on their way to Ireland and a military road was built from near Gretna to Portpatrick via Dumfries, Castle Douglas, Newton Stewart, Glenluce, Castle Kennedy and Stranraer. This particular part went along Old Port Patrick Road until it joined the present A77 and entered Portpatrick.

At the next junction (300 m farther on) there is a good view of Stranraer. The Way now turns right (and past the farm of Ochtrelure) but walkers wanting to visit Stranraer should continue heading north-east towards the town.

Stranraer (off the Way)

The road down to Stranraer gives a superb view over the whole town. A major crossroads is met about 1·5 km after leaving the Way; go straight ahead and walk down High Street and George Street into the centre of the town. This road eventually leads to the ferry terminal and the Tourist Information Centre. Stranraer is the district's biggest town and it has all the facilities (including a railway station) needed by the walker. The campsite is on London Road, to the south-east of the ferry terminal.

Stranraer was created a burgh in 1596 and the rich agricultural land around it and its sheltered position in Loch Ryan have been important factors in its growth. The beginning of Stranraer's real prosperity can perhaps be taken as 1860 when the first steam locomotive arrived: this allowed the ferry service to Larne to develop into its present-day importance to the town's economy. The ferries operate around the clock with about half a dozen return sailings each day.

The Old Town Hall (now the local museum) is at 55 George Street; the building was opened in 1791 and added to in 1820. It bears the town's insignia and the motto '*Tutissima statio*' ('Safest harbour'). The building is topped by a clock tower and a weathercock. There are some interesting nineteenth-century hotels nearby.

Stranraer Castle is met farther down George Street. It was built by Adair of Kinhilt around 1500 and came into the possession of the Kennedy family in 1590. For a while after 1682 it was the headquarters of John Graham of Claverhouse, or 'Bloody Clavers' as he was known during the 'Killing Times'. It was originally built with three storeys; the top storey was added in 1820 and then the castle contained a courtroom, cells and an exercise yard at parapet level. The very thick walls contain a network of passages.

Very near the castle is an elaborately designed cast-iron drinking-well bearing the words: 'Erected by the town council in commemoration of Queen Victoria's record reign 1897.' The town's insignia are also portrayed as well as a piece of advice to thirsty people: 'Keep the pavement dry.'

Just opposite the ferry terminal is the North West Castle Hotel, an elaborate building of 1820 that was the home of Rear-Admiral Sir John Ross (1777–1856). Its name celebrates his search for the 'north-west passage', the long-sought-for sea route through the Arctic waters north of Canada. Some of his exploits in the far north were described in his book *Narrative of a Second Voyage in search of a North-West Passage, including the discovery of the North Magnetic Pole* (1835).

To the west of the ferry terminal is a harbour and beyond that is Agnew Park which has a memorial cairn dedicated to those who died when the *Princess Victoria* sank.

Ochtrelure to Castle Kennedy (8·5 km)

Ochtrelure to the A77 (2·5 km)

The Way passes to the left of the farm of Ochtrelure and follows a straight minor road that gives a good view over the low-lying ground on the left. The large wooded area around Castle Kennedy can be seen about 6 km away to the north-east; the Way will be going through this at the start of the next section. The road bends to the left and at the next bend (which is to the right) continue north-eastwards by taking a path (on the left) that runs down to the house of Lee Nook.

Turn right at the road and 600 m later bear left when the road bends to the right. The route of the dismantled Stranraer–Portpatrick railway line is crossed 300 m later and then the road passes the large farm of Whiteleys before meeting the A77 (Glasgow–Stranraer–Portpatrick). The hamlet of Lochans (which has a hotel) is 1·5 km to the right.

The A77 to Loch Magillie (4·5 km)

Turn left at a tall waymarker to walk along the A77 towards Stranraer and then turn right at a track after 100 m. The track passes to the left of a Nissen hut. These buildings are becoming rare now, but during the Second World War thousands of them were dotted around the countryside and used as shelters for soldiers and equipment. The huts are easily erected as they are made from corrugated-iron sections that are bolted together; this one has a protective outer layer of concrete for extra protection against air attack. Some brick and concrete gun emplacements are soon seen on both sides of the track. These date back to the Second World War too and they housed anti-aircraft guns that protected the ships anchored in Loch Ryan.

Turn right when a road is met, then left 150 m later at a narrow farm road and pass a bungalow and some farm buildings. The road heads towards the farm of Culhorn Mains, but turn left at a T-junction and walk along the track that skirts the little wood of birches and conifers on the right. Turn into the wood about 350 m after the T-junction.

Culhorn Loch is passed on the left but this small sheet of water is generally obscured by the trees around it. The next wood that is walked through has many mature trees, a great number of which are heavily overgrown with ivy; this is less noticeable in the summer when there is more foliage on the trees.

The track ends at a little gatehouse at a minor road (another part of the old military road). Turn right at the tall waymarker and pass an unmanned railway crossing on the Glasgow–Ayr– Stranraer line.

The road ends at a T-junction beside a railway bridge; the Way turns left and under the bridge, but on the right can be seen Loch Magillie. Just beyond this loch is Soulseat Loch. Soulseat Abbey once stood on a promontory on the south-western shore of this loch. It was founded before *c.* 1150 by Fergus, Lord of Galloway for

Premonstratensian monks and it was a ruin by 1684. This was the order's first establishment in Scotland and it was the 'mother' abbey of the more famous priory at Whithorn. The site is now occupied by a house called Meadowsweet which offers bed and breakfast accommodation. The house has a walled garden that once belonged to the abbey and the Meadowsweet Herb Garden is open to the public during the summer.

Loch Magillie to Castle Kennedy village (1·5 km)

After passing under the railway bridge and walking a few tens of metres, take a stile on the right on to a narrow path that runs parallel to the railway line. The Way goes through a little wood with numerous conifers, beeches and brambles and the path ends at a stile near some houses in Castle Kennedy village. Continue walking straight ahead and pass between an oil distribution depot and Castle Kennedy School. Turn left at a T-junction where the house on the left is called Old Toll Cottage.

Pass to the left of a petrol station and the section ends when the A75 is met. This junction is opposite the entrance to Castle Kennedy Gardens (which are not signposted outside the tourist season). The A75 connects Stranraer to the A74 (Glasgow–Carlisle) and there are always huge lorries on the road going to or coming from the ferries.

Castle Kennedy

The village is called after the castle of the same name which is passed during the next section. The oldest houses in Castle Kennedy village are found to the south of Old Toll Cottage; these are few in number and most of the houses are quite modern. There are few facilities in the village – just a general store/post office, beside which is a public telephone box. There are no public toilets nearby.

The general store can be reached from where the Way meets the village or from the petrol station. From where the houses are first met, turn left instead of going past the school and follow this road;

from the petrol station, walk towards Stranraer and take the first turning on the left.

The Eynhallow Hotel is on the A75, just 600 m south-east of the petrol station. Bed and breakfast accommodation is available at Serendipity Cottage; this is the last house along the road that runs southwards from the petrol station. There is a small café at Castle Kennedy Gardens (see p. 85).

Section 2 Castle Kennedy to New Luce

Information

Start of section: On the A75 at the entrance to Castle Kennedy Gardens (NX108598).

Diversion: It was originally intended that this section would end at a point 2 km east of New Luce. The original route went from Glenwhan Moor to the waterfall known as the Loups of Barnshangan; this route was to the south of New Luce and passed Cruise farm and Kilhern. This route would have crossed the railway line that is to the west of Cruise but as a bridge has not yet been built, the Way has been diverted along the Castle Kennedy–New Luce road and the section now ends at New Luce.

Walkers following the present route (i.e. the diversion) should follow the instructions given in the stage entitled 'Glenwhan Moor to New Luce' but when the bridge has been built the instructions in 'Glenwhan Moor to Cruise' and 'Cruise to the Loups of Barnshangan' can be followed. The section will then end 2 km east of New Luce – which is not at all convenient for accommodation.

There are notice-boards at various points on the route that explain the diversion; their locations are mentioned in the text. If walkers find no notice-boards at these locations then they can assume that the bridge over the railway line has been built and that the original route can be followed.

End of section:
1. At the junction of a track and the road heading east from New Luce (near the Loups of Barnshangan) (NX191650) (original route) or
2. At the village hall in New Luce (NX175645) (via the diversion).

Distance: 15·5 km (9½ miles) to the Loups of Barnshangan (original route) or 9·5 km (6 miles) to New Luce (via the diversion).

Stages:
1. Castle Kennedy village to Glenwhan Moor (4·5 km).
2. Glenwhan Moor to Cruise (original route) (6·5 km).
3. Cruise to the Loups of Barnshangan (original route) (4·5 km).
4. Glenwhan Moor to New Luce (diversion) (5 km).
5. New Luce.
6. Glenluce (off the Way).

Breaks in route:

1. Glenwhan Moor (to New Luce).
2. Cruise (to New Luce or Glenluce).

Conditions: This section is quite fast as the present (i.e. diverted) route follows a road for a few kilometres. This allows enough time for a visit to Castle Kennedy Gardens.

The original route via Cruise is longer and is over more difficult terrain so it is much slower.

The moorland between Cruise and Kilhern is very open and may be boggy after heavy rain.

Points of interest: Castle Kennedy and Castle Kennedy Gardens, Caves of Kilhern, Glenluce Abbey (off the Way).

Maps:

1. Ordnance Survey no. 82.
2. Bartholomew no. 37.

Transport: There is a bus service between Stranraer and New Luce. Glenluce is on the Dumfries–Stranraer bus route (see p. 55).

Car parking: On route: at Castle Kennedy Gardens, at the start of Glenwhan Moor. At the Loups of Barshangan: at the side of the narrow road. At New Luce: at the village hall.

Accommodation: Milton of Larg, New Luce (various), Galdenoch farm, Glenluce (off the Way; various).

Notes: Some walkers may want to start Section 3 immediately after reaching New Luce or the Loups of Barnshangan and perhaps stop at Derry. However, the moorland before Derry is very exposed and it should not be tackled late in the day, especially if the weather is poor. The beginning of Glenwhan Moor is taken to be at the junction of a road and a track at NX141619. There are no shops until New Luce.

Castle Kennedy village to Glenwhan Moor (4·5 km)

Castle Kennedy village to Castle Kennedy Gardens (1 km)
This section starts at the A75, beside a petrol station and opposite the entrance to Castle Kennedy Gardens; cross the road and walk along the straight driveway towards the gardens. A stone gatehouse

at the roadside is painted in estate colours and has some interesting woodwork on its front. The driveway is flanked by some fine mature trees and many rhododendron bushes. The White Loch lies ahead and the ruin of Castle Kennedy can be seen near the eastern side of the loch; the castle is described below.

Once the loch has been reached, Lochinch Castle can be seen in the parkland on the northern shore. This castle was completed in 1867 to replace Castle Kennedy which was accidentally burned down in 1716. It is built in Scottish Baronial style and is situated in a commanding position overlooking the White Loch; it is not open to the public.

The White Loch (also known as the Loch of Inch) is in an attractive wooded setting. No streams flow into the loch but it is connected to the Black Loch (which is less than 1 km farther along the Way) by a canal. The thickly wooded island of Inch Crindil can be seen near the western shore of the loch, and on the shore (just to the left of the island) are the ruins of the old Inch Church. It dates from the end of the seventeenth century and the adjacent graveyard has gravestones from around that time. Greylag geese and Canada geese may be seen (and heard) at the northern end of the loch. Tufted ducks, mallard and teal frequent both lochs.

The lochside road leads to the gate to Castle Kennedy Gardens where the Way turns right.

Castle Kennedy Gardens and Castle Kennedy
The road to the gardens and the castle goes to the left, through the wrought-iron gates, and crosses a little bridge over the canal that joins the two lochs. The ticket office (and a café) at the gardens' entrance is a little farther on and the castle can be seen from there. The gardens are very extensive and are worth visiting. They were built by the second Earl of Stair (1673–1747) who was the British ambassador to France from 1715 to 1720 and his idea for the gardens' design was inspired by Versailles. The gardens are arranged on a series of terraces and the great amount of earth-moving that was necessary to create the new landscape was done by soldiers of the Royal Scots Greys and the Inniskilling Fusiliers – who were meant to be chasing Covenanters at the time!

As well as colourful trees, shrubs and flowers, there are features such as a sunken garden, a large circular lily pond and an avenue of tall monkey-puzzle trees. The rhododendrons and azaleas are particularly beautiful.

The main part of Castle Kennedy is a roofless four-storey ruin with two wings. The entrance is very small (for easy defence) and it faces the gardens' ticket office. Two narrow towers that were once seven storeys high stand behind the main building and the two three-storey buildings at the side are later additions. There are few architectural embellishments though there is a nice dormer window and pedestal on the north side of the building, and some circular gun holes can be seen in the walls.

The lands around the castle came into the hands of the powerful Kennedy family in 1482, and in 1607 the fifth Earl of Cassillis started building the castle on what was then an island. The family's support for the Covenant led them to lose their lands and in about 1677 the estate was taken over by Sir James Dalrymple (1619–95) who in 1690 became Viscount Stair. In 1641, while serving in the army, he became a professor at Glasgow University but later left both the army and the university to practise law. In 1657, during Cromwell's Commonwealth, he became a judge of the reformed Court of Session and after the Restoration (the accession of Charles II in 1660) he became immersed in the affairs of state. During the time of the Covenant he attempted to counter what he saw as the excesses of the government in harrying the Covenanters and in 1684 he left Scotland as a precaution against arrest. He returned home in 1688 with William of Orange (later William III) and once again took a role in British politics.

His son, John Dalrymple (1648–1707), was created the first Earl of Stair in 1703 and he is remembered in Scotland for the part he played in the Massacre of Glencoe when he held the office of Secretary of State. The story of the massacre is one of Scotland's saddest tales. William III was then on the throne and he and his lieutenants in Scotland were determined to subdue the recalcitrant Highlanders. The clan chiefs were ordered to take an oath of

Castle Kennedy.

allegiance to the throne before 1 January 1692 and MacDonald of
Glencoe's lateness in giving his word was used as an excuse to teach
the Highlanders a lesson. A party of government troops was
quartered with the MacDonalds and on the night of 13 February the
soldiers turned on their guests and thirty-eight people were put to
death. The fact that many of the soldiers were Campbells fuelled
the animosity that already existed between the two clans.

It was John Dalrymple's son (the second Earl of Stair) who laid
out the gardens.

Castle Kennedy Gardens to Glenwhan Moor (3·5 km)
The Way climbs away from the gardens' gate and passes to the left
of a pair of charming little cottages. There is now a view over the
Black Loch, also known as Loch Crindil. The well-wooded Heron
Isle was adopted by herons after their favourite trees on Inch
Crindil were felled in 1821. This island contains the remains of an
Iron Age crannog which was investigated in 1870–1 and a series of
pointed wooden stakes were found in the water around the crannog.
The central part of the structure had a wooden floor about 15 m in
diameter.

Continue along the track, passing to the right of an old water
tower, until the Castle Kennedy village–New Luce road is met; turn
left.

On the other side of the road can be seen Cults Loch, a rather
small sheet of water surrounded by fields. A crannog built on stones
was investigated near its western shore in 1872 and a number of
stakes were found along the shore. To the right of the loch are
buildings that were associated with the airfield that was once there,
and farther along the road (towards Castle Kennedy) there are large
aircraft hangars that are now used for storage and industrial
purposes.

As the road heads towards the north-east, the slopes below the
wooded hills ahead would have been sea-cliffs at the time when the
land around Castle Kennedy was under the sea and the Rhins of
Galloway was an island. After following the road for about 700 m,
the Way turns right at a tall waymarker and passes in front of
Balnab. Join another track that comes down from the left and cross

the Chlenry Burn in front of the farm of Chlenry. Go through the gate that is in front and follow the track past the farm buildings. Pass to the right of a conifer wood and bear right when the track divides just before two gates. Follow the dyke that is on the left. The view to the south-west now opens out; Cults Loch lies in the low ground and beyond it are the moorlands on the Rhins of Galloway that were crossed in Section 1.

Turn left at a gate just before the end of the field, then turn right to go over a stile. Follow a track as it runs beside a dyke and leads to a tall waymarker and a stile at a gate beside the Castle Kennedy–New Luce road. Turn right and follow the road uphill. After about 600 m there is a tall waymarker at a large lay-by on the right.

This is the beginning of Glenwhan Moor and there are two routes from this point; see 'Diversion' on p. 30. A notice at the lay-by explains the diversion.

Glenwhan Moor to Cruise (6·5 km) (original route)

Glenwhan Moor to Craig Fell (4 km)
Cross the stile at the gate, follow the track over the moorland and enter the forest on Glenwhan Moor. The next 3 km of forest track passes through the highest diversity of conifer species seen on the Way. Lodgepole pine, Sitka spruce, Corsican pine, Scots pine, larch and Norway spruce are all nearby. Turn right at a waymarker and follow a fire-break. About 450 m later a tall waymarker is met at the edge of the forest and at a point 400 m south of Craig Fell (164 m).

The view from Craig Fell
There is now a fine view towards Luce Bay; Glenluce Abbey and Castle of Park can be seen 2·5 km and 4 km respectively down the Water of Luce. Glenluce Abbey was founded about 1190 as a Cistercian monastery. In the sixteenth century the Earl of Cassillis took advantage of the Church's threatened position and gained possession of the abbey. To do this, he persuaded a monk to forge a lease of the abbey, complete with the signature of the previous

abbot. To safeguard his position, the Earl hired an assassin called Carnochan to kill the monk and then got this fellow hanged for his evil deed – such was life in those troubled times!

The abbey's church was cruciform in shape and had other buildings joined on to it so that the whole group enclosed an open space known as a 'cloister'. The best-preserved part of the abbey is the chapter house, which has a fine vaulted ceiling. Some walls and parts of later buildings are still standing and the site has been in the care of the State since 1933.

There is a small museum beside the abbey where tickets and a guide to the abbey are available.

Castle of Park was started in 1590 and it is a fine example of a tower house. It is an L-shaped structure and its builder, Thomas Hay, pulled down parts of Glenluce Abbey in order to obtain suitable building stones.

Craig Fell to the railway line (1·5 km)
Turn left and follow another fire-break; keep to the right of a dyke for 250 m then turn right at a waymarker and go through a narrow fire-break between the larches. The summit of Craig Fell is out of sight on the right. The Way then crosses two narrow fire-breaks and a left turn is taken in order to make a steep descent on a path that winds its way through the trees. A wide path is then met a short distance from the railway line. Turn left and walk parallel to the line.

Cross the attractive Craig Burn at a wooden bridge, go over a little wooded hill which has a great jumble of mossy boulders on it and bear right to walk near the railway line. Bear left after passing a little brick building, then follow a track and cross a stile over the fence on the right. Go through a gap in a broken-down dyke and walk through the very pleasant Airyolland Wood. Cross a stile at a gate to enter a field and the bridge over the railway line should (when it is built) be on the right.

The railway line to Cruise (1 km)
Bear right after crossing the railway line and head across the field to reach the bridge over the Water of Luce. The first part of the field is

an old terrace formed when a river cut into sediment dumped by a previous river. Cross the wooden suspension bridge (the Huftanny Bridge) which was built specially for the Way. A plaque on it records that it was constructed by 33 (Indep) Field Squadron, a group of Royal Engineers based at Antrim in Northern Ireland. The bridge's unusual name came from the soldiers who built it. During the work, they were often visited by their Squadron Sergeant Major who insisted that the men were correctly dressed at all times – including the wearing of berets. After his departure, they continued to wear head-dress, but substituted 'funny hats' for berets. The bridge's name is an anagram of 'Funny Hat Bridge'!

Walk under an electrical transmission line and cross a stile near the left-hand side of the trees that are ahead. Cross a stream and walk up the side of a field to the stile at the road that runs between New Luce (2 km to the north) and Glenluce (6 km to the south). At present, a notice at the stile informs that the route across the railway line is closed.

Galdenoch farm, which is only 500 m to the south, offers bed and breakfast accommodation.

Head northwards on the road and walk 250 m to Cruise farm.

Cruise to the Loups of Barnshangan (4·5 km) (original route)

Cruise to Kilhern (3 km)

Across the road from Cruise farm is a track at the beginning of which is a stile, a tall waymarker and a notice explaining the local diversion. The track climbs towards the farm's upper fields and leads to a stile; cross this and follow the dyke on the left. After the next stile, take the track that runs straight ahead. The ground on this part of the moor can be very wet so progress might be slow, especially if it has been raining recently.

The farmland and green fields are now left behind as the straight track crosses the bare and exposed moor; this is a very pleasant walk. The moor has little shelter and few signs of recent habitation, though one old ruined building is seen on the left near two trees. Kilhern Moss stretches away to the right and it rises to 205 m at

Bught Fell. This hill has many remains of old structures dotted around it including cairns, hut circles (the huts were about 4 m in diameter) and numerous walls. Some of the walls may be what is left of 'bughts' or small pens into which ewes were driven to be milked; hence the name of the hill.

Soon the abandoned farmhouse of Kilhern can be seen ahead. A stile is crossed and a track on the right should be ignored. The farmhouse at Kilhern is abandoned but it is still surrounded by numerous drystane dykes that have stood the test of time.

Kilhern to the Loups of Barnshangan (1·5 km)

Turn left at the farmhouse in order to walk to the left of the building and then follow a track that runs between two drystane dykes. Cross a stile to the left of some sheep enclosures and pass a little greywacke quarry before ascending to another stile.

Before crossing this stile, some walkers may wish to visit the ancient and very interesting burial cairn known as the Caves of Kilhern. Look north-east along the dyke that is to be crossed: about 400 m away (and very close to the dyke) there is a small rise on which can be seen some large boulders. There are four main graves in the cairn, the most prominent one being on the northern side. The walls of its body-size compartment were built with large flat stones and it was topped by the massive cap-stone that is still in place. The three other main graves have similar compartments and there are a few other prominent stones which may also have been associated with burials. The cairn was undoubtedly much larger than it is now as many of its large stones were probably used by farmers who were more concerned with obtaining building material than conserving Scotland's archaeological heritage.

After crossing the stile near the Caves of Kilhern, follow the track and cross a stile at a gate on the right. Descend the hill, passing to the right of a little conifer wood. The Cross Water of Luce can be seen ahead, and to the right of it is the minor road along which the Way will soon go. The track runs downhill and meets this road at a tall waymarker and a notice giving details about the local diversion.

Kilhern. This lonely abandoned farmhouse stands on an open, windswept moor.

The waterfall known as the Loups of Barnshangan may be heard nearby and it is described on p. 102.

The Way now turns right to begin Section 3, but those walkers seeking sustenance or accommodation at New Luce or Glenluce should turn left. New Luce is 2 km away and Glenluce is 10 km away.

Glenwhan Moor to New Luce (5 km) (diversion)

Glenwhan Moor to Milton of Larg (3 km)

Continue on the Castle Kennedy–New Luce road. Soon there is a view over the moorlands to the Galloway hills; Glen Trool lies to the right of the highest hills that can be seen. About 800 m after the start of the diversion there is a milestone on the left with 'N2' and 'S7' written on it, informing that this point is 2 miles from New Luce and 7 miles from Stranraer.

The standing stones of Glenterrow are near this milestone and walkers who wish to visit them should go through the gate on the left just before the milestone. Then bear left, heading to the left of a large conifer plantation. The stones are found on a broad grassy rise and are about 200 m from the gate. The stones (four of them near each other and one just a little distance away) are about 50 cm high and they may be the remains of a double concentric stone circle.

The road passes to the right of the disused farm buildings at Auchmantle. After another milestone (with 'N1' and 'S8' on it) are the deserted Milton Cottages, from which it is possible to see the route taken by the Way between Cruise and Kilhern (see p. 91). The farm of Cruise is about 1·5 km away to the south-east. The Way climbs the moors to the east of Cruise and passes the abandoned farmhouse of Kilhern which can be seen 4 km away to the east.

The road to the farm of Milton of Larg (which offers bed and breakfast accommodation) is then passed.

The Caves of Kilhern, an ancient burial site on the open moorland.

Milton of Larg to New Luce (2 km)

About 250 m after Milton of Larg, there is a small hillock on the right. The large boulders around it are the remains of a cairn that was some 20 m in diameter. The railway line is the next significant feature; this is the same line as was seen just before Castle Kennedy and this part of it follows the Water of Luce towards the coast. The high ground over which the Way has just crossed has forced the line to take this route down the valley but once the coast is reached it crosses the low-lying land between Luce Bay and Loch Ryan on its way to Stranraer.

As the road makes its descent to New Luce it passes above an intricate pattern of drumlins in the fields on the right. The road crosses the Main Water Bridge over the Main Water of Luce which rises some 14 km from New Luce. This river is joined by the Cross Water of Luce near the centre of the village and the enlarged river is then called the Water of Luce.

Pass the general store/post office and turn right at the main road through the village; on the other side of the road is a waymarker and a notice about the local diversion. This road runs between Barrhill (18 km to the north) and Glenluce (8 km to the south). Follow the Glenluce road, passing a cottage called The Old Smithy which is on the left. The Kenmuir Arms Hotel is just before the bridge over the Cross Water of Luce.

The end of the section is at the village hall which is found on the left; on it is the inscription 'New Luce War Memorial 1914–1918'.

New Luce

New Luce is a pleasant little village that nestles comfortably between the hills. In 1839 it boasted a population of 180, three inns and three shops but today it is a much smaller community. Many of the village's cottages are small and a number have recently been renovated.

The local church is just south of the village hall and it was built about 1821. Alexander Peden (see below) preached here in an earlier building. The church is simple in design and has few embellishments – a little bell-tower and some stained glass windows. There are a number of eighteenth-century gravestones in the graveyard. A sandstone war memorial in the shape of a Celtic cross stands in front of the church.

The most famous person associated with New Luce is Alexander Peden (1626–86), known as 'Peden the prophet' for his ability to foretell the future. He was the local minister from 1659 to 1662 when he was ejected. Peden then wandered around Scotland until he was arrested in 1673 and sentenced to four years and three months on the Bass Rock and fifteen months in the Tolbooth in Edinburgh. In 1678 he was sentenced to banishment to Virginia in America but he gained his freedom in London and spent the remainder of his eventful life in Scotland and Ireland.

The village hall has a car-park and public toilets. There is a public telephone box opposite the general store/post office. The village has a hotel and some houses offer bed and breakfast accommodation.

Glenluce (off the Way)

Although only a village, Glenluce has numerous hotels, bed and breakfast establishments and a few shops. There is a campsite in the village and one at Whitecairn, to the north of Glenluce.

The Glenluce Motor Museum is open during the summer. The village's local tourist attraction is Glenluce Abbey.

Section 3 New Luce to Bargrennan

Information

Diversion: The diversion in Section 2 affects the start of this
section; see 'Diversion' on p. 30.

Start of section:
1. At the junction of a track and the road leading east from New
Luce (near the Loups of Barnshangan) (NX191650) (the end of
Section 2's original route) or
2. At the village hall in New Luce (NX175645) (the end of Section
2's diversion).

End of section: At the car-park at the northern end of the bridge
over the River Cree at Bargrennan (NX349765).

Distance: 26 km (16 miles) from near the Loups of Barnshangan
(the end of Section 2's original route) or 28 km (17½ miles) from
New Luce (the end of Section 2's diversion, i.e. using the present
route).

Stages:
1. New Luce to Laggangarn (9·5 km).
2. Laggangarn to Derry (5·5 km).
3. Derry to Knowe (6 km).
4. Knowe to Bargrennan (7 km).
5. Bargrennan.
6. Newton Stewart (off the Way).

Break in route: Knowe (to Newton Stewart).

Conditions: In bad weather this long section can be difficult and
very tiring as conditions underfoot could be atrocious. Route
finding in poor visibility should not be difficult except for the stretch
between Balmurrie and the new forestry plantation.

The Way follows a road from New Luce to Balmurrie and this
allows height to be gained quite quickly. Then there is a very nice
walk for 5 km over an open moor to Laggangarn. Maps may not
show the new plantation that extends from before Mulnigarroch or

See page 100 for the continuation of this section of the route.

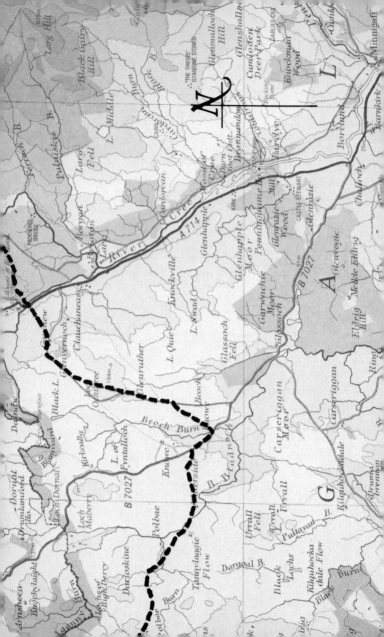

Purgatory Burn to Laggangarn, nor the new track that runs through this plantation.

The route over Craigairie Fell (from Laggangarn to the junction with a forest track) follows fire-breaks for 3 km; in wet conditions it could be exceptionally boggy and very slow. Most of the rest of the section is on tracks or roads and is fast.

Points of interest: Views from the moorlands before and after Craigairie Fell, the Standing Stones of Laggangarn, the Wells o' the Rees, Newton Stewart (off the Way).

Maps:
1. Ordnance Survey nos. 82, 76.
2. Bartholomew no. 37.

Transport: There is a bus service between Newton Stewart and Girvan via Bargrennan. Newton Stewart is on the Dumfries–Stranraer bus route (see p. 55).

Car parking: On route: on the road up to Balmurrie, on the road near Derry, at Knowe, at Loch Ochiltree. At Bargrennan: at the car-park beside the local hall.

Accommodation: Derry, Knowe, Bargrennan, Caldons Campsite (next section), Newton Stewart (off the Way; various).

Notes: In bad weather it may be a real comfort to know about the accommodation available at Derry and Knowe. It should be borne in mind that there is only one break (at Knowe) and this is on a very quiet minor road. There are no shops until St John's Town of Dalry.

New Luce to Laggangarn (9·5 km)

New Luce to the Loups of Barnshangan (2 km)

This section starts from the village hall at New Luce. Walk along the road towards Glenluce and turn left after the church. The road follows the valley of the Cross Water of Luce and as height is gained there are views over the village and the district's pleasant farming land. About 2 km after the village, a track goes off to the right and there is a tall waymarker to the left of the road. This marks the end of the Cruise to the Loups of Barnshangan stage (see p. 94); a notice explains the local diversion.

Keep on the road. About 150 m after the track is the small waterfall in the river known as the Loups of Barnshangan. There is a good view of it from a small iron bridge across the river just below the waterfall; the path to the bridge starts from a stone stile set into the roadside dyke. The farm of Barnshangan can be seen on the opposite side of the river.

The Loups of Barnshangan to Laggangarn (7·5 km)

Continue along the road but bear left at a tall waymarker when the road bends to the right to go the farm of Dranigower.

Pass to the left of the farmhouse at Balmurrie. The surface now deteriorates as the Way goes along a rough track that leads to Kilmacfadzean, the farm that is seen over to the left. Rolling grassy moorlands lie to the north and one interesting feature on them is the tall cairn called Cairn na Gath; it can be seen to the right of the sheep pens that are ahead. Go straight ahead when the track splits and then pass to the left of the complex of sheep pens. Keep near the dyke on the right and cross it at a stile about 100 m after the pens. Turn left and follow the path as it runs beside the dyke.

This is the start of a 5 km stretch of open and very pleasant moorland with no shelter available until the forest at Laggangarn is reached. The new plantation near Mulniegarroch or Purgatory Burn was planted only in 1984 and it will be some years before it can offer protection from the elements. Care must be taken with route finding in poor visibility.

Over to the right is Balmurrie Fell (246 m) and from the next stile Cairn na Gath is about 400 m away to the right. The cairn lies on a north–south axis and it has a prominent pile of boulders at its southern end. Old walls and enclosures have been discovered around the cairn. Bear right after the stile and head towards a small hill on which waymarkers can be seen. The summit of this hill offers an excellent view over to the Galloway Hills. The rocky summit of Craigairie Fell can be seen 6 km away to the east of north; the Way will be passing to the right of its summit. Luce Bay can be seen beyond Balmurrie and the hills of England's Lake District can be seen across the Solway Firth.

Descend the hill, bearing left towards the new plantation. The

Way goes through a gap in the dyke and over a stile. On the left is a rack containing beaters that can be used to put out a small forest fire. Walk through a fire-break and cross Mulniegarroch or Purgatory Burn by means of a wooden bridge. Bear left when the path splits after passing a dyke on the right. A waymarker and a sign with 'Southern Upland Way' on it are soon met at a new forest track and a right turn is made.

The Way leaves the track at a fire-break on the right; another 'Southern Upland Way' sign stands near this junction. This fire-break can be boggy, especially at a point where it descends to meet a dyke. Turn left at this dyke and go through a gap in it about 50 m farther on, then bear left. A junction of two dykes is now met; go through gaps in both of them (while bearing to the right) and walk along another fire-break. Pass to the left of the ruined cottage of Laggangarn (or Laggangairn).

Laggangarn

The Way soon meets two standing stones that were originally erected by pagans but were later adopted by Christians. Beside them is a notice bearing the words: 'Laggangairn. These 2 early Christian memorial stones of about the 8th century AD mark a now deserted settlement. Each stone has an incised cross with a simple cross in each of the angles.' The sandstone pillars are nearly 2 m tall and are all that remain of the thirteen that were said to be here at one time; others were removed to be used locally as gate-posts or lintels.

At the top of the small rise behind the stones is a small pillar-shaped stone that was reputed to mark the grave of a farmer who died at Laggangarn. He was suffering from hydrophobia and was smothered at his own request. It was also said that his misfortune occurred because he had removed stones from the nearby monument. From the rise it may be possible to see the ruined cottage of Killgallioch; this is 600 m to the east and is surrounded by forest. To the south-east can be seen Eldrig Fell (226 m) which has a cairn on its summit.

Laggangarn to Derry (5·5 km)

Laggangarn to Linn's Tomb (4 km)
The path now meets the wooden bridge over the Tarf Water. Beside the bridge is a plaque with '2 troop 130.FD.SQN.RE(V). June 1983' on it. This refers to the builders – a troop of soldiers from Camberley in Surrey. Bear left after the bridge and head uphill along a fire-break, passing a sign with 'Knowe village 7 miles. Meals. B&B. Camping' on it; an accommodation leaflet box stands just beside it. The Way now begins to climb up the eastern flank of Craigairie Fell. From this point until the forest track is met (3 km farther on) there are some marker posts (similar in size to waymarkers) that indicate the route between the forest track and the standing stones; these posts can be followed. Ignore any fire-breaks to the left or right. Many parts of this stretch of forest can be very boggy and the going may be very slow and unpleasant if there has been a lot of rain. Flocks of crossbills can sometimes be heard above the forest.

As height is gained the view to the south gradually opens out. A suitable place for admiring the view is beside the sign pointing towards the standing stones and the Wells o' the Rees ('ree' = 'sheepfold'). The boulder beside the sign has many small circular indentations on it – these are also found on other boulders and outcrops nearby and seem to be natural features rather than man-made markings.

Those walkers who wish to visit the wells should cut through the gap in the dyke below the path and continue downhill for less than 100 m until another sign to the wells is met. There are three wells after the sign. Each is a 1 m high dome of unmortared boulders, with the well at ground level and a small recess above it.

Continue along the fire-break. Soon there is a cairn on an outcrop on the right and this gives an excellent view of the Galloway Hills and across the Solway Firth to the Lake District.

The summit of Craigairie Fell (320 m) can be seen directly ahead during the next stretch of the path; ignore any fire-breaks to the left

The standing stones of Laggangarn, ancient pagan memorials later used by Christians. Incised crosses can be seen on the stones.

or right. The path descends and meets a forest track at a waymarker. On the left is a sign informing that the track boasts the name 'Killgallioch road East' and another sign points to the wells and the standing stones. Turn right at the track and soon the rocky Craigmoddie Fell (248 m) can be seen in front. Walkers with binoculars may be able to see the walled structure known as Linn's Tomb (see below); it is to the left of the summit and below some crags.

About 1 km after the start of the track and at a little break in the trees on the right is a tall signpost pointing to Linn's tomb.

Linn's Tomb

Those walkers who want to visit this reminder of the violent Covenanting times should go through the nearby gate and follow an indistinct track/path that runs more or less in the same direction as the sign points. A small cairn will be found to the left of this track after about 100 m and from there it is possible to see the tomb and to start cutting across the moorland towards it. Look towards the highest and rockiest outcrop on the hill and the tomb will be seen below and to the right of that. The tomb is about 500 m away from the small cairn and it sits in a rocky gully that faces the Galloway Hills.

The tomb is a well-maintained walled structure with various sandstone tablets set into its inner wall. The main tablet carries the inscription '*Memento Mori* [remember death]. Here lies the body of Alex' Linn who was surprised and instantly shot to death on this place by Liewt General Drummond for his adherence to Scotlands Reformation Covenants National Solemn League 1685'. The tomb's various restorations are recorded on the tablets. A little rose bush grows inside the tomb and entry is by means of a substantial stile formed out of large blocks of stone. A religious service is held here every three years.

There is a fine view of the Galloway Hills from near the tomb and the Solway Firth can also be seen. Loch Derry (see below) can be

Linn's Tomb and the Galloway Hills. The tomb is a short distance off the Way.

seen 1 km away to the north-east. An even better view can be obtained by climbing to the summit of Craigmoddie Fell. The outcrops on the hill have evidence of having been scored by the passage of ice over them. These 'striations' were produced by the rubbing of boulders frozen within the ice when the glacier moved over the bare rock.

Linn's Tomb to Derry (1·5 km)
About 400 m after the signpost to Linn's Tomb there is a break in the trees on both sides of the track and on the left is a gate leading to Loch Derry. The loch is at the edge of the forest and bare moorland lies to the north of it. The moorland has the place-name of Eldrig of Liberland ('liberland' = 'leperland') on the Ordnance Survey map as there may have been a leper colony there at one time. Leprosy was so feared a disease that sufferers were isolated in incredibly lonely places such as this.

The farm of Derry is soon seen through a gap in the forest on the right; conifer plantations stretch away into the distance and beyond that are the beckoning Galloway Hills. Belted Galloway cattle may be seen near the farm. These very distinctive animals have a broad white belt across their black bodies.

Various signs confront the walker just before Derry farm is reached. One is a request for dogs to be kept on a lead and another informs that the track leads back to the tomb, the wells and the standing stones. The notice that will be most welcome to many walkers, especially if they are ready for rest or food, is the one informing that the farm offers bed and breakfast, evening meals, snacks and lunches; it also has a campsite.

Derry to Knowe (6 km)

Derry to the River Bladnoch (4 km)
Continue on the track past Derry, bearing left when the track to the farm is met; on the right is the ruin of a shepherd's house. Soon the track gives way to a metalled road and this surface continues to Knowe. The road winds through the seemingly never-ending

conifer plantations and at one point it bends round a large boggy depression on the right that has the place-name Calder Loch on the Ordnance Survey map. Polbae Burn is soon seen on the right and this is crossed at the substantial Darloskine Bridge where the road bends to the right. A tall waymarker and a ruined house stand to the left of the bend. The large house of Polbae is seen downstream of the bridge. There are many fine trees standing in its grounds and their variety is in stark contrast to the monotonous conifer plantations that are found elsewhere in this district.

The road passes the farm of Tannylaggie and then crosses the River Bladnoch.

The River Bladnoch to Knowe (2 km)

The Way passes the farm of Waterside and meets the B7027. This road runs between Barrhill (13 km to the north-west) and Challoch (9 km to the south-east). Newton Stewart is 3 km beyond Challoch. Turn right, walk along the Newton Stewart road and pass the tall waymarker on the right.

The tiny hamlet of Knowe (which has only three houses) is met 600 m after the road junction.

Knowe

Knowe was a little village of about a hundred people at the beginning of the twentieth century and in 1891 the local school had an average attendance of twenty-three pupils. The walls of many ruined houses can be seen by the roadside and the village mill was behind the ruins that are on the left after the two houses on that side. There is a public telephone box near the houses.

Overnight camping and bed and breakfast accommodation is available at the house on the right; food is also available for sale. This building was once the Snap Inn, an old posthouse in the days of horse-drawn transport. The ruinous building beside it has the date 1856 above a doorway and beside this building is a milestone indicating that Newton Stewart is 8 miles away and Girvan is 22 miles away.

Knowe to Bargrennan (7 km)

Knowe to Loch Ochiltree (3 km)
The road passes the campsite and crosses the Beoch Burn; the
bridge is dated 1933 and carries an Ordnance Survey bench-mark.
Turn left at the tall waymarker beside the road and follow a
fire-break through the forest for 1.5 km.

Turn right at the end of the forest in order to cross a stile over a
fence and then pass to the left of the old peat cuttings that are in
front. Head for the right-hand edge of the group of mature beeches
beside Glenruther Lodge. A tall waymarker is found beside the
single track road; turn left.

Pass to the right of Glenruther farm and 700 m later take a path
on the right to ascend the Hill of Ochiltree (184 m); the start of the
path is found just after a cattle grid and is marked by a tall
waymarker. The Way rejoins the road 1·5 km farther on, so if
conditions are bad or if time is at a premium then it may be best to
keep to the road. There is a better view of Loch Ochiltree from the
road than from the Hill of Ochiltree.

Loch Ochiltree can be seen to the north-west. Its charm lies in its
small wooded islands: their vegetation is rich compared to the
moorland around its shores since sheep cannot graze on them. The
larger of the two small islands at the south end of the loch has a
cairn on it that is about 8 m in diameter. To the south-west of Loch
Ochiltree is the small Loch of Fyntalloch.

Loch Ochiltree to Bargrennan (4 km)
Head uphill and bear left to reach the trig point at the summit. On
the side of the trig point can be seen a metal insert with a
bench-mark inscribed on it. This is used by surveyors wishing to find
the altitude of any point in the surrounding area as the position and
altitude of the bench-mark is accurately known.

The Solway Firth and the Lake District can be seen to the
south-east. There is a good view to the north-east towards Glen
Trool and to its left are Benyellary (719 m), The Merrick (843 m)
and Kirriereoch (786 m). The caravan site near Bargrennan can be
seen 4 km to the north-east. The path heads northwards after the

summit and meets the single-track road at a tall waymarker; turn right.

A long straight stretch of the road heads directly towards The Merrick, the highest of the Galloway Hills. There are nice birch trees in the Garchew Wood and some well-built sheep enclosures on the right before the farm of Garchew. Immediately before the farm buildings are some interesting rocks that owe their shape to the passage of ice over them. As a glacier advanced over them, the ice smoothed their upstream ends and then roughened their downstream ends by plucking chunks out of the rocks. The curious French name of '*roches moutonnées*' ('sheep rocks') that is given to them is due to the rocks' supposed similarity in shape to recumbent sheep.

Turn left at a tall waymarker about 100 m after the farm and cross the stile. Follow the fence on the right for a while and then bear left to meet a stile over the fine drystane dyke that is now on the right. Bear left to another stile and then right to yet another stile in order to climb a little rise. Head to the right of Brigend cottage and meet the A714. This road runs between Girvan (which is on the west coast) and Port William (which is in Luce Bay); Newton Stewart is 13 km away to the south. On the other side of the road is the important River Cree which rises at Loch Moan (9 km to the north) and flows past Newton Stewart on its way to Wigton Bay in the Solway Firth.

Turn left at the tall waymarker and cross the narrow single-arch Middle Bridge of Cree. On the left is the local hall; the car-park beside it marks the end of this section.

Bargrennan

Bargrennan is a small collection of houses on the important A714 cross-country route. The only building of note nearby is Bargrennan Parish Church which sits on a little hill to the west of the car-park. It is a plain-looking greywacke structure built in 1839.

The nearest settlement of any size is Glentrool Village (2 km away) and this is found by going northwards along the road for

200 m and then bearing right. This is a Forestry Commission village and it has a general store/post office and a public telephone box. Along the Glentrool Village road are the House O'Hill Hotel and the Merrick Caravan Park (which takes tents); these places are 300 m and 900 m respectively from the A714. There is a telephone in the House O'Hill Hotel.

There are no shops, public toilets or public telephone box near Bargrennan.

Newton Stewart (off the Way)

Newton Stewart is a little market town that is an important focus for commerce, shopping and social life in the district; Wednesdays and Fridays are market-days. The town has a good selection of hotels and places offering bed and breakfast accommodation. Minnigaff Youth Hostel is very close to Newton Stewart and it is found by crossing the bridge over to the east bank of the River Cree, turning first left and continuing for about 600 m to a former school on the left. The Creebridge Caravan Park (which takes tents) is on the B7079, about 1 km from the bridge over the River Cree.

Newton Stewart Museum is housed in the former St John's Church in York Road (west of the main street); it is normally open in the afternoons and has a collection of local material. The Tourist Information Centre is found on the right when walking southwards along the main street towards the market; it is opposite the McMillan Hall (1881). One surprising and welcome feature about the town is that it has a cinema that shows current films.

The town is pleasantly situated on the west bank of the River Cree. It owes its foundation to a ford across the river and the village at the crossing became known as Fordhouse of Cree. The first bridge was built in 1745 but this was wrecked by the River Cree when it was in spate and the present handsome five-arch bridge was erected in 1813.

One building of note in the main street is the eighteenth-century former town house; it has a square clock tower topped by a cupola roof and a weathercock.

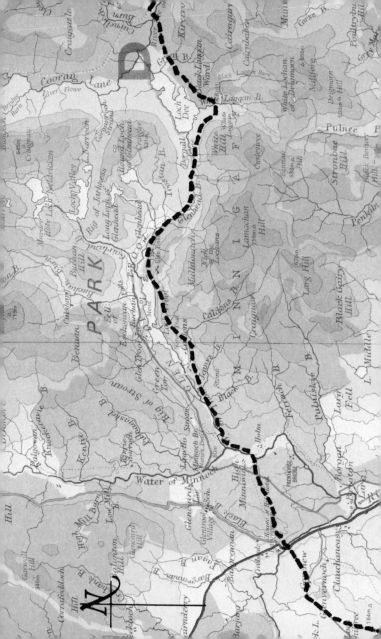

Section 4 Bargrennan to St John's Town of Dalry

Information

Start of section: At the car-park at the northern end of the bridge over the River Cree at Bargrennan (NX349765).

End of section: At the fountain at the junction of the A713 and the A702 in St John's Town of Dalry (NX619812).

Distance: 36 km (22½ miles).

Stages:

1. Bargrennan to Caldons (6·5 km).
2. Caldons to the River Dee (11·5 km).
3. The River Dee to Clenrie (9·5 km).
4. Clenrie to St John's Town of Dalry (8·5 km).
5. St John's Town of Dalry.

Breaks in route:

1. Stroan Bridge (to Glentrool Village).
2. Caldons Campsite (to the north side of Glen Trool).
3. Glenhead (to the north side of Glen Trool).
4. The River Dee (to the west side of Clatteringshaws Loch and the A712).
5. Near Mid Garrary (to the east side of Clatteringshaws Loch and the A712).

Conditions: This is another very long walk, much of it through the Galloway Forest Park which is a popular recreation and holiday area. The Park is entered at Bargrennan. Quite a bit of the route is exposed and so this should be regarded as a difficult section in bad weather.

Most of the route between Bargrennan and Glenhead is along paths and the going can be slow, especially after rain.

After Glenhead, a path leads to a forest track that passes Loch Dee and reaches the River Dee; this stretch is quite high and exposed. A forest track then goes past Clatteringshaws Loch to the perimeter of the forest park.

The walk from Mid Garrary over Shield Rig to Clenrie is on a grassy path across nice open moorland; exposure will be a real

See page 116 for the continuation of this section of the route.

problem in bad weather. The descent from Clenrie to Garroch Bridge is on track and road. There is then a mixture of surfaces to the end of the section.

Points of interest: Views of Loch Trool, Loch Dee, St John's Town of Dalry.

Maps:

1. Ordnance Survey nos. 76, 77.
2. Bartholomew no. 37.

Transport: There is a bus service between Ayr and Castle Douglas (via St John's Town of Dalry). Castle Douglas is on the Dumfries – Stranraer bus route (see p. 55).

Car parking: On route: near the track to Holm, at Caldons Campsite, at Craigencallie (off the Way), near Mid Garrary, at Drumbuie. At St John's Town of Dalry: in Main Street.

Accommodation: Caldons Campsite, White Laggan Bothy, Talnotry Campsite (off the Way), St John's Town of Dalry (various).

Notes: An unofficial alternative route has been described from Caldons to Glenhead Burn (see p. 120). Accommodation in the middle of this section is a particular problem. Local signposts shorten the name 'St John's Town of Dalry' to 'Dalry'. There are no shops until St John's Town of Dalry.

Bargrennan to Caldons (6·5 km)

Bargrennan to the Water of Trool (3·5 km)

This section starts at the car-park to the north of the Middle Bridge of Cree at Bargrennan. Cross the road to a tall waymarker and enter the forest. Crossbills and siskins may be seen here.

Follow the track as it narrows to a path and bends round to the north. Turn right at a dyke; House O'Hill Hotel may be seen about 300 m over to the left. Go through a gap in the dyke and then keep to the left side of the dyke as it goes over Rig of the Cairn. Turn left at a junction of dykes and follow the dyke that is now on the right until a minor road (and a car-parking area) is met. Turn left at the road and turn first right where there is a sign to the farm of Holm.

Bear left immediately after crossing the concrete bridge over the Water of Minnoch, a tributary of the River Cree. Walkers may find that there is a new route between the minor road and the Water of Minnoch.

The Way follows the east bank of the river, crossing stiles and little footbridges. The route is generally straightforward and no turns are taken away from the river. Any other marker posts that are seen here have been erected by the Forestry Commission to mark local paths for the many visitors who walk in this area.

The river-bed is composed mainly of round water-worn granite pebbles and boulders, and beside the river can be seen man-made embankments that have been built to prevent flooding. The river is fished for trout and at one point there is a notice with 'Poachers pool' on it. The confluence of the Water of Minnoch and the Water of Trool is met and there is a handy seat at this point from which to admire the fine trees standing by the banks of the two rivers.

The Water of Trool to the Martyrs' Tomb (2·5 km)
The path now follows the Water of Trool and passes a small waterfall before arriving at Stroan Bridge. The Way does not cross the bridge, but it can be used as a means of reaching the public road that runs between Bargrennan, Glentrool Village and the north side of Loch Trool. The bridge is built on substantial foundations and its deck is well above the normal summer level of the river.

The view in front soon opens out; Buchan Hill (493 m) is prominent to the north-east and the Fell of Eschoncan (360 m) is to its left. On the south side of Glen Trool, Craignaw (540 m) is the nearest hill and behind it is a curving ridge whose highest peak is Lamachan Hill (716 m). The Way crosses a number of streams running into the river and passes some rounded moraines that were dumped by a receding glacier. As the Way moves away from the river it goes through a little deciduous wood; at one point bear to the left when the path forks at a sign with 'Forest Trail' on it; the path then leads to a stile after which a right turn should be taken. A notice with 'Stroan Bridge 2¼ miles' on it is found after the stile. The Way now meets the walled structure known as the Martyrs' Tomb.

The Martyrs' Tomb

Inside the tomb a granite tablet carries the words: 'Here lyes James and Robert Duns, Thomas and John Stevensons, James McClive, Andrew McCall, who were surprised at prayer in this house by Colnell Douglas, Lievtnant Livingston, and Cornet James Douglas, and by them most impiously and cruelly murthered for their adherence to Scotlands Reformation Covenants National and Solemn League 1685'. A cornet was a junior officer who carried the troop's flag. Another plaque gives a few more details of this bloody encounter and a modern notice just before the tomb informs that the tablet replaces one erected by Old Mortality.

Old Mortality was the stonemason Robert Paterson (1715–1801) who came from near Hawick. His house was plundered by Jacobites in 1745 and he was held prisoner by them for a time. He later spent some forty years cutting and erecting stones at the graves of Covenanters. Sir Walter Scott took his deeds as the inspiration for the book *Old Mortality* (1816).

The Martyrs' Tomb to Caldons (0·5 km)

Turn left after passing the tomb. Bear right to a waymarker and then turn left, on a more distinct path. The path heads directly towards the Forestry Commission's Caldons Campsite, but turn right just before the camping area is reached. The Way then meets a track and tall waymarker.

The Way follows the fence on the right and turns right just before the Caldons Burn, but those walkers who wish to visit the campsite or the other side of Loch Trool should turn left when the track is met.

The campsite is the main recreation centre in the Galloway Forest Park and the site's office/shop is on the other side of the burn. The park is very extensive (600 sq km) and it includes forestry plantations, moorland, rugged hills and farmland. The first plantations were started in 1922 and a wide variety of conifers have been planted, including Sitka spruce, Lodgepole pine, Japanese larch and Scots pine.

The park's many different types of landscape provide suitable habitats for many birds. Parts of the park are very 'highland' in appearance and numerous birds of prey such as golden eagle, peregrine falcon, merlin and hen harrier roam the skies looking for prey. Ravens in search of carrion may be seen (and heard) in the sky.

Caldons to Glenhead Burn (4·5 km)
(unofficial alternative route via the north side of Loch Trool)
The route followed by the Way along the southern side of the loch is slow and there are few views of the loch, so some walkers might prefer to walk along the northern shore in order to enjoy open views of the very fine scenery. Beautiful deciduous woods, waterfalls and Bruce's Stone are added attractions to this route, but the traffic on this narrow road may be rather busy at the height of the tourist season.

   To follow this alternative (and longer) route, turn left along the track that was met just before Caldons Campsite, pass a Way notice-board and meet the lochside road. Turn right and walk 2·5 km to the car-park; Bruce's Stone is on a knoll to the right of this. Continue on a track that runs to the left of Buchan and heads towards Glenhead. Once Glenhead Burn is on the right, look for a sign with 'Forest Trail' on it; bear right and follow the burn upstream to a wooden bridge. A waymarker is found on the far side of the bridge; turn left and rejoin the Way (see p. 123).

Caldons to the River Dee (11·5 km)

Caldons to Glenhead Burn (3 km)
Follow the Caldons Burn upstream, passing the house of Caldons which is on the opposite side of the burn. The Way now gains height quickly as it follows a well-used path through the forest. Turn left at a forest track and cross the burn. The track narrows to a path and few waymarkers are encountered from now until Glenhead Burn is reached. A number of 'forest walk' or 'forest trail' signs are

The northern side of Loch Trool. The Fell of Esconcan is on the left and the Buchan Burn is in the middle of the picture.

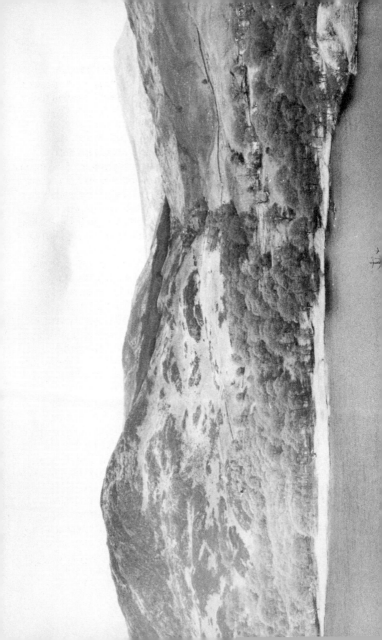

seen beside the path and these can be followed to Glenhead Burn.

A great jumble of rocks at one stretch may make the going rather slow, but the difficulties are nothing compared to the problems faced by Sir Aymer de Valence, then the Guardian of Scotland, when he was here in 1307 in pursuit of Robert the Bruce. He led 2,000 English troops in single file along the narrow path but unknown to them Bruce and his small band of men were lying in wait. Bruce commanded his men from the opposite side of the loch and when he saw that the Englishmen were in their most vulnerable position below the steep slopes of Mulldonach he blew three blasts on his horn as a signal that a huge pile of boulders should be pushed downhill to cause a landslide above the soldiers. Many that were not crushed or drowned in the loch were finished off by the Scots. This famous encounter is called the Battle o' the Steps o' Trool. Bruce had earlier been in hiding in Glen Trool and he spent his time hunting deer as recorded in *The Bruce*, which was completed by John Barbour in 1376.

Unfortunately there are no views over Loch Trool until near its eastern end; however, the view from there is really worth all the effort. The two most prominent hills in view are the Fell of Eschoncan and Buchan Hill, while Benyellary lies between them but much farther back. The Merrick lies beyond Benyellary. Below the Fell of Eschoncan can be seen a car-park and to the right of that is a knoll on which stands Bruce's Stone. The stone carries the inscription: 'In loyal remembrance of Robert the Bruce, king of Scots, whose victory in this glen over an English force in March, 1307, opened the campaign of independence which he brought to a decisive close at Bannockburn on 24th June, 1314.' The stone was erected in 1929 on the 600th anniversary of Bruce's death and there is a superb view of the loch from it.

The steep slopes on each side of the loch were formed when the valley was 'over-deepened' by a glacier that flowed from east to west, and on either side of Buchan Hill can be seen 'hanging valleys' which at one time had tributary glaciers that fed the main glacier. When the ice finally melted, these hanging valleys were left high above the loch. The one to the left of Buchan Hill carries the

Buchan Burn and the one to the right carries the Gairland Burn. They both have fine waterfalls and there are some beautiful trees where the burns meet the loch.

The path now begins to descend and the forest on the left ends; the path runs parallel to the dyke and fence on the left. Cross a stile over the fence and follow the dyke as it turns to the left and leads to another stile. The Way now meets Glenhead Burn at a bridge. The Way turns right, while the forest trail crosses the bridge in order to reach the lochside road that runs from Glenhead farm to Glentrool Village and Bargrennan. The flat land on the left is known as the Soldiers' Holm, where those Englishmen who died in the 1307 battle are said to be buried.

The bridge marks the end of the unofficial alternative route from Caldons to Glenhead Burn (see p. 120).

Glenhead Burn to the White Laggan Bothy (5 km)

Follow the southern bank of the burn and bear right at a junction of dykes to keep beside the conifers that are on the right. Cross the fence on the right at a stile and follow the Sheil Burn into the forest; one early stretch could be very boggy. The path climbs through the forest before meeting a forest track; turn left.

Moorland soon takes over from the forest and after a climb there is a good view to the north-west where The Merrick, the highest hill in southern Scotland, is prominent. The track soon gets to the top of the col that was cut by the ice as it moved from Loch Dee to Loch Trool.

There is now a pleasant view forward as the track makes its descent to Loch Dee. Craiglee (531 m) stands above the north-western shore of the loch, while the southern and eastern shores have plantations on them. A few sandy beaches can be seen along the shore.

The loch is stocked with brown trout and it is popular with fishermen. After passing a track that runs to the shore, a little box on a pedestal is passed on the left of the track; this was erected by the Forestry Commission as part of a research project. The fishing in the loch is being improved by stocking it with acid-tolerant fish and fishermen are asked to leave in the box a record of the size of the fish that they catch, together with a sample of the scales from the fish (to determine their age).

The track crosses the White Laggan Burn, but just before doing so, a path on the right leads up to the White Laggan Bothy which is only 300 m off the track; this provides welcome shelter to walkers. The cottage was in a bad condition until it was repaired and opened in June 1973 under the care of the Mountain Bothies Association. It has accommodation for about eight people.

The White Laggan Bothy to the River Dee (3·5 km)

The track then passes the ruin of the shepherd's cottage of Black Laggan. A track on the right (1 km later) should be ignored. There is soon a view northwards into the wilderness area behind Craiglee that stretches up to Loch Macaterick, some 12 km away. To its right are the afforested hills of the Rhinns of Kells, whose nearest peak is Meikle Millyea (746 m).

The hills in this district are an important range that have an interesting geological history. At one time a huge hot mass of rock lay under this area and as it moved slowly upwards through the earth's crust it heated the rocks around it. This hot rock eventually cooled to become granite and around it were the baked greywackes and shales that had become even harder than the granite. The change that they had undergone made them more resistant to erosion than the granite and during the Ice Age, when this district was one of the most important centres of ice accumulation in southern Scotland, the ice found it easier to erode the granite than the hardened rocks. So today the low ground is where the granite is found and this is surrounded by a ring of rugged hills such as The Merrick and the Rhinns of Kells.

The track now splits at a waymarker and the Way turns left, but the track on the right can be followed in order to reach the A712 (Newton Stewart–New Galloway) which is 9·5 km away. Cars can be taken to Craigencallie which is only 2 km from the Way. The track now descends to the concrete bridge over the River Dee (also called the Black Water of Dee). The river flows from Loch Dee through Clatteringshaws Loch and Loch Ken before entering the Solway Firth at Kirkcudbright.

The River Dee to Clenrie (9·5 km)

The River Dee to Clatteringshaws Loch (4 km)
Keep to the right and follow the river downstream to
Clatteringshaws Loch. On the far side of the loch it is possible to see
Benniguinea (387 m) and Cairnsmore (493 m).

The next part of the walk is along a fairly straight forest track
through a plantation of very tall trees which at present restrict the
view towards the loch. The track passes under a National Grid
electricity transmission line. This is connected to Kendoon Power
Station which will be passed later on. The farm of Mid Garrary can
be seen through the gap in the trees on the left. There is soon a view
of Clatteringshaws Loch.

Clatteringshaws Loch
Clatteringshaws Loch is a storage reservoir and is part of the
Galloway Hydro-electric Scheme which was opened in 1936. The
scheme's other main reservoirs are Loch Dee, Loch Doon and Loch
Ken. Water from Clatteringshaws Loch leaves at its eastern shore
through a 6 km long pipeline and feeds Glenlee Power Station
which will be seen near the end of the section. The supply from
Loch Doon feeds the Kendoon, Carsfad and Earlstoun Power
Stations. Water from all the power stations then gathers in Loch
Ken and feeds Tongland Power Station, just north of
Kirkcudbright. The walker will see a number of these power
stations. If they are not easily spotted then look for the tall
cylindrical surge towers built above their generators; these contain
water and are used to dampen fluctuations in the flow of water.

The reservoir's dam is 3 km to the south of the track, and to the
left of the dam (and partially hidden in a stand of trees) is the
Galloway Deer Museum. The museum was opened in 1971 and it is
well worth visiting. It has good displays covering such subjects as
local forestry, archaeology, flora, fauna and geology. In 1974, when
Clatteringshaws Loch was lowered for maintenance, two hut-circles
were found, and a reconstruction of a primitive Romano-British hut
from around AD 200–300 has been built near the museum.

Less than 1 km north of the museum is another Bruce's Stone.

This one is cared for by the National Trust for Scotland and it celebrates a victory over the English in 1307 at Raploch Moss. Farther west along the A712 from Clatteringshaws Loch are the Deer Park, the Wild Goat Park and the Forestry Commission's Talnotry Campsite.

Clatteringshaws Loch to Clenrie (5·5 km)
The track now heads away from the loch and meets a gate at the perimeter of the Galloway Forest Park; cars can be parked at the gate. A tall waymarker is met at a T-junction. The Way goes left but a right turn leads to the A712 (3 km away).

Head uphill towards Mid Garrary, but turn right at a tall waymarker 400 m later and cross a stile. Keep near the dyke on the left and go through a gap in it after about 20 m; walk beside the dyke that is now on the left. Cross another stile, pass an accommodation leaflet box and follow the dyke as the path follows a fire-break.

After climbing well above Mid Garrary, go through a gap in the dyke on the left at a junction of dykes. A waymarker and a post supporting a number of fire beaters stand at the gap. After walking along another fire-break, cross the stream called Hog Park Strand and pass a large circular sheep enclosure that is on the left. The fire-break then meets the edge of the forest. A stile and a gate lead out on to the open moorland.

Pass to the left of a circular sheep enclosure and follow the path as it runs north-eastwards beneath Shield Rig (328 m). The forests and hills of the Galloway Forest Park are now left behind as the path climbs on to the grassy moor and past many ice-smoothed outcrops. Many of these are similar in shape to the *roches moutonnées* seen at Garchew. In poor visibility, care should be taken to keep fairly near the summit ridge in order not to stray on to the moorland on the right.

Looking towards St John's Town of Dalry from Waterside Hill. On the right can be seen the suspension bridge over the Water of Ken, Dalry Motte and Dalry Parish Church.

The route may become a little more indistinct as it descends from the hill, but head east of north, towards the farm of Clenrie. The path nears the dyke that will be seen on the left and then crosses a bridge over the Garroch Burn. Bear right to join the track that runs past the farmhouse and the conifer plantation on Snab Hill.

Clenrie to St John's Town of Dalry (8·5 km)

Clenrie to Waterside Hill (6 km)

The rough track continues until a single-track road is met at a tall waymarker opposite the road to Drumbuie farm. A notice beside the road gives a reminder about the danger of forest fire in the Forrest Estate. Largmore farm is passed on the right and a little later a sign at a track on the left has 'Thomas Olsen Road' on it. This owes its name to the Norwegian ownership of Forrest Estate. As the conifer plantation ends, the road nears the Garroch Burn which has some very pleasant deciduous trees standing by its banks. Highland cattle may be seen in the fields near Knocksheen. Those walkers who are seeing these shaggy beasts for the first time may think that they are quite fearsome-looking; however, they are generally exceptionally docile – and very photogenic!

Deciduous trees soon line both sides of the road – a welcome change from the conifers. This very pleasant mixed wood has oak, ash, birch and hazel and it is protected by its status as a 'Site of Special Scientific Interest'. Summer visiting birds such as redstart, pied flycatcher and wood warbler can be seen here.

About 350 m after the road crosses the Garroch Bridge, a tall waymarker on the left indicates that the Way leaves the road on that side and enters a small wood. Follow the burn then cross it at a wooden bridge. Turn right and follow the burn to a stile over the dyke on the left. The Way now meets Waterside Hill. There is a nice view from it but care is needed in route finding if the visibility is poor.

Waterside Hill to the Water of Ken (2·5 km)

Head uphill, bearing to the right. As the hill is climbed the long water-pipe that feeds Glenlee Power Station can be seen over to the right; this station produces 24,000 kW.

Keep on the southern flank of Waterside Hill, generally heading eastwards, and pass to the right of a lone tree. St John's Town of Dalry can now be seen in the valley but first the Way must cross the bridge that can be seen over the Water of Ken. Head downhill (in the direction of the village) towards a dyke and bear left, passing between a prominent outcrop and the sheep enclosure that is beside the dyke. Follow the dyke and walk under three electrical transmission lines.

The dyke leads to a gate beside Earlstoun Power Station. Walk down the track beside the power station. On the left is the fish ladder which enables salmon to swim upstream, bypassing the generators. Meet a tall waymarker at the A762, part of the route between Ayr and Kirkcudbright.

The power station produces 14,000 kW and the building has the words 'The Galloway Water Power Scheme. Earlstoun Power Station. 1936' on it; the bridge over the outflow is dated 1935. Water comes to the power station from the dam on Earlstoun Loch which is 600 m farther up the Water of Ken. Nearly all the loch's water is taken into the power station via a pipeline, so the river between the dam and the power station is often so low that it would be possible to jump across in one leap. The dam can be reached by taking a left turn on the road and then bearing left when the A713 is met.

Turn right at the A762 and 500 m later a tall waymarker and a stile take the Way to the left, towards the Water of Ken. A broad grassy haugh lies ahead and beyond it can be seen the suspension bridge. Follow the track beside the fence to the wide gravelly area at the riverside and cross the river. Beside the bridge is a notice warning that the river is 'liable to sudden rise due to hydro operations' – a 50 cm rise in a few minutes can occur! The bridge certainly seems anchored quite securely and a notice on its far side informs that it was repaired in July 1985 by a troop of Royal Engineers from Newcastle.

The Water of Ken to Dalry Parish Church (20 m)
Once the eastern bank has been gained it is only a few minutes'
walk to the end of the section, but there are three places worth
seeing before finishing: the motte, the church and the Town Hall.

On the left is Dalry Motte. It is 8 m high, about 35 m in diameter
and it was encircled by a ditch which was broadest on the east side
where it was about 7 m wide. The top commands a fine view,
especially to the south where there is the grassy Holm of Dalry. On
either bank can be seen the embankments that were built to protect
the agricultural land from erosion by the river.

Dalry Parish Church
On the right is Dalry Parish Church. It can be reached either from
the main road or, more immediately, by three stone steps built into
the perimeter wall. The present church, built of greywacke and
sandstone, was erected in 1831. It has a square three-storey
bell-tower and some curious blocked-up windows.

There are lots of old tombstones in the graveyard, many of them
dating back to the eighteenth century; some sport a skull and
crossbones or an hourglass. One particular gravestone is well
known and is worth looking at; it is lying horizontal and is in the
corner of the graveyard nearest the bridge. It is dedicated to Robert
Stewart and John Grierson 'who were murdered by Graham of
Claverhouse *anno* 1684 for their adherence to Scotlands
Reformation and Covenants National and Solemn League'. These
two 'Auchencloy martyrs' were killed during the 'Killing Times' by
Claverhouse when he trapped them on Auchencloy Hill (12 km
south of St John's Town of Dalry) after the shooting of the
Episcopalian minister from the village of Carsphairn. The text on
the gravestone explains that Claverhouse 'his rage pursued even
such when dead and in the tombs of their ancestors laid – causing
their corps be rais'd out of the same, discharging in churchyard to
bury them'. The two bodies were thus taken out of their families'
graves and were reburied in this northern corner of the churchyard,
traditionally the place where criminals were interred.

The most interesting structure in the church's grounds is the
Gordon Aisle which is on the south-eastern side of the church.

Inside this roofless shell is a paved floor and a plaque bearing the words: 'This aisle and the vaults below were built by Sir James and Lady Gordon 1546. Restored by their descendants Charles and Jean Forbes 1939.' The phrase *'Ora pro nobis'* on the plaque means 'Pray for us'. The south wall has a crow-stepped gable and a window covered with a strong iron grille. Above that is a rather worn stone shield with three boars' heads (for the Gordon family) and a lion rampant (for the Crichton family). Above the shield are the initials 'IG' and 'MC' and a date, believed to be 1546. The arms and initials 'IG' refer to James Gordon of Lochinvar. He was the King's Chamberlain for part of Galloway and was killed in the battle of Pinkie (which is to the east of Edinburgh) in 1547. 'MC' refers to his wife Margaret Crichton.

To the east of the old chapel is the Session House, dated 1880. The driveway from the church to the main road is sheltered by a fine avenue of lime trees that was planted in 1828 and outside the gate is a granite war memorial in the form of a Celtic cross. A left turn at the memorial leads to the fountain at the end of the section (see below).

Dalry Parish Church to St John's Town of Dalry (120 m)
Continue along the path from the bridge. The Way passes the Town Hall which is an impressive building for such a small community. It has a clock tower with a pyramidal roof and above the main door is a stone plaque with a coat of arms, the date 1897 and the words *'Hinc mihi salus'* ('Hence comes my salvation').

The Way now meets the junction of the A713 (Ayr–Castle Douglas) and the A702 (St John's Town of Dalry–Thornhill). The section ends at the granite fountain at the junction. This is McNaught's Fountain and a brass plaque on it explains that it was erected in 1917 as a 'gift to the inhabitants of St John's Clachan of Dalry'. This is an old name for the village and the word 'clachan' means 'kirk-town'. Hence the name of the Clachan Inn which stands just to the west of the fountain.

St John's Town of Dalry

St John's Town of Dalry, whose name is derived from the dedication of the local church to John the Baptist, is a neat little village with many small whitewashed houses. The village has hotels, bed and breakfast accommodation, a post office, general stores and a café. There is a public telephone box a short distance along the Ayr road from the fountain, and the public toilets are behind the Town Hall.

The most famous historical event associated with the village was the incident that led to the Pentland Rising. This happened in 1666 during the time when soldiers were billeted in many towns and villages in order to impose the King's will in the dispute over Church organisation. As part of the attempts to impose bishops on the people, fines were imposed for non-attendance at church and many people who absented themselves from church incurred large debts as a consequence. On 13 November 1666, John Maclellan and three fellow fugitive Covenanters arrived at the village to be told that some soldiers were holding an old farmer called Grier. He had not paid his church fines and it was rumoured that he was going to be roasted on a gridiron (a metal frame on which meat was roasted). The four men confronted the soldiers (though Maclellan's pistol was loaded with a plug of tobacco for want of bullets!) and the soldiers were overpowered.

News of the incident spread quickly and in Balmaclellan, some 4 km away, Covenanters attacked a local garrison. Soon a company of about 200 men advanced on Dumfries and captured the soldiers' commander, Lieutenant-Colonel Sir James Turner. They then marched on Edinburgh, hoping to use their captive as a bargaining weapon. They never reached the capital and were completely defeated at Rullion Green in the Pentlands. Many prisoners were executed and others who had helped or supported the rebellion were severely punished.

St John's Town of Dalry. McNaught's Fountain can be seen at the bottom of Main Street.

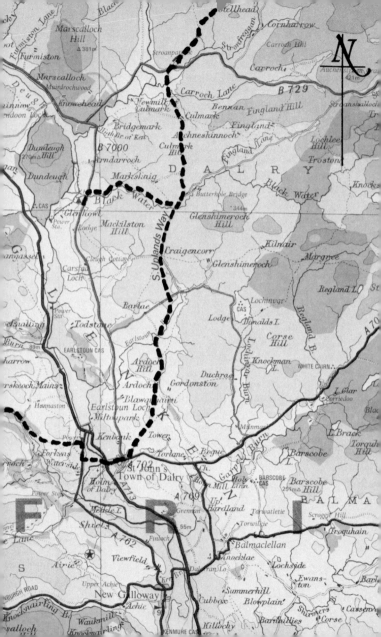

Section 5 St John's Town of Dalry to Sanquhar

Information

Start of section: At the fountain at the junction of the A713 and the A702 in St John's Town of Dalry (NX619812).
End of section: At the junction of the A76 and Leven Road in Sanquhar (NS784096).
Distance: 41·5 km (25½ miles).
Stages:
1. St John's Town of Dalry to Butterhole Bridge (8 km).
2. Butterhole Bridge to Kendoon Youth Hostel (spur) (2·5 km).
3. Butterhole Bridge to the B729 (4 km).
4. The B729 to Polskeoch (15 km).
5. Polskeoch to Sanquhar (14·5 km).
6. Sanquhar.
Spur: There is a waymarked spur from Butterhole Bridge to Kendoon Youth Hostel; see p. 140.
Breaks in route:
1. At the road junction after Barlaes (to the B7000 and Kendoon Youth Hostel).
2. Butterhole Bridge (to Kendoon Youth Hostel or Moniaive).
3. Stroanpatrick (to the B7000 and Kendoon Youth Hostel or to Moniaive).
4. Polskeoch (to Lorg).
5. Polgown (to Penpont).
Conditions: This can be one of the most enjoyable sections of the whole Way as it crosses a number of prominent hills and there are superb views over the countryside. However, it is also the longest and most difficult section and anyone attempting the whole of it in one day should be aware of the problems that may arise, especially if the weather is bad, as the route is mainly over open moorland and there is very little accommodation available. This is not a section to take lightly.

The stretch from St John's Town of Dalry to Stroanpatrick is on paths over farmland and moorland and is pleasant, though exposed.

See pages 136 and 138 for the continuation of this section of the route.

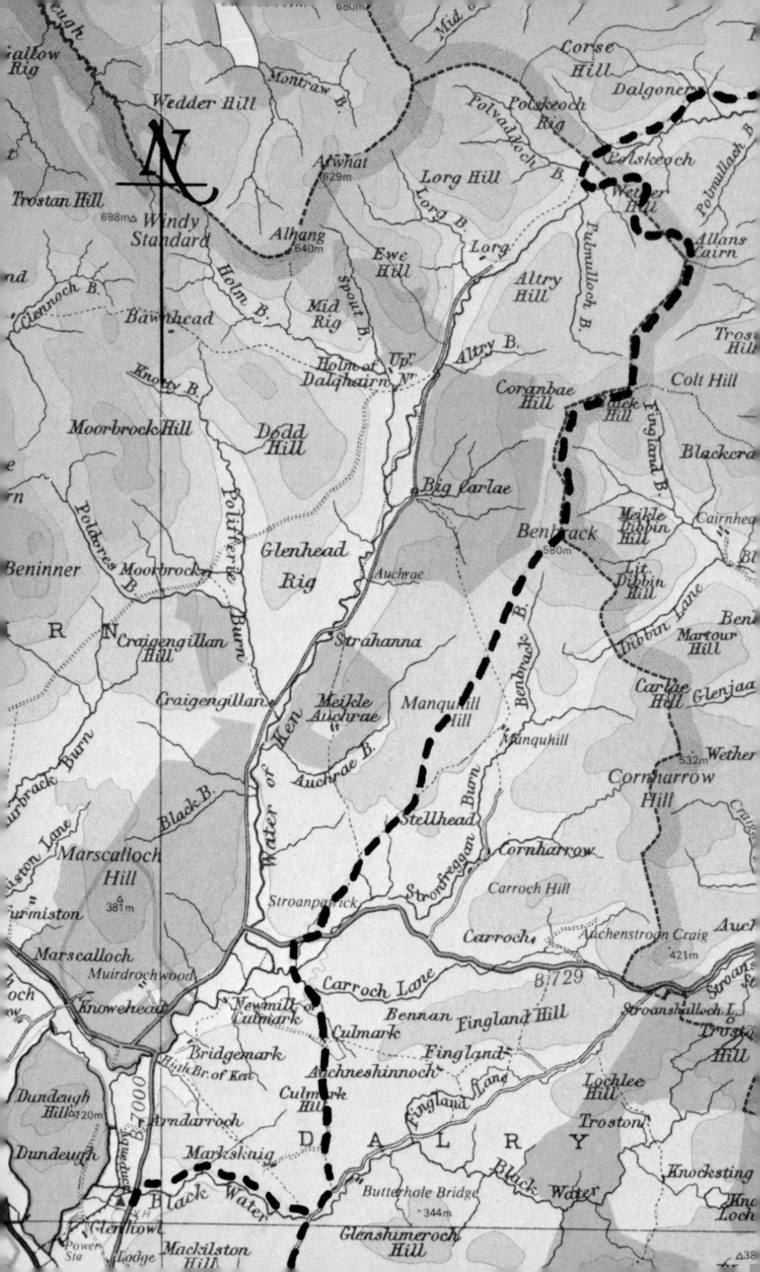

Gallow Rig
Wedder Hill
Montraw B.
Mid
Corse Hill
Dalgoner
Polvaddoch B.
Polskeoch Rig
Polskeoch
Polmullach B.
N
Atwhat
629m
Lorg Hill
Trostan Hill
698m
Windy Standard
Alhang
640m
Lorg B.
Lorg
Wether Hill
Allans Cairn
Ewe Hill
Holm B.
Spout B.
Altry Hill
Clennoch B.
Bawnhead
Mid Rig
Pulmullock B.
Altry B.
Holm of Dalqhairn
Up. Nr.
Knotty B.
Coranbae Hill
Colt Hill
Black Hill
Moorbrock Hill
Dodd Hill
Fingland B.
Blackcra
Big Carlae
Polifferie Burn
Meikle Dibbin Hill
Cairnhea
Poldores B.
Benbrack
580m
Glenhead Rig
Beninner
Moorbrock
Auchrae
Lit. Dibbin Hill
Dibbin Lane
Craigengillan Hill
Strahanna
Benbrack B.
Martour Hill
Craigengillan
Meikle Auchrae
Manquhill Hill
Carlae Hill
Glenjaa
Manquhill
Water of Ken
Auchrae B.
532m
Wether
Black B.
Stellhead
Stronfreggan Burn
Cornharrow Hill
Marscalloch Hill
381m
Cornharrow
Carroch Hill
Stroanpatrick
Furmiston
Carroch
Auchenstroan Craig
421m
Marscalloch
Muirdrochwood
Carroch Lane
B 729
Knowehead
Newmill of Culmark
Bennan
Fingland Hill
Stroanshalloch
Culmark
Bridgemark
Fingland
Trostan Hill
High Br. of Ken
Auchneshinnoch
Dundeugh Hill
420m
B 7000
Culmark Hill
Fingland Lane
Lochlee Hill
Troston
Dundeugh
Markskaig
D A L R Y
Knocksting
Black Water
Butterhole Bridge
344m
Glenhowl
Power Sta
Lodge
Mackilston Hill
Glenshimeroch Hill

From Stroanpatrick to Polskeoch there is a long climb as the Way ascends Manquhill Hill, Benbrack and High Countam; this stretch gives superb walking but is exceptionally exposed. A forest track and a road takes the Way from just after Allan's Cairn to Polgown. The excellent walk over the hills from Polgown to Sanquhar is exposed and there is the added problem of tiredness at the end of a long day.

The text gives warnings about a number of places where route finding needs great care.

Points of interest: Superb views from the hills (especially Benbrack), Allan's Cairn, Sanquhar.

Maps:
1. Ordnance Survey nos. 77, 78.
2. Bartholomew nos. 37, 40.

Transport: There is a bus service from Dumfries to Kirkconnel via Thornhill and Sanquhar. Kirkconnel is on the Glasgow–Carlisle (via Dumfries) railway line; Thornhill is on the Edinburgh–Dumfries bus route (via the A702). There is also a bus service between Kilmarnock and Dumfries via Sanquhar; Kilmarnock is connected to Glasgow by train and bus.

Car parking: On route: on the road to Lochinvar, at Butterhole Bridge, on the A729, at Lorg Bridge (off the Way), at Polskeoch, near Polgown, near Ulzieside. At Sanquhar: on the A76.

Accommodation: Kendoon Youth Hostel (off the Way), Moniaive (off the Way; various), Polskeoch Bothy, Sanquhar (various).

Notes: Be prepared to make a tactical retreat before starting a moorland walk if the weather is poor. Note that the 'breaks' to low ground often involve long walks. An unofficial alternative route is described in order to avoid Manquhill Hill, Benbrack and High Countam if the weather is bad (see p. 144). There are no shops until Sanquhar.

See page 138 for the continuation of this section of the route.

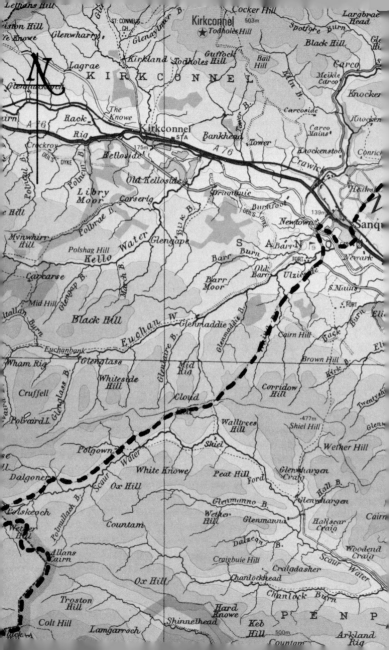

St John's Town of Dalry to Butterhole Bridge (8 km)

St John's Town of Dalry to Ardoch (3 km)

This section starts at the fountain at the junction of the A713 and the A702. Follow Main Street uphill, passing the post office, the local library and a public telephone box. A crossroads is now met and a Victorian letter-box (with the letters 'VR' on it) will be seen on the right. Queen Victoria reigned from 1837 to 1901 and letter-boxes of this reign are seldom seen outside the country districts. The road on the left is the B7000 to Carsphairn; Kendoon Youth Hostel is on this road, 7·5 km away. Go uphill along Midtown to a Y-junction where there is a tall waymarker.

Just to the right of the waymarker is a little stone seat called St John the Baptist's Chair. Little is known about the history of this unusual object but it was hidden for a while after a friend of Sir Walter Scott tried to take it for Scott's collection.

Bear left at the junction and then follow the track that is to the right of Townhead Crescent. As the track straightens, the house on the left (Craighead) has on its southern gable-end a stone plaque with three carved animals and the letters 'WC'. Above the windows that overlook the Way are carvings of a crescent and three or, in one case, four stars.

As the track climbs there is a good view over to Meikle Millyea and the other peaks of the Rhinns of Kells. After passing to the left of Creaganfois and a curious outbuilding with large windows, the track leads to a stile and passes to the right of School House Plantation.

The Way now reaches the pastures above the village and there are good views over the pleasant countryside; Glenlee Power Station can be seen over to the south-west. Follow the dyke on the left, cross a stile and follow the dyke again. Cross the dyke at a stile at the end of the field and then bear right. Cut across the field and head towards the right-hand side of the farm of Ardoch; cross a stone stile over a dyke. Ascend the hill to join a track that runs to the left of the farm.

Ardoch to Butterhole Bridge (5 km)

Turn left at a T-junction, pass some sheep enclosures and turn right to walk along another track. Bear right after a gate to walk high above Ardoch Glen. Bear to the left after passing the end of a dyke on the left, cross a stile beside a gate and then bear left. As Ardoch Hill is rounded there is a good view to the north, where the highest and most prominent hill is Cairnsmore of Carsphairn (797 m).

Cross a stile over a dyke, head to the right-hand side of Barlaes farm and take care to avoid a boggy patch where drainage water gathers from the new plantation on the right. Waymarkers lead to a stile over a dyke. Bear left, cross a small stream and bear right towards some trees, but turn left before they are reached to cross a wooden bridge over the Earlstoun Burn. Turn right and follow the stream, crossing a stile at a fence. Follow the fence and a dyke then bear left in order to climb a little hill. The path now heads in the direction of Cairnsmore of Carsphairn and then bears a little to the right of this direction to go due north. This stretch is waymarked, but care should be taken with route finding in poor visibility. On the right can be seen the road to Lochinvar.

The Way meets a single-track road at a T-junction where the road to the right is signposted to Lochinvar. This lonely little loch is about 3 km away and is now a reservoir surrounded by moors. Lochinvar Castle used to stand on an island in the loch until it was covered when the reservoir was filled. The loch's name is widely known because of the character Young Lochinvar in Sir Walter Scott's *Marmion*. A left turn at this junction leads to the B7000 (2·5 km away); Kendoon Youth Hostel is then 3 km to the north.

Cross the road at the junction and pass the tall waymarker that is on the right. The road crosses moorland and after 1·5 km it arrives at Butterhole Bridge over the Black Water.

Butterhole Bridge to Kendoon Youth Hostel (2·5 km) (spur)

Turn left after the cattle grid at Butterhole Bridge; walk across the moor, following the dyke on the left. The route is waymarked but any path between the waymarkers may be indistinct; however, the route keeps within 50 m or so of the Black Water which is on the left. Drainage channels have been dug in this stretch of moorland so care should be taken, especially if visibility is poor.

Two stiles are crossed during this walk and after the second the Way bears left. The river now flows through a rocky gorge so in misty conditions watch out for cliffs and steep slopes. Keep to the high ground after the gorge and then keep to the left of a drystane dyke. The dyke leads down to a stile and a tall waymarker at the B7000 (which was previously met at St John's Town of Dalry). Turn left, cross the Blackwater Bridge and the hostel is the little wooden building on the right. It is a small and rather basic hostel but is a very pleasant resting place.

Behind the hostel is a dam that stores water from the Black Water and from Kendoon Loch. The water is then fed to Kendoon Power Station, whose tall cylindrical surge tower can be seen about 1·5 km south-west of the hostel. The power station produces 24,000 kW.

Butterhole Bridge to the B729 (4 km)

Butterhole Bridge to Stroanfreggan Burn (3·5 km)
Continue on the road after Butterhole Bridge. It runs parallel to the Black Water and passes a tall waymarker and the track to the farm of Marskaig. About 500 m after the bridge there is a tall waymarker on the right and the Way turns left just before three prominent trees. Ascend the flank of Marskaig Hill, keeping to the right of the highest ground. The Way bears right to a dyke, crosses a stile over a fence and then follows the dyke. Bear left at a waymarker and cross a stile over a dyke. Bear left (and go to the left of a prominent rise) to reach the top of Culmark Hill from where there is a fine view.

The prominent hills to the west of north with steep east-facing slopes are Beninner Gairy (left, 710 m) and Moorbrock Hill (right, 650 m). Behind them is Cairnsmore of Carsphairn.

To the south-west can be seen the tall surge tower of Kendoon Power Station. To its left (and much nearer) are two small buildings; the one on the right is Kendoon Youth Hostel. The Rhinns of Kells are the hills on the western skyline. Meikle Millyea

is the prominent hill behind and just to the left of the surge tower. Corserine (814 m), the highest hill in the Rhinns of Kells, stands to the west and to its right is Carlin's Cairn (808 m). It is said that this hill's name originates from an incident involving Robert the Bruce. When he was being pursued by his enemies a woman called Carlin hid him for a few days so that he might elude capture. In thanks for this deed, Bruce later gave her a present of some land in the district and in gratitude for the gift she built the huge cairn (17 m in diameter and 3 m high) on the summit of the hill.

Continue heading northwards and towards Culmark farm. Head for the left-hand side of the sheep enclosures behind the farm and cross the stile beside them. Follow the track that runs past the farm. The Way crosses an unusual-looking bridge (five concrete pipes lying side by side) over the Stroanfreggan Burn. The burn and its tributary on the right have been eroding the opposite bank and it has had to be strengthened by a concrete embankment that is now almost completely grassed over.

Stroanfreggan Burn to the B729 (0·5 km)
On the right of the track are the remains of Stroanfreggan Cairn which stands on a slight rise. This cairn once covered a circle some 23 m in diameter but much of the material has been removed, no doubt for some practical building purpose. Three large boulders mark the original perimeter of the cairn and there are also some holes in the ground where other such boulders once lay. A cist (a stone coffin) was found in the cairn in 1910 and the huge cap-stone that covered the cist can be seen in place. On the other side of the track is a little hill of very regular shape; this is Stroanfreggan Motte, an ancient fortification.

The hill that stands directly in front is Stroanfreggan Craig; a couple of cairns may be seen on it. The hill also has the remains of a large hill-fort that was once about 40 m in diameter. This general area is a good place to see wheatears.

The track now meets a tall waymarker at the B729; the

Culmark farm is in the foreground. After crossing the B729, the Way climbs the long ridge behind Stroanpatrick.

picturesque village of Moniaive is 15 km away to the right. The Way is soon going to cross high open moorland over Manquhill Hill, Benbrack and High Countam and the next public road that will be reached is at Polskeoch, 15 km farther on.

If weather conditions are bad then a tactical retreat can be made to the left to find accommodation. Kendoon Youth Hostel is about 6 km away – go left at the B729 and left again when the B7000 is met.

The B729 to Polskeoch (12·5 km)
(unofficial alternative route, avoiding Manquhill Hill, Benbrack and High Countam)
It is possible to reach Polskeoch by another and much lower (and shorter) route. Turn left at the B729 and take the first turn on the right (after 800 m) to follow the Water of Ken. After another 10 km the track crosses Lorg Bridge and goes left to the farm of Lorg. Leave the track after this bridge, join a path that follows the Water of Ken (which is on the right) and go through a fire-break in the forest. The Way is rejoined near the Polskeoch Bothy (see p. 147).

The B729 to Polskeoch (15 km)

The B729 to Manquhill Hill (4 km)
Turn right at the B729 and then left at a tall waymarker 300 m later to walk up the track to Stroanpatrick farm. Bear left just before the gate to the farmhouse. Cross a stile and turn right, following the dyke on the right as it runs behind the farmhouse and gradually goes uphill. The path eventually moves away from the dyke and passes to the right of two prominent trees that are beside some old ruined walls. The summit of Manquhill Hill (421 m) now lies straight ahead; great care must be taken in poor visibility.

The Way follows the dyke that is now found on the right, passes some sheep enclosures and then goes uphill to a T-junction of dykes. Cross the stile and keep to the right of the outcrop that is seen ahead. The waymarked path gradually bears to the left after the outcrop and reaches the top of a knoll. Now walk almost due north to a waymarker; it can be seen on the skyline. As you pass this waymarker on your left, the next one should be seen straight ahead on an outcrop. Over to the left is the forest on Auchrae Hill and behind that is the previously mentioned road that runs up to Lorg.

Bear right at the waymarker on the outcrop and follow the ridge to the next waymarker. The summit of Manquhill Hill now lies straight ahead and the Way ascends the north-west shoulder of the hill, passing just to the left of the summit. It is worth ascending the hill's summit for the view.

Manquhill Hill to Benbrack (3 km)

The Way now heads north-east almost directly towards Benbrack (580 m), the next summit to be climbed. The route is indistinct and great care must be taken in poor visibility, in which case it may be safer to keep to the left (towards the forest) to avoid the possibility of straying on to the slopes on the right.

From a waymarker at the north-eastern end of Manquhill Hill, a more distinct path heads downhill and passes to the left of a prominent knoll. Pass to the left of an outcrop that is found soon after the knoll and head in the direction of the top of the forest on the left. Pass to the left of a pile of stones, cross Craigencarse Burn and go over a stile on a fence. Bear left as the path gradually nears the forest on the very steep and seemingly relentless climb up the Shoulder of Corlae to the top of Benbrack. The fence beside the forest runs up to the trig point at the summit.

The view from the summit is quite superb in all directions, indeed this is one of the finest viewpoints on the whole of the Way. The 'golf ball' structures of the radar station on Lowther Hill (725 m) are 25 km away to the north-east. Lowther Hill is the highest point on the Way and is climbed in Section 7. Two landmarks that are roughly to the south-east are the village of Moniaive (12 km away) and the prominent hill of Criffel (659 m, 45 km away), which is to the south of Dumfries.

Winter walkers may be lucky enough to see snow buntings near here. They are winter visitors from the Arctic.

Benbrack to Allan's Cairn (4·5 km)

Cross the stile beside the trig point and turn left. Keep near the
fence on the left as it guides the path northwards down the hillside.
The fence marks the boundary between the districts of Stewartry (to
the west) and Nithsdale (to the east) and the Way follows the
boundary to Allan's Cairn (see later). Soon more forest is seen on
both sides of the route, but fortunately the trees do not obscure the
wide views over the hills. Just after the path begins to make another
ascent, it moves away from the fence for a while but then rejoins it
and follows it up to the summit of Black Hill where there is a
waymarker – and a good view. Colt Hill (598 m) is to the east.

Turn left and follow the fence. The Way soon turns left at a
waymarker, goes over a stile and runs between a fence (on the left)
and a conifer plantation. This direction is followed until the fence
bears right at High Countam, except for a curious (and quite short)
loop into the forest. When the fence ends, the path becomes a track
and this leads to a T-junction beside which there is a tall waymarker
and a signpost to Allan's Cairn. If the weather is poor or if time is
short then the walk to the cairn can be omitted and instead a left
turn can be taken at this junction as the Way will be meeting this
track again (800 m down the track, see later) after visiting the cairn.

Cross the junction and follow the path to Allan's Cairn, taking
care to avoid the very boggy patch (and its deep pools) that will
soon be found. In a clearing is Allan's Cairn, a sandstone pillar
encircled by an iron railing. This is another Covenanting monument
and it was erected in memory of George Allan and Margaret Gracie
who (the text explains) 'were shot by the dragoons of Coupland and
Lagg, near the fawns of Altry in the days of the Covenant'
('fawns' = ' a rough wet place on a hill'). The pillar was erected on
the '2d Sabbath [Sunday] of July 1857' and it stands at an altitude of
497 m.

Allan's Cairn to Polskeoch (3·5 km)

Turn left at the cairn and follow a fire-break (which later bends
round to the left) down to a waymarker at the forest track referred
to earlier; turn right. The track makes a rapid but twisting descent
and passes the Polskeoch Bothy. This simple new bothy offers good

shelter, a fireplace – and running water! It was specially built in 1986 for walkers on the Way. It was constructed by army engineers based in Ripon in Yorkshire and it will be a welcome sight to many a weary person coming off the hills; it can accommodate about eight people.

The track now crosses the Polvaddoch Burn; the end of the unofficial alternative route via Lorg Bridge is then passed. The track soon splits. Bear right and pass the house of Polskeoch.

Short-eared owls, kestrels and blackcock may be seen in the area on the right.

Polskeoch to Sanquhar (14·5 km)

Polskeoch to Polgown (4 km)

A narrow tarmac road starts at Polskeoch and this is followed down to Polgown. To the left and right are new plantations in the Forestry Commission's Nithsdale Forest. The forest ends just before Dalgonar farm and over to the right can be seen the Polskeoch Burn and (farther away) the Polmullach Burn. Both burns have numerous meanders as they flow through the sand and gravel base of the valley. The next farm is Polgown and the Way now leaves the road. The road continues to Penpont which is on the A702.

Polgown to Ulzieside Plantation (6 km)

After crossing the stream at Polgown, turn left at a tall waymarker and walk behind the sheep enclosures. Great care must be taken from now until Ulzieside if the visibility is poor. Follow the fence that is now on the right; this is soon crossed at a stile. Keep following the fence again until it is recrossed at another stile beside a gate. There is soon a good view down the beautiful but very lonely valley of the Scaur Water (or Scar Water), with the spurs of the hills on either side locking into each other to provide an interesting landscape. To the south of east stands Cairnkinna Hill (552 m) which has a cairn on its summit, and to its left (and rather nearer) is Glenwhargen Craig.

After the stile, follow the distinct path that runs to the waymarker on the skyline. Meet a fence that comes up from the right and after a few tens of metres bear left at a fork in the path. Bear right at another fork soon after a waymarker is passed. The path now continues along the hillside with height being gained gradually. The view down the valley slowly opens out and becomes even more superb. The route crosses a stile at a gate and continues along the side of Cloud Hill.

A dyke runs along the top of Cloud Hill, and more or less parallel to the Way, but the path does not get near the dyke until the dyke has descended from Cloud Hill's summit and has climbed a prominent knoll that is seen on the left. The path bears left after passing this knoll and crosses the dyke at a stile.

Bear right, gradually gaining height and keeping fairly near the slope on the left. The sharply defined valley of the Euchan Water can be seen on the left and beyond this is the important communications route of Nithsdale which connects Ayrshire and Dumfries. A mast can be seen on Todholes Hill (480 m) to the north and the village of Kirkconnel lies below it. The path later heads to the right, towards a gate where there is a stile. Turn left after the stile and follow the fence to another waymarker. Sanquhar lies straight ahead and its castle can be seen to the right of the town. Lowther Hill can be seen to the north of east; to its left is Green Lowther (732 m) with its own array of aerials. To the left of Green Lowther is the Mennock Pass which connects Wanlockhead to Nithsdale.

Head north-eastwards down the ridge towards Sanquhar. Waymarkers show the route, but care should be taken in poor visibility as there is no one definite path. Indeed, the broad grassy ridge has a maze of paths and tracks (and some drainage ditches) on it. Do not stray towards the right as the valley of the Whing Burn has some very steep gullies, so if the waymarkers cannot be seen it is safer to keep to the left of the ridge where the Ulzieside Plantation should be seen.

Ulzieside Plantation to Sanquhar Castle (4 km)
When the Mains Plantation is on the right, an ancient construction called the Deil's Dyke can be seen on the hillside between the

plantation and the hill to the south of it, Cairn Hill. The dyke is in the form of a bank and it may have marked a boundary in late Iron Age or later times.

The Way nears the Whing Burn and crosses a fence that runs from Ulzieside Plantation. Turn right, pass a waymarker and then bear left, away from the fence, to meet another waymarker where a right turn should be made towards some trees by the burn. Cross the burn at a wooden bridge and then go over a stile above the bank. Bear left and pass to the right of some sheep enclosures. Head towards the dyke on the left and cross it at a stile. Two more stiles are crossed then follow the dyke on the right and join a track just before a gate.

The track passes to the left of the farm of Ulzieside and a tall waymarker is met at a minor road where a left turn should be taken. The Euchan Water is crossed at the sandstone Euchan Bridge which has the date 1819 engraved on two of its pillars; there is also a bench-mark on the right parapet. The road then passes a number of telegraph poles, two of which bear an old notice which reads: 'Persons throwing stones at the telegraphs will be prosecuted.'

Sanquhar Golf Club is passed on the left and then a tall waymarker is met at a crossroads; turn right and cross Blackaddie Bridge over the River Nith. The three-arch bridge is made of sandstone and has the date 1885 engraved on it. The River Nith is 115 km long; it rises to the north of Cairnsmore of Carsphairn and flows though Dumfries on its way to the Solway Firth.

Turn right at a tall waymarker immediately after the bridge and follow the path that runs along the river-bank. Ascend a flight of steps, pass some industrial buildings, and go under an electrical transmission line that spans the river. Keep high above the river and go through a little gate on the left. Keep to the right of the fence that runs round the housing scheme on the left. Cross a gully after passing the houses and follow the fence on the left in order to reach Sanquhar Castle.

Sanquhar Castle

This ruinous castle measures about 50 m by 40 m and it is protected by steep embankments and ditches. The Way climbs up into the outer courtyard and on the right is a fifteenth-century building through which a pend (an arched passageway) runs. To its right is a circular tower which contained the well chamber. The pend leads to the inner courtyard to the right of which is an early fifteenth-century four-storey square tower. The tower has been greatly altered and little remains of the original structure. Points of interest in it include the vaulted basement, the windows and the spiral staircase.

The castle was built by the Ross family but in 1639 it was sold to the Douglases of Drumlanrig. William Douglas, the first Duke of Queensberry (1637–95) built the fine mansion of Drumlanrig (12 km south-east of Sanquhar) but spent only one night at that place and retired to Sanquhar Castle.

Sanquhar Castle to Sanquhar (0·5km)
Leave the castle from the corner nearest the housing scheme. Cross the castle's defensive ditch and walk through an avenue of trees. A Way notice-board is found on the left, just before the A76 (Kilmarnock–Dumfries) is met at a tall waymarker. There is a campsite at the Castleview Service Station which is just across the road.

Turn left at the A76 and walk along Castle Street. The houses here are mainly single-storeyed. A Victorian letter-box is on the wall of the house at number 18 and the two-storey building opposite it is dated 1890. Pass the church of St Ninians and the end of the section is at the junction of the A76 and the first turning on the right (Leven Road). Two signs at the junction bear the words 'Southern Upland Way'.

Sanquhar

Sanquhar's history goes back many centuries and it became a royal burgh in 1598. Although there is much farming land around it, it has the air of an industrial village, and mining and manufacturing industries were important in its development.

Sanquhar tolbooth.

There is an interesting walk along the A76 through the village to the tolbooth. After passing Leven Road (where Section 6 starts, see p. 157), a tall granite obelisk will be seen on the right-hand side of High Street. This carries the date 1864 and the inscription: 'In commemoration of the two famous Sanquhar Declarations which were published on this spot where stood the ancient cross of the Burgh [the mercat-cross]; the one by the Rev. Richard Cameron, on the 22nd of June 1680; the other by the Rev. James Renwick, on the 25th of May 1685; "The Killing Time".' These two Covenanting proclamations were issued against Charles II and James VII (II of Great Britain) respectively.

Opposite the obelisk is Sanquhar Library, beside which is a house given to Sanquhar in October 1925. On this building's wall is a plaque to Robert Nivison, one of the benefactors. Also on the wall is a barometer and thermometer with a small plaque bearing the words: 'Presented to the Burgh of Sanquhar by William Ewart Esqr. M.P. for the Dumfries Burghs.' Continue past The Crown (established 1738). Sanquhar Post Office is at 41 High Street and is claimed as Britain's oldest post office (1763).

The main road is greatly narrowed as it squeezes past the tolbooth, a fine Georgian building topped by a clock tower, an octagonal cupola and a weathercock. A double-sided staircase leads to a first-floor entrance, above which is the date 1735. An old water pump stands just outside the vaulted pend that runs through the building. There are plans to use the tolbooth as a Tourist Information Centre.

The village has quite a few hotels and houses offering bed and breakfast accommodation; there are also a number of shops. There are campsites at the Castleview Service Station and at the Blackaddie House Hotel (on the left after crossing Blackaddie Bridge). Public toilets are situated to the west of the tolbooth. There is a public telephone opposite The Crown.

Section 6 Sanquhar to Wanlockhead

Information

Start of section: At the junction of the A76 and Leven Road in
Sanquhar (NS784096).
End of section: At the Museum of Scottish Lead Mining in
Wanlockhead (NS872129).
Alternative route: There are two routes between the deserted
cottage of Cogshead and the ruined Meadowfoot Smelt Mill. The
original route is directly across the open moors while the alternative
route is along a forest track and past the farm of Duntercleuch. This
longer northern route has been established to avoid the moors
during the lambing and grouse-breeding season (from the beginning
of April to the beginning of June) and when there may be
grouse-shooting parties on the moors.
Distance: 12·5 km (8 miles) (original route) or 16 km (10 miles)
(alternative route).
Stages:
1. Sanquhar to Cogshead (6·5 km).
2. Cogshead to Meadowfoot Smelt Mill (original route) (3·5 km).
3. Cogshead to Meadowfoot Smelt Mill (alternative route via
   Duntercleuch) (7 km).
4. Meadowfoot Smelt Mill to Wanlockhead (2·5 km).
5. Wanlockhead.
6. Leadhills (off the Way).
Break in route: At Dinanrig Plantation (to Sanquhar).
Conditions: This short section is quite fast as much of it is on track.
The route up to Bog is mainly on road and track. The route is then
over moorland and is very exposed on the steep climb over the
south-east flank of Conrig Hill.

   The original route from Cogshead to Meadowfoot Smelt Mill is
over open moorland and is very pleasant. The alternative route (see
above) from Cogshead to Meadowfoot Smelt Mill is on a good
forest track but the trees restrict the views.

   The Way follows good tracks and paths from the Meadowfoot
Smelt Mill to Wanlockhead.
Points of interest: The lead-mining remains at Wanlockhead

including the beam engine, Loch Nell Mine and the mining
museum.

Maps:

1. Ordnance Survey no. 78.
2. Bartholomew no. 40.

Transport: There is a bus service between Sanquhar and Leadhills.

Car parking: On route: near Bog, at Meadowfoot Smelt Mill. At
Wanlockhead: near the mining museum.

Accommodation: Wanlockhead (various), Leadhills (off the Way;
various).

Notes: The original route after Cogshead goes over a grouse moor
where there might be shooting. The industrial remains at
Wanlockhead are described in some detail as they are quite
fascinating and many walkers will want to spend some time looking
at them. A short unofficial detour is included to see the
Wanlockhead Beam Engine (see p. 167). There are no shops until
Wanlockhead.

Sanquhar to Cogshead (6·5 km)

Sanquhar to Bog (3 km)

This section starts at the junction of the A76 and Leven Road near
the middle of Sanquhar. Walk up Leven Road and pass a sign with
'Southern Upland Way' on it. The road soon splits, so bear left in
order to pass some brick buildings. The local fire station will be seen
on the right. The Way now passes under the Glasgow–Carlisle (via
Dumfries) railway line. This was opened in 1850 and passes through
Kilmarnock which is 45 km to the north-west. Sanquhar has no
railway station, but there is one at Kirkconnel.

Just before the track narrows to a path there is a view of the
house of Eliock; it is amongst some trees about 3 km to the
south-east. This was the birthplace of the legendary James Crichton

Looking back towards Sanquhar from Cow's Wynd. Ulzieside Plantation can be seen
on the right; the Way passes to the left of this as it descends to Sanquhar (at the end of
Section 5).

(1560–82) who earned the nickname 'Admirable Crichton' for his prodigious intellectual powers. It was said that he spoke at least ten languages and had a command of philosophy and mathematics. This amazing young man was killed in a street quarrel by the young Italian prince to whom he was tutor.

The Way climbs Cow's Wynd to get high above Sanquhar. There is now a good view over the village to the hills behind it. The route that was taken by the Way in Section 5 can be seen as it runs between Ulzieside Plantation and the Whing Burn. The village of Kirkconnel is about 6 km farther up Nithsdale and unsightly pit bings can be seen near this village, on either side of the railway line.

A narrow minor road is met; bear right and follow this uphill. It soon deteriorates into a track and passes to the right of a water supply installation. Leave this track when it bends to the right and take a rougher track that heads straight towards Conrig Hill (485 m). The Way will climb the south-eastern flank of this hill before descending to Cogshead. The aerials on Lowther Hill can be seen 10 km to the east. The track leads to a gate where there is a notice informing that 'Dogs must be kept on a lead or they will be shot' – a stern warning indeed!

Follow the well-made dyke on the left until it meets a stile at a conifer plantation. The stretch before the trees may be very boggy, so it might be easier to take a higher route on the right; watch out for a ditch. Cross the stile and walk through a fire-break to another stile. Keep heading in the same direction until a track is found – this bears left and heads towards Dinanrig Plantation. Descend to a gate and a tall waymarker at a minor road. A left turn at the road leads back to Sanquhar, but the Way turns right, towards the hills.

Walk along the road to a tall waymarker at a T-junction where there is a seat for a rest. To the south of the junction (and standing by a stream) is a doocot. For the non-Scots, 'doo' is the Scots word for 'pigeon'. Turn right and head towards the farms of Brandleys and Bog, then bear left when the track splits.

Bog to Cogshead (3·5 km)
Turn left at a path just before the track meets Bog Plantation on the right. The Way now heads north of east over the grassy moors.

Farms and isolated stands of conifers are dotted around the pleasant landscape. The Way is now well above Nithsdale, and Kirkconnel can be seen over to the west.

The path leads to a stile beside a gate and a small rise is then climbed. Follow a fence that is met on the right; the next steep stretch leads to a stile at a junction of fences. Now follow the fence on the right, climb to the col and cross a stile at a fence.

The rather steep route taken by the Way follows a 'coffin route' along which the deceased's coffin was carried from the Wanlockhead district down to Nithsdale for burial. Coal from Sanquhar was also carried along this route to the lead mines. The Mennock Pass cart road was built about 1742 to replace this long-established route.

The Way now follows the edge of the steep gully on the left and descends to meet a forest. The ruinous building that can be seen ahead is Cogshead. Turn left when the trees are met and enter the forest at a stile beside a gate. Turn right at a track and cross the Cog Burn. Just after the end of the forest on the right there is a tall waymarker and a notice explaining the local alternative route (see p. 162).

Cogshead to Meadowfoot Smelt Mill (3·5 km) (original route)

Cross the stile beside the tall waymarker and follow a track towards the old cottage of Cogshead. In very bad weather this building could give some shelter. Turn left at the dyke just before Cogshead and follow this up to a stile. Turn right and a track/path heads generally north of east across the flank of Lowmill Knowe. The Cog Burn is on the right and a wind-powered generator will be seen by its banks. To the south-east are smooth grassy hills that are rent by numerous gullies; behind them is the Mennock Pass.

Cross two streams at small bridges and cross a stile at a gate. Bear left and follow a path going north of east and passing between Highmill Knowe (on the left) and Glengaber Hill (on the right); this path leads to a stile at a gate. Lowther Hill can be seen to the south of east. Bear right and pick up a grassy track that runs downhill to the Wanlock Water. The cottage of Duntercleuch will soon be seen over to the left; the Way's alternative route runs past it.

One interesting landmark that can be seen is Tinto (707 m), 24 km to the north-east. It has a massive cairn on its summit which may have been associated with pagan rituals. Tinto is one of southern Scotland's most conspicuous hills as it stands quite apart from other hills. It is made of red felsite which gives it a special character all of its own.

On the other side of the Wanlock Water is Sowen Dod (544 m), whose eastern flank has huge bare patches that were caused by poisonous lead fumes (see later). The ruins of the Meadowfoot Smelt Mill lie just below the hill.

As the track winds its way downhill there is a view up the Wanlock Water towards Wanlockhead and the remains of the old lead mines. Green Lowther and Lowther Hill stand behind the village. The Way passes some shooting butts and descends to the Wanlock Water, crossing it at a wooden bridge. The route then meets the track to Wanlockhead near a tall waymarker; turn right.

Meadowfoot Smelt Mill

This mill was built in 1843 to replace the Pates Knowes Smelt Mill (see p. 164). The mills used water-power and this one's lower position enabled it to take advantage of a greater volume of water at a higher pressure. The mill produced lead from a mixture of the ore (galena) and lime. Originally there were three hearths (two more were added in 1910) and peat and coked coals were used as fuels. Air was blown into the hearths using power supplied by a large waterwheel.

The hearths were enclosed and in 1867 a complex of wood-lined flues was built in order to take the fumes away. These led to a chimney on the hill of Sowen Dod behind the mill. The remains of these flues can be seen just above the mill and the ground around the wooden posts is devoid of vegetation, so poisonous were the

Sowen Dod and the Meadowfoot Smelt Mill. This is the view from the route via Cogshead. The bare patches on the hill were caused by poisonous lead fumes from the smelt mill.

lead fumes. The flues were washed out twice a year, enabling more lead (12 per cent of total production) to be recovered. Silver could also be recovered from the lead ore and between 1842 and 1910 some 14,000 kg of silver were refined out of a total lead production of about 76,000 tonnes. The plant was finally closed in the 1930s and part of the demolition work on the buildings was done by the army during artillery practice on it during the Second World war.

The history of the mines at Wanlockhead is described later.

Cogshead to Meadowfoot Smelt Mill (7 km) (alternative route via Duntercleuch)

The forest track follows the Cog Burn, ascends the western flank of Lowmill Knowe and then descends to the Glensalloch Burn. It goes round Well Hill, passing to the east of Wedder Dod. The track meets a T-junction where a right turn should be made. Yet another long descent and ascent are made in order to pass to the south of Duntercleuch Rig.

The forest ends at a gate and the track curves round to the right and follows the valley of the Wanlock Water. Lowther Hill can now be seen ahead. The farm of Duntercleuch is passed and there is a small wind-powered electrical generator just after it. The Way then crosses the Wanlock Water at a little wooden bridge beside a ford. The track runs all the way to Wanlockhead.

The scenery on either side of the river becomes barer as Wanlockhead is approached. Spoil heaps from the lead mines lie scattered about and old tramways and cart tracks can be seen at different levels above the banks of the river.

Cross a stile at a gate and the remains of the Meadowfoot Smelt Mill are then passed; the mill is described on p. 160.

A tall waymarker and a notice about the alternative route are in front of the mill. On the right is a small bridge over the river. This is where the Way's original route from Cogshead meets the track to Wanlockhead.

Meadowfoot Smelt Mill to Wanlockhead (2·5 km)

Meadowfoot Smelt Mill to Meadowfoot (1 km)

On the left (and above the level of the Way) is the track of an old tramway and a little farther on are the remains of an ore-dressing plant. This was built in 1843 and in it dirt was removed and the ore was broken into smaller fragments before being taken to the Meadowfoot Smelt Mill.

The hillsides above the valley have a patchwork look about them as they are grouse moors and there is periodic burning of the heather. Shooting butts can be seen and grouse may be heard. Wanlockhead is one of the few places in the west of the Southern Uplands where red grouse are very common and even from within the village they can be heard calling from the heather-clad hillsides.

The hamlet of Meadowfoot is reached and after it is a cemetery. Many of those buried here are described on the gravestones as 'miner, Wanlockhead' and in view of the risks to their lives while working in and living near the mines, the relative longevity of some of the men is surprising. One grave by the northern corner of the graveyard is that of Charles Nelson who was 'accidently killed in the lead mines, Wanlockhead' as recently as 21 October 1953.

On the other side of the river are the remains of the New Glencrieff Mine, with its piles of spoil and the sad sight of industrial decay and dereliction. This was the deepest mine in the district and its workings went down to the astonishing depth of 150 m below sea level! It was used mainly in the second half of the nineteenth century and was closed in 1938. In the 1950s the workings were drained and ore was extracted for a few years, but the low price of lead made the new undertaking uneconomic.

Meadowfoot to Pates Knowes Smelt Mill (0·5 km)

The Way continues along the track, but on the left and only a few tens of metres after the graveyard a little path beside a stream leads uphill to the remains of the Bay Mine. A short distance up this path is a deep stone-lined pit in which there was once a large waterwheel that pumped water out of the mine. The mine was built in 1789 and it had a revolutionary steam pumping engine. Its use has been commemorated by a metal plaque on a tall stone pillar at the mine head which carries the words: 'Site of William Symington's improved atmospheric pumping engine 1789'. Symington (1764–1831) was born in neighbouring Leadhills (see p. 172) and brought up in Wanlockhead. He later developed a steam engine for the tugboat *Charlotte Dundas* which worked on the Forth and Clyde Canal.

Unfortunately the mine closed after only ten years but it was reopened in the second half of the nineteenth century and continued in production until about 1910. The pillar was erected when the mine was reopened in order to support a water-powered pump. The use of this type of pump was a technological step back from the steam-driven apparatus of Symington but it was much cheaper to make and operate. Beside the pillar is a large concrete base for the headgear that was used in the 1950s during an attempt to drain the mine.

The Way continues on the track for a while, but turns right at a tall waymarker and descends to the remains of the Pates Knowes Smelt Mill. This was built in 1764 and enlarged in 1789; in 1842 it was dismantled in order to provide materials for the Meadowfoot Smelt Mill. During the years 1785 to 1835 it smelted about 64,000 tonnes of lead. Its four hearths were fired by burning peat and coal, and two of them have been partially reconstructed. Beside each of the hearths was a smaller 'slag hearth' in which the slag was reheated at a higher temperature in order to recover more of the lead. A vaulted roof above each of the four hearths funnelled the fumes upwards into large chimneys.

The two sets of hearths were built facing opposite directions and between the two sets was a huge overshot waterwheel. This powered the eight pairs of bellows that blew air into the hearths. The waterwheel's pit has been excavated and the water outlet can be seen at the side of the pit. The little shed facing the hearths was where the ore was physically broken down into manageable pieces and dirt was removed by sieving and washing. A plaque above the site has a drawing which shows how the mill once looked.

The Pates Knowes Smelt Mill, showing the reconstructed hearths. A large heap of waste material stands at the site of the New Glencrieff Mine.

Pates Knowes Smelt Mill to the Wanlockhead Mining Museum (1 km)

Turn right at a waymarker, cross the culverted burn and turn left to walk along the route of an old narrow gauge railway. The path passes a plaque on which there is a 'representation of a drawing made at this spot by John Clerk of Eldin in 1775 and which shows the waterwheel pumping engines on the Straitsteps Mine'. On the left can be seen an old shaft and a reconstructed windlass similar to the type used in the 1780s to lift men and materials up and down a shaft. The large Wanlockhead Beam Engine can be seen a little farther away.

From the plaque there is only 0·5 km to the end of the section and the walker can either continue on the Way as it follows the railway track bed to the museum or follow a short detour in order to have a closer look at some other items of interest. The detour is described below (see 'Detour via the Wanlockhead Beam Engine').

Those walkers who are continuing on the Way will cross the burn once more and pass a plaque on the right. It bears the words: 'North Portal. Mennockhass water tunnel. Cut 1763–1774. Length 1385 m.' Water was essential to the efficient operation of the mines: it was needed by the waterwheels and for washing the ore and so the construction of this water channel was of great importance.

The path ends at a tall waymarker and across the road is the Museum of Scottish Lead Mining. A Way notice-board on its wall marks the end of this section.

Detour via the Wanlockhead Beam Engine (0·5 km)
(unofficial detour)

Those walkers who wish to follow the short detour should bear left after passing the windlass. Cross the burn and pass a wagonway. On the left will be seen two cottages that have been renovated by the Museum Trust. Their interiors have been reconstructed to show living conditions in 1740 and 1890.

The Wanlockhead Beam Engine is then reached. This large

The Wanlockhead Beam Engine. A horse gin is in front of the beam engine; the cottages on the left have reconstructed interiors.

structure was water-powered and was used to drain water from abandoned workings in the Straitsteps Mine; it performed this task from the late 1870s until the early 1900s. It has a huge wooden beam which is balanced on a tall sandstone pillar. On the right arm of the beam was suspended a bucket which was filled with water from a cistern. The bucket dropped when it was sufficiently full, thus raising the other arm which was connected to pumping equipment located in the mine workings 30 m below. At the end of each stroke the water in the bucket was automatically released into a drainage channel and so the bucket was raised to start a new cycle; each cycle lasted about thirty seconds. The engine is protected as an Ancient Monument as it is the only water-powered beam engine of its type in Britain.

In front of the beam engine are the remains of a horse gin with the circular track round which the horses walked. The horses turned a vertical axle on which there was a large drum. A rope was wound round this and passed over pulleys to enable ore and spoil to be hauled out of the mine.

Pass to the left of the church, an unadorned building that was built in 1848. Bear right immediately after the church and keep to the right of a fence in order to reach the entrance to the Loch Nell Mine.

This mine was opened in 1710 but was later abandoned from the 1760s to 1793. Then it produced ore until the 1860s when the cost of pumping water from deep shafts became prohibitive. After that it was used to provide access to other mines and today guided trips 200 m into the mine are available at certain times; tickets can be obtained from the museum.

Cross the burn and turn left to rejoin the Way.

Wanlockhead

Wanlockhead is Scotland's highest village and it lies at the considerable altitude of 467 m. Its weather is often just what would be expected at such a height! The houses generally date from the nineteenth century and although there are a few rows of houses,

many of the buildings are dotted about the hillsides in a rather
haphazard manner. This is mainly because the mining companies'
buildings were built on the flattest and best land available and the
miners' houses had to be built on whatever suitable plots remained.
Many of the houses are small single-storey cottages that have
retained many original external features and their whitewashed
walls contrast strongly with the sombre greys and browns of the
surrounding hills.

The road that runs behind the museum leads to the old school
(now a community and outdoor centre), the war memorial, the
Miners' Library and Wanlockhead Youth Hostel.

The Miners' Library is on the left of this road and opposite the
war memorial. The gable-end of the library is dated 1850 and on its
front wall are two plaques. The granite one is inscribed:
'Wanlockhead library instituted 1 Nov 1756'. Below that is a metal
plaque with a bust of the local poet Robert Reid and the words:
'Robert Reid (Rob Wanlock) author of "Kirkbride", "Moorland
Rhymes", etc. Born at Wanlockhead 1850. Died at Montreal 1922.
A great lover of this "auld gray glen" and the kindly dwellers in it.'
The library has about 2,500 books and it was the second
subscription library to be formed in Britain (Leadhills was the first).
It may be open during the busiest part of the tourist season.

The village has a general store/post office which is south-west of
the museum. There is another small shop just above the entrance to
Loch Nell Mine. The Walk Inn (for location, see p. 177) has a
tea-room. The public toilets outside the museum are open during
the summer months and there is a public telephone box near the
library.

Lead mining in Wanlockhead
Lead ore was probably mined in the Wanlockhead district in
Roman times but the first records of 'modern' lead mining go back
to 1675. The first smelt mill was constructed in 1682 but it was
closed after only two years' use. The area saw much bloodshed
during the late seventeenth century's 'Killing Times' so this turmoil
may have greatly hampered the mining operations. New enterprises
were started in 1691 and 1710 and a smelt mill was built in the

middle of the village. The effect on everyone's health doesn't bear thinking about! Rich ore was later found in the New Glencrieff Mine and during the period 1756–65 some 3,434 tonnes of ore were extracted. The ore was processed in two smelters which were constructed near where Pates Knowes Smelt Mill was built in 1764.

However, lead prices were falling and the plants at Wanlockhead were not keeping up with the new technology being used elsewhere. The landowner, the Duke of Buccleuch and Queensberry, took over the operation in 1842. The Meadowfoot Smelt Mill was constructed and production was increased. In 1902 a railway line was built which linked the village with Leadhills and Elvanfoot (Elvanfoot is on the present-day main railway line). More investments were made in the years that followed and new deep shafts were sunk but the mines were unable to survive the Depression of the 1930s and were closed down. The New Glencrieff Mine was reopened for a short time in the 1950s but the ore was smelted outside the district.

Gold has also been discovered in the burns at Wanlockhead. The largest piece found was nearly 200 g in weight and is now in the British Museum.

Public interest in the fascinating industrial history of Wanlockhead led to the setting up of the Wanlockhead Museum Trust and its main attractions are the museum, the industrial relics and the Miners' Library. The museum, which was originally a smithy, was opened in 1976 and it has an interesting display of local minerals, mining equipment, a working model of the beam engine and displays outlining the history and operation of the mines. It is open during the summer months.

A new (and separately run) tourist attraction associated with the mines is planned – a narrow-gauge railway (see p. 178).

Wanlockhead from Lowther Hill. The Way comes over the hills on the left before following the valley of the Wanlock Water into Wanlockhead.

Leadhills (off the Way)

Leadhills is a nearby village and, as its name suggests, it was also connected with the lead-mining industry, though it has none of the substantial remains that Wanlockhead possesses. It is about 2 km north of Wanlockhead along the B797. Its main street has a hotel (The Hopetoun Arms), general stores and a post office; bed and breakfast accommodation is available in the village.

Opposite the post office is the Miners' Library that was started in 1741 by a local poet, Allan Ramsay (1686–1758). Near the centre of the village (and to the west of the main street) is a tall wooden structure with a large bell suspended from it. This was rung at the start of shifts, at funerals and to muster search parties for people missing on the hills. Near the north-western end of the village is a tall granite obelisk erected in 1891 to William Symington 'the inventor of steam navigation'. He also constructed the 'atmospheric pumping engine' at the Bay Mine in Wanlockhead.

Behind the obelisk is the local cemetery and one of the tombstones (it is very close to the obelisk) is that of 'John Taylor who died in this place at the remarkable age of 137 years'. He is said to have worked as a miner for about a hundred years.

Section 7 Wanlockhead to Beattock

Information

Start of section: At the Museum of Scottish Lead Mining in Wanlockhead (NS872129).
End of section: At the Old Brig Inn, Beattock (NT077028).
Distance: 31·5 km (19½ miles).
Stages:
1. Wanlockhead to Over Fingland (8 km).
2. Over Fingland to Daer Water Reservoir (7 km).
3. Daer Water Reservoir to Easter Earshaig (13 km).
4. Easter Earshaig to Beattock (3·5 km).
5. Beattock.
6. Moffat (off the Way).
Breaks in route:
1. Over Fingland (to Elvanfoot).
2. Daer Water Reservoir (to the A702 and Elvanfoot).
3. Mosshope (to the A74).
4. Rivox (to the A74).
5. Holmshaw (to the A74).
Conditions: This is a long and tiring section but one which offers superb scenery over two different ranges of hills. The section starts high up at Wanlockhead and climbs to the Way's highest point at Lowther Hill; it is not downhill from then though, as this is the Way's hilliest section. This means interesting changes of view but all the ups and downs will take their toll on the time taken to complete the section, to say nothing of what they might do to some walkers' knees.

The first stretch (Wanlockhead to Over Fingland) is very hilly and exposed. In good weather it is a marvellous walk, but in wet or windy weather it can be very unpleasant and in bad weather it could be downright treacherous.

From Over Fingland to Daer Water Reservoir the route follows a road and a forest track and the forest offers shelter for much of the distance. After Daer Water Reservoir the Way goes over more

See page 176 for the continuation of this section of the route.

exposed high ground but the shelter of the forest is reached after Beld Knowe. The walk from Holmshaw to Easter Earshaig is through forest. The final stretch to Beattock is on a road and is mainly downhill.

Points of interest: Very fine views from Lowther Hill to Laght Hill and on the hills after Daer Water Reservoir; Moffat.

Maps:
1. Ordnance Survey no. 78.
2. Bartholomew no. 40.

Transport: See p. 55 for services to Beattock and Moffat. There is a bus service between Edinburgh and Dumfries via Crawford and Thornhill; the bus goes along the A702.

Car parking: On route: on the A702 after Over Fingland, before Daer Water Reservoir, near Mosshope, near Rivox, near Easter Earshaig. At Beattock: near the Old Brig Inn.

Accommodation: Beattock (various), Moffat (off the Way; various), Barnhill Springs Country Guest House (next section).

Notes: This is a difficult section – the terrain and the lack of accommodation pose problems – and these factors should be borne in mind if the weather is deteriorating. Moffat is dealt with in this section as it offers more accommodation and shops than Beattock. The end of this section is more than half-way along the Way – less than half the Way to go! There are no shops until Beattock.

Wanlockhead to Over Fingland (8 km)

Wanlockhead to Lowther Hill (3 km)

This section starts at the mining museum in the middle of Wanlockhead. Walk through the museum's car-park, cross a burn and ascend a flight of steps. Pass to the right of some trees and cross a track and the B797 (Sanquhar–Abington). Pass to the right of a tall waymarker and a sign with 'Public footpath by the Enterkin Pass to Carronbridge' on it. On the left is a new graveyard and directly ahead are some buildings that were originally built to house people working at Lowther Hill Radar Station. These are now occupied by the Walk Inn (hotel, bunk-house and tea-room) and a school's field centre.

Just in front of the hotel is a sign with 'Lowthers Railway Society.
Wanlockhead Station' on it. Up until 1938 a railway line associated
with the lead mines ran from Wanlockhead to Elvanfoot, where it
joined the Glasgow–Carlisle line. Now, a long time after the track
was ripped up, local enthusiasts have started to build a two foot
narrow-gauge line that will run between Leadhills and
Wanlockhead. It will run on the existing track bed and at one
point will climb an incredibly steep 1 in 40 gradient!

Ascend the track that runs to the right of the hotel and follow the
direction taken by the fence on the right. The Way now climbs on to
the moor on the western side of Stake Hill. On the right is the
picturesque Mennock Pass which is particularly fine in autumn
when the heather and bracken are changing colour. The green
valley of Nithsdale will be seen at the western end of the pass.

The path heads towards the aerials on Green Lowther then it
crosses the Mossy Burn, turns to the right and heads in the direction
of Lowther Hill. Turn right when the road is met. The tall snow
poles beside the road are reminders that the weather can be very
harsh at this altitude and that snow may still be lying well after
Easter. The road is followed for about 1 km; Tinto can be seen
25 km away to the north-east.

The Way leaves the road at a path on the left a little after a
prominent right-hand bend; keep to the right of a fence. The road is
met twice again; cross it the first time and turn right at it the second
time it is met. The Way now follows the road for about 100 m but
when the road bends to the left the Way goes right in order to cross
a stile over a fence. However, since it is only a short walk to the
radar station, it is worth the effort to see the unusual buildings that
are there.

The radar station was opened just after the Second World War
and it is used by the Civil Aviation Authority to track civil
aeroplanes flying within 290 km of the station. Large aerials revolve
inside the two 'golf ball' buildings that are so conspicuous from far

Lowther Hill. The two 'golf ball' buildings on its summit are visible from far away.

away. Other small aerials that are used for ground-to-air
communications are scattered about the site.

Green Lowther is about 1·5 km to the north-east and its large
steel gantry supports an array of aerials used by British Telecom for
telephone communications; the summit gives a superb view.

Lowther Hill to Laght Hill (3·5 km)
After crossing the stile, turn left and pass to the left of a little hut
that might provide shelter in bad weather. Bear right after the hut
and pass to the left of a waymarker. In poor visibility, keep close to
the radar station's fence which is on the left and follow it to a stile
(see below). The Solway Firth can be seen to the south and to its
right is Criffel (569 m); the Galloway Hills are to the south-west.
Walkers will be pleased to know that this is the highest point of the
Way (710 m) – but it is not downhill all the way to Cockburnspath!

Lowther Hill used to be the last resting place for people who
committed suicide. In the nineteenth century and before, suicides
were treated with great shame. The bodies of local suicides were
taken to this lonely and windswept hillside and buried, without
ceremony, in the clothes in which they were found. The cart that
was used to haul the body up the hill and the horse's harness were
left to rot as they were considered accursed.

The Way now meets the fence which runs due south from the
summit of Lowther Hill and which marks the boundary between
Dumfries and Galloway Region and Strathclyde Region. Daer
Water Reservoir can be seen over to the south-east; the Way will be
passing behind the reservoir later in the section. Cross the fence
(into Strathclyde) at a stile; turn right and keep near the fence.
Even though visibility may be bad (there is often mist on Lowther
Hill) the Way keeps to the left of fences (and dykes) for the next
9·5 km and only crosses a fence just before the descent to the A702.

As the Way follows the fence there is a marvellous view of the
hills in front – they are smooth in outline and cleft with numerous
gullies. The summits to the south-east are generally about
600–700 m high. During the Ice Age, the glaciers on these hills
planed the land to around this level, leaving the post-glacial rivers
to continue the work of cutting the gullies that do so much to

enhance the scenery. To the west is the head of the Enterkin Burn. The Enterkin Pass follows its course and it is remembered in history as the place where (in 1684) a party of dragoons was ambushed and its six Covenanter prisoners rescued.

The fence bears left and the slope steepens. A little bridge takes the Way across a gully before a steep climb to the summit of Cold Moss (628 m); from its summit there is a view of the Dalveen Pass on the right. It was the route taken by a Roman road (see later) and Dalveen Castle used to stand farther down the pass.

The path continues to the next summit, Comb Head (609 m). On the left is a fascinating series of gullies that have been cut in the south-eastern flanks of Lowther Hill and Green Lowther. During the very late stages of the last Ice Age these gullies harboured three glaciers that descended to an altitude of 400 m, so on a geological timescale, this landscape is very 'new'. The water flowing through the gullies gathers in the Potrenick Burn. This burn will be crossed farther on, when the Way is following the A702. Some sheep enclosures can be seen near the stream, just before it starts a series of meanders.

An old dyke (a precursor to the fence that has been followed) starts on the right. Another steep descent/ascent is made to reach the final summit of the Lowther Hills – Laght Hill. The western top of Laght Hill is met at a junction of dykes and fences. The regional boundary now heads south-west but the Way bears left and follows the dyke/fence that goes north-east.

Laght Hill to Over Finland (1·5 km)

The Way descends from the high moors and passes to the right of a prominent rise; cross a stile on the right at a junction of dykes and fences. Follow the dyke/fence on the left and descend to pass the farm of Over Finland (or Upper Finland). The Way crosses the route of a Roman road a few tens of metres before the A702 (Elvanfoot–Carronbridge) is met. The Roman road came north from Nithsdale on a route just south of the Dalveen Pass. From Over Finland it followed the modern road to near Elvanfoot where it met the important highway from Beattock (see p. 198).

The Way meets a tall waymarker at the A702; turn left.

Over Fingland to Daer Water Reservoir (7 km)

Walk northwards on the A702, pass a cottage and then the driveway
to Over Fingland where there is a sign with 'No access to Southern
Upland Way' on it. Another of these notices is found at a lay-by
400 m later. The road crosses the Potrenick Burn which has a little
sluice gate just downstream of the bridge. Turn right at a tall
waymarker 200 m after the bridge; go through the small gate and
bear left. Head towards the forest, passing to the right of some old
broken-down dykes and a fence. The path then follows the Potrail
Water downstream to a wooden bridge.

Turn left after the bridge and cross a stile at the edge of the
forest. Follow the river for about 100 m then turn right at a
fire-break through Watermeetings Forest. Turn right at a tall
waymarker when a forest track is met and keep on this main track.
A well-built circular sheep enclosure stands to the right of the gate
at the end of the forest.

There is soon a good view of the undulating hills to the
north-east. The valley in front of them is that of the Daer Water, a
head-water of the River Clyde, one of Scotland's most important
rivers. Comb Law (643 m) stands to the south of the track. When
the Way re-enters the forest it meets a tall waymarker on the right;
keep to the main track and ignore a track seen on the right.

Less than 1 km after the forest is re-entered the track meets a
waymarker at the single-track road that runs along the western side
of Daer Water Reservoir. The road surface has the traditional red
colour of Lanarkshire roads as the stone chips are made of felsite
which is quarried at Cairngryffe Hill, just north of Tinto. Turn left
at the road and later pass the end of another track to Watermeetings
Forest. Cross the Daer Water and turn right at the road that runs
from the A702 to the reservoir. Cross the Hapturnell Burn and turn
left at a tall waymarker just after the bridge.

The Daer Water Reservoir.

Daer Water Reservoir

The grassed-over embankment of the reservoir's dam is seen to the south-east and below it are the buildings that house the water treatment plant. The post-Second World War house-building programme in industrial Lanarkshire necessitated the construction of this very large reservoir which supplies about 100 million litres (22 million gallons) of water each day to that area.

Beside the road is a large commemorative stone on which is a plaque bearing the words: 'Her Majesty Queen Elizabeth II inaugurated this reservoir on October sixteenth 1956.' The plaque also shows the coat of arms of the Daer Water Board and those of the local authorities that took part in this project. The five coats of arms are (from the left): Hamilton, Motherwell and Wishaw, Lanark County, Coatbridge, and Airdrie.

Daer Water Reservoir to Easter Earshaig (13 km)

Daer Water Reservoir to Mosshope (7 km)

Leave the commemorative stone and walk to the right of the two huge pipes that carry water away to storage reservoirs farther north. Follow the fence that goes round the plantation on the right; this leads to a good view over the reservoir. The reservoir is surrounded on most sides by grassy moors that sweep gently up to summits of over 550 m. The single-track road that was followed earlier can be seen at the southern end of the reservoir.

Cross a stile over the dyke that is met and turn left. Follow the dyke uphill. Stiles are crossed as this dyke (and later a fence) is followed all the way up the very long and steady climb over Sweetshaw Brae to the summit of an unnamed hill (567 m). The summit is marked by a junction of fences and it offers a superb view over the countryside. Lowther Hill and Green Lowther are both to the west and Tinto is to the north. The A74 (4 km to the north-east) can be seen running through the forest as it follows the valley of the Evan Water.

The Way now follows the fence that marks the boundary between the regions of Strathclyde and Dumfries and Galloway. It makes its way to Hods Hill (561 m) where the fence bears to the right and descends. Forest soon appears on the left but there is still a fine view over the moorland and the reservoir on the right. A dyke is followed down a steep descent then back up to the summit of Beld Knowe (507 m) where the dyke and the Way turn to the left.

Continue going straight ahead when the dyke makes another turn to the left, but take a left turn at a waymarker which is found only a few tens of metres after leaving the dyke. Care should be taken in this area if visibility is poor. The path that is now followed may be indistinct but it runs between some mounds; it heads south of east and leads to a stile at a gate. In case of difficulty, look for the dyke that was last seen on the left and follow it to the stile.

The Way has now re-entered Dumfries and Galloway Region and follows a track downhill through a large forest. Some tall white poles are seen beside the track. These mark the route of a gas pipeline which the Way will be following for quite some distance. The poles are deliberately conspicuous in order that the pipeline can be checked quickly by helicopter. About 2 km after the start of the forest, the Way turns right and crosses a stile beside a gate. Two buildings stand near here; to the right is Brattleburn Bothy (see below) and to the left is Mosshope. As the track is followed downhill, a tall, isolated, upright stone will be seen on the left; on it is inscribed: 'J Wat died 1794.' This marks the spot where a shepherd perished in a snowstorm and he was buried where he was found. The Way now crosses a track that runs downhill past the deserted cottage of Mosshope and meets the A74 after about 3 km.

Brattleburn Bothy is about 500 m to the right. Walkers wishing to visit it should follow the track that the Way crosses and bear left after passing an old ruined building. The bothy is then on the far side of a stream. At times of high water it may be better to cross the stream by keeping to the Way and turning right after the Cloffin Burn (see below). This excellent shelter has been renovated and is under the care of the MBA; it will accommodate about eight people.

Mosshope to Easter Earshaig (6 km)

Cross the Cloffin Burn and ascend a wide fire-break to reach the summit of Craig Hill (360 m). At the start of the next descent, Rivox can be seen 700 m away to the south-east and Holmshaw is rather farther away (and to the left of Rivox); the Way will be passing to the right of Holmshaw. The Way now crosses two tracks; the A74 can be reached by going left on either of them. It may now be possible to hear the sound of the traffic on the A74.

Continue on the fire-break and soon Holmshaw will be seen ahead. Cross a stream at a wooden bridge and then go over a stile at a dyke. Head towards the wide fire-break that is seen to the right of Holmshaw. Climb a small rise and then a bridge takes the Way over the Garpol Water. The bridge has a plaque with 'Foy's Bridge' on it and just after it is a little memorial on which is written: 'This plaque was presented by apprentices at ICI Wilton in memory of L/Cpl Foy V erected by 1 Troop 118 Sqn RE TA September 1982.' Vince Foy was an apprentice at Wilton and he was killed in a motor-cycle accident just before he went away to an army camp.

In bad weather conditions it may be an advantage to take the track that runs from Holmshaw to the A74; this goes near the Auchen Castle Hotel.

Bear left and cross a dyke at a stile. Follow the broad fire-break that goes steeply uphill. The fire-break may be overgrown and boggy, and care should be taken when crossing ditches. Bear right at a waymarker at a prominent junction of fire-breaks. Pass through a gap in a dyke and later take a waymarked turn to the right. This fire-break narrows to a small gap through the trees after which a waymarker on another fire-break takes the Way to the left.

The Way passes a pond and the forest soon ends at a gate. Follow a track for a few tens of metres then bear right in order to go through a gate on which there is a 'no dogs allowed' sign. The public road is now met and the farm of Easter Earshaig is seen on the right; turn left.

Easter Earshaig to Beattock (3·5 km)

Easter Earshaig to Beattock Hill (1·5 km)

The road is followed all the way to Beattock. The Way soon enters more forest and just before it leaves the forest at a gate, a little memorial will be seen on the left. A sandstone pillar carries the words: 'Ben Wilson of Holmshaw killed by lightning on the 11th August 1897.' This tragic incident happened in the early hours of the morning when he was collecting lambs during a terrible storm. A notice on the other side of the road lets walkers know that they have been through the Earshaig part of the Forestry Commission's Moffat Forest.

The road begins its descent to Beattock and there is soon a good view over the important valley of Annandale. For those walkers with a bit of energy left after the long walk from Wanlockhead, an even better view of the surrounding district can be obtained by climbing Beattock Hill (259 m).

The view from Beattock Hill

Beattock Hill is to the left of the road and the summit is reached by turning left immediately after passing the gate to the local rubbish tip. While walking to the summit, the walker will cross the remains of a hill-fort that once stood there. Beattock Hill Fort was oval in shape and about 40 m by 20 m in size. It had two walls, the outer one being quite massive, and the entrance to the fort was to the south-west of the hill's summit. This is the most important of a number of hill-forts that are found on this moorland.

The village of Beattock lies to the east of the summit; it lies between the railway line and the A74. Farther away still is the Evan Water which soon joins up with the River Annan. From the southern end of the fort it is possible to see Lochouse Tower (see below) which stands beside the Beattock–Moffat road.

Moffat lies in a sheltered spot 4 km to the north-east. To the right of Moffat is the valley of the Moffat Water; the Way will start heading up this valley in Section 8. To the left of the valley are the Moffat Hills. Their highest point is on the broad summit of Hart Fell (808 m) which can be seen to the left of Moffat.

Beattock Hill to Beattock (2 km)

Continue walking down the road, passing some water supply installations. There is now a much better view of Lochouse Tower. This handsome three-storey tower was built as a fortified house in the troubled times of the sixteenth century. It has been renovated and it is occupied.

The road now crosses the railway line; this is the main west-coast line linking Glasgow and London. It was opened in 1847 and the steepest part of the route was up to Beattock Summit which is 15 km to the north of Beattock and 309 m above sea-level. The construction of the line over the summit involved the building of about sixty bridges and culverts and the making of three cuttings through solid rock. The line climbs a gradient of about 1 in 75 over a distance of 16 km and in the early days two railway engines were often needed to haul the load up this tortuous incline. In 1849 the journey from Glasgow to London by express train took 12 hours and 30 minutes; today it takes just over 5 hours. Passenger services to Beattock were stopped in 1954 and the nearest station is at Lockerbie, 22 km to the south.

Numerous sheds are passed at Beattock farm. A rather nice circular building near the road once housed a horse gin where horses walking round and round in a circle were used to power a mill. The Way soon reaches the bottom of Crooked Brae and meets the A701 (Broughton–Dumfries). Opposite the road-end is the entrance to the Beattock House Hotel (which has a campsite), while the road to the right leads to the village of Beattock (see later).

The Way turns left at a tall waymarker and crosses the Evan Water by means of the single-arch sandstone Beattock Bridge. At the beginning of the bridge is a plaque set into the wall that bears the inscription: 'This bridge was built by John MacDonald from a plan by Thomas Telford in the year 1819.' To the right of this is a more modern plaque with the inscription: 'widened 1951'. The bridge is a minor example of the work of Thomas Telford (1757–1834).

Telford was born in Westerkirk in Eskdale, just 26 km south-east of the bridge. After working in Langholm as a stonemason he began designing houses and eventually moved into large-scale civil engineering projects. He will be remembered the length and breadth of Britain as one of the greatest engineers of his time as he was responsible for the designs of such structures as the Caledonian Canal, numerous highland roads, the Menai Straits Bridge and St Katherine's Docks in London.

The Old Brig Inn is then met on the left; it marks the end of this section.

The Old Brig Inn

The inn was also designed by Telford and it was opened as the Beattock Inn in 1822. It was built as a coaching inn and the innkeeper had about forty horses which were used as fresh replacements for the coaches that stopped here. The inn was on the new Glasgow–Carlisle route which had opened in 1820, bypassing the previous route through Moffat. The last mail-coach to Glasgow left the inn on 14 February 1848, though other coaches on the Edinburgh–Dumfries route still called. The arrival of the railway age forced the inn to close in 1889. It was then used as a farmhouse but was reopened as a hotel in 1975.

The name 'Lochhouse' on the gate dates back to the time when the inn was used as a farmhouse. Behind the main building are the old stables and the traditional arched gateway through which the coaches passed when going into the courtyard.

Beattock

The village has some attractive little cottages that were built in the nineteenth century and a number of them were erected when the railway was being built.

The village has a café and a general store/post office; there are no public toilets in Beattock. Beattock Caravan Park (which takes tents) is passed on the left when walking into the village. At the far end of the village is a junction where the A701 bears to the right and to the left of this junction is a public telephone box. Continue on the A701 to reach the Graigielands Country Park (which takes tents); it is on the right after going under the railway line.

Moffat (off the Way)

The easiest way to get to Moffat from the Old Brig Inn is to cross
the A701 and follow it northwards; pass under the A74 and Moffat
will be reached after 2 km. The Tourist Information Centre is on the
right just after the Mercury Motor Inn. The village is an important
tourist centre and it has a good selection of shops and
accommodation. The Hammerlands Farm campsite is found behind
the Silver Birches public house, which is on the A708.

Moffat is a handsome village, its most noteworthy feature being
its exceptionally wide main street. This was described in 1805 as
'wide and spacious, handsomely formed and gravelled . . . and is a
most agreeable walk to the inhabitants, and to the company that
comes for goat's whey or the mineral waters'.

Moffat's prosperity stemmed from Rachel Whitford's discovery
in 1633 of sulphurous springs just 2 km outside the town at Moffat
Well. A little farther away is Hartfell Spa which is a source of
chalybeate waters which are rich in iron. Before long the village
became a noted spa and tourist centre and in the eighteenth and
nineteenth centuries it became a fashionable resort. Many of the
present-day hotels date back to the spa and coaching days and many
of the hotel frontages have the traditional arched gateway through
which the coaches passed.

Although the spa water could be taken in the Baths House, it was
generally held that it should be drunk at its source as the water
might lose some of its curative properties *en route* to the town.
Descriptions of the taste and smell of the water varied, one writer
comparing it to a 'slightly putrescent egg'. Nevertheless, thousands
flocked to the wells to cure themselves of afflictions such as lung
infections, rheumatism and dyspepsia.

Moffat's most impressive building is the Moffat House Hotel
which is found on the west side of the main street; it was designed as
Moffat House by James Adam in 1751 for the Earl of Hopetoun.
When James MacPherson was staying there in 1759 he showed the
so-called 'Ossian' verses to John Hume. MacPherson claimed that
he had discovered these 'ancient' Gaelic poems and they were
published as long-lost originals and named after Ossian, son of the

third-century Irish hero Fingal. The poems started off a great literary controversy and MacPherson never produced the originals, thus bolstering the opinion of those who claimed that he had written them himself. So heated was the debate surrounding the affair that at one point MacPherson challenged the famous writer and critic Dr Johnson to a duel!

The Baths House where the waters were taken stands just south of the Moffat House Hotel. It carries the date 1827 above the inscription denoting its present use: 'Town Hall'. The local library (and public toilets) are situated behind it.

The Colvin Fountain stands in the middle of the main street and on top of it stands the bronze statue known as the Moffat Ram. The fountain was erected in 1875 and its prominent position reflects the importance of sheep farming to the local economy.

At the southern end of the main street are the roads to St Mary's Loch and Selkirk (A708) and to Beattock (A701). Near the start of the Beattock road stands St Andrew's Parish Church, a Gothic building erected in 1885–7 and with a tower 33 m high. Opposite it stand three buildings of interest to the visitor: the local museum, the Black Bull Hotel and the Tourist Information Centre.

Moffat Museum has a collection of local material covering the landscape, history and crafts of the area. It is open at Easter and on most days from Whit to September.

The Black Bull Hotel is one of the town's oldest buildings, dating back to 1568. In the late seventeenth century it was used as a base by Graham of Claverhouse during the 'Killing Times' when he ruthlessly hunted and butchered the Covenanters. Robert Burns also visited the inn in 1789 and scratched the poem 'Epigram on Miss Davies' on one of the window panes.

Robert Burns (1759–96) is Scotland's greatest poet and his works have been translated into the world's major languages. He was born in Ayrshire and received little formal education. The farms he and his family worked were very poor and he considered emigrating to the West Indies. In 1786 he had just had published the Kilmarnock edition of his poems, including 'The Twa Dogs' and 'To a Mouse', when he was persuaded to go to Edinburgh to publish a further edition. His new source of income allowed him, in 1788, to settle at

Ellisland on the Nith where he wrote 'Auld Lang Syne' and 'Tam o'
Shanter'. In 1789 he took up a post as an excise officer, moving later
to Dumfries. In Nithsdale he wrote his greatest collection of
Scottish songs. However, his health was failing and he died at the
age of thirty-seven.

The walker may wish to ponder on how many of the world's poets
have their words sung by tens of millions of people of different
nationalities. The best-known of his songs is 'Auld Lang Syne'
which is popular in so many different countries, particularly at the
end of happy gatherings:

>Should auld acquaintance be forgot,
>   And never brought to min'?
>Should auld aquaintance be forgot,
>   And days o' lang syne?
>
>   For auld lang syne, my dear,
>   For auld lang syne,
>   We'll tak a cup o' kindness yet,
>   For auld lang syne!

Section 8 Beattock to St Mary's Loch

Information

Start of section: At the Old Brig Inn, Beattock (NT077028).
End of section: At Tibbie Shiels Inn at the southern end of St Mary's Loch (NT240205).
Alternative route: There is an alternative route around Aik Rig during the lambing season; see p. 200.
Distance: 32 km (20 miles) or 32·5 km (20 miles) taking the alternative route.
Stages:
1. Beattock to Dumcrieff Bridge (2·5 km or 3 km taking the alternative route).
2. Dumcrieff Bridge to Craigmichan Scar (8·5 km).
3. Craigmichan Scar to Over Phawhope (4 km).
4. Over Phawhope to Scabcleuch (9·5 km).
5. Scabcleuch to St Mary's Loch (7·5 km).
6. St Mary's Loch.
Breaks in route:
1. The River Annan (to Moffat).
2. Dumcrieff Bridge (to Moffat)
3. Belshaw Bridge (to the A708).
4. Craigmichan Scar (to Selcoth and the A708).
5. Scabcleuch (to Ettrick).
6. Pikestone Rig (to the Loch of the Lowes).
Conditions: This is a rather long section but it is reasonably fast as much of it is on track or road. Two good stretches on moorland (especially the one at Pikestone Rig) need great care in poor weather as they are very exposed.

   The pleasant walk from Beattock to Belshaw Bridge is generally along minor roads and good paths. The forest track from the Moffat Water to Birch Hill allows height to be gained easily and quickly. The path from Birch Hill to Ettrick Head is nice and very open and needs care from Craigmichan Scar onwards. The walk down the Ettrick Valley to Scabcleuch is exposed but is on good track and

See page 196 for the continuation of this section of the route.

road. The path from Scabcleuch to the Captain's Road is over high moors on Pikestone Rig. It is nice but in bad weather it could be very difficult.

Points of interest: Views of the Moffat Water, Craigmichan Scar, St Mary's Loch.

Maps:
1. Ordnance Survey nos. 78, 79, 73.
2. Bartholomew no. 41.

Transport: There is a bus service between Ettrick and Selkirk. There are services between the Glen Café and Peebles, Selkirk and Moffat.

Car parking: On route: near Dumcrieff Bridge, near Belshaw Bridge, at the end of the public road up the Ettrick Valley, near Scabcleuch. At St Mary's Loch: near Tibbie Shiels Inn and near the Glen Café.

Accommodation: Barnhill Springs Country Guest House, Moffat (off the Way; various), Craigbeck Hope, Cossarshill, Angecroft Caravan Park (off the Way), Honey Cottage Caravan Park (off the Way), Tushielaw (off the Way), Ettrick Bridge (off the Way), Tibbie Shiels Inn, Rodono Country Hotel (off the Way).

Notes: This is another very pleasant walk, except that there are too many conifers at some points. Walkers who visit Moffat can rejoin the Way just after the beginning of Section 8. By going along the A708 and taking a road on the right, the Way can be met near Aik Rig or at Belshaw Bridge. A map should be studied for the details. There are no shops until Galashiels.

Beattock to Dumcrieff Bridge (2·5 km, or 3 km taking the alternative route)

Beattock to Aik Rig (1·5 km)

This section starts at the Old Brig Inn in Beattock. Cross the A701 and walk along a little lane between two fields; a tall waymarker stands to the left of the lane. This blocked-off and overgrown minor road leads towards the A74. This is one of Scotland's busiest roads and, although not a motorway, it is one of the country's most important highways as it links central Scotland with Carlisle and north-west England. There are plans to upgrade the road to a motorway.

Fortunately, the walker does not have to cross the A74 as a narrow path on the right descends to the Evan Water. This is not a big river, but is an historically important one as its route was followed by the Romans, the railway builders and the modern roadmakers as they each tried to find a route from north-west England into Scotland. The Evan Water joins the River Annan about 2 km farther downstream.

The path takes the Way under the A74, past a little wood and then on to a minor road where a right turn should be taken; beware of traffic as this road leads to the A74. Although the road now leads through pleasant rural scenery, the roar of the vehicles on the A74 will be in the ears of the walker for quite some time.

About 500 m after joining the road, the Way crosses the route of a Roman road. The line of this road can be seen running through two farm gates that are directly opposite each other. A Roman fortlet stood about 2 km to the south of the Way and the road went past it, through these gates, past Lochouse Tower and then over Coats Hill (which stands to the west of Moffat). From there it kept to high ground before swinging north-westwards to a camp at Beattock Summit. The route then continued to Glasgow via Carstairs or Edinburgh via Biggar.

The top of Lochouse Tower (see p. 187) can be seen about 500 m away to the left. The Way passes Barnhill Springs Country Guest House on the left and in the field opposite it is an old Nissen hut.

The next river to be met is the River Annan, one of the region's most important rivers. It starts at a large and well-known gully north of Moffat called the Devil's Beef Tub, once a noted place for hiding stolen cattle. The river runs through the important agricultural valley of Annandale and passes through the town of Annan before flowing into the Solway Firth, some 38 km below this point.

The most famous historical figure connected with Annandale is King Robert the Bruce (1274–1329), whose family held the title of Lord of Annandale. Bruce spent much of his youth at the court of

Edward I and was at peace with Edward as late as 1302. Bruce was not involved in William Wallace's battles at Stirling Bridge and Falkirk but after Wallace's execution in 1305, Bruce took up arms against Edward. He was crowned King of Scotland that year and spent the next eight years inflicting defeats on English-held positions in Scotland. This culminated in the Battle of Bannockburn in 1314 when the English army was routed. Hostilities continued until 1327 and the Treaty of Edinburgh was signed with Edward III on 17 March 1328.

The river is crossed by a Bailey bridge which is made of a lattice of steel bars; this type of bridge is named after its inventor Donald Bailey, a Yorkshire engineer. Just in the manner that engineers do things, his initial design was sketched on the back of an envelope while he was on his way to a conference. The design was put to great use during the Second World War as its simplicity and robustness allowed it to be erected quickly so that heavy vehicles could cross rivers with minimum delay.

The road soon comes to a T-junction and this is where the alternative route starts. On the opposite side of the road there is a stile, a tall waymarker and a notice informing the walker that this next part of the Way (over Aik Rig) is closed from 15 March to 15 May each year during the lambing season. The alternative route (see below) follows the road on the right.

The road on the left at the junction leads to Moffat which is about 3 km away.

The route over Aik Rig (0·5 km)
(original route)
Those walkers who are following the Way over Aik Rig should cross the stile and head uphill, bearing leftwards and heading towards a stile at a fence. The Way then follows the dyke on the right.

At this point, walkers may wish to detour slightly up to the left to reach the summit of Aik Rig as it offers a good view of Moffat and Annandale. The wooded hill to the right of Moffat is Gallow Hill (254 m), where local criminals were dispatched. From this vantage point there is also a view (to the north-east) of the valley of the Moffat Water. On the descent of Aik Rig there is a sighting (also to the north-east) of the mansion of Dumcrieff (see below).

The Way meets the alternative route around Aik Rig at a roadside stile; turn left and follow the Moffat Water. A post beside the stile carries the same notice about the diversion as was seen earlier.

The route around Aik Rig (1 km)
(alternative route)
Those walkers who take the alternative route should turn right at the T-junction and follow the River Annan downstream. Its banks have been strengthened to prevent flooding of the low-lying fields. Oakriggside is passed; it has a fine display of broom and rhododendron bushes. As the road curves round to the left, a notice with 'toot' on it will be seen on the right, so drivers can give a warning signal to other road users on this tight bend. The house beside the bend is called Three Waters as three rivers (the Evan Water, the River Annan and the Moffat Water) meet just south of it.

The road follows the Moffat Water upstream and the end of the route over Aik Rig is met on the left about 700 m after Three Waters.

Aik Rig to Dumcrieff Bridge (0·5 km)
From the junction of the routes over Aik Rig and around it, the walker should follow the Moffat Water upstream to the T-junction at Dumcrieff Bridge. The road on the left at this junction goes to Moffat, about 2·5 km away. There is a fine view of Dumcrieff just before the bridge is crossed.

The house's best-known occupant was John Loudon McAdam (1756–1836), who lived there in 1783–4. He was an Ayrshire inventor who gave his name to the system of road-making known as 'macadamizing'. His first attempts at the new methods were made (while he was still at school) between Maybole and Kirkoswald, which are south of Ayr. His roads consisted of two layers: the lower one was made of crushed rock to support the load while the upper one used a lighter stone to absorb wear and to shed surface water. He is buried in the old graveyard in Moffat.

Robert Burns' first biographer, Dr James Currie (1756–1805), owned Dumcrieff in the late eighteenth century and the house was rebuilt in the early nineteenth century by Dr John Rogerson (1741–1823), who had earlier been the court physician to Catherine the Great of Russia for nearly fifty years.

Dumcrieff Bridge to Craigmichan Scar (8·5 km)

Dumcrieff Bridge to Belshaw Bridge (1·5 km)

Turn right and cross Dumcrieff Bridge. The Way follows the road for a short distance, then crosses a stile on the left to enter Dumcrieff Wood; this is found just before a minor road is met on the left. This is the finest beech wood in the whole of Annandale and the woodland walk is very pleasant, with mature trees rising high above the path. The route generally runs parallel to the just-mentioned minor road which is now on the right, then swings leftwards when a roadside cottage can be seen on the right. In autumn the path may be obscured by a deep layer of leaves.

The Way now crosses a small stream and a stile to meet the Moffat Water once more. Dippers, goosander and grey wagtails may be seen. Follow the river upstream to a stile beside Belshaw Bridge; a large flat grassy haugh is on the right. A minor road is now met. The A708 can be reached by turning left and walking about 500 m, but the Way crosses the road to a tall waymarker beside a gate and follows a track.

As the track is followed alongside the river there is a good view up the valley of the Moffat Water.

The valley of the Moffat Water

The valley has the classic U-shape of a glaciated valley. It is situated on a geological fault and this accounts for its straightness as the weakness of the rock along this fault made it easier for the ice to cut its way down the valley. On either side of the main valley are a number of hanging valleys that held tributaries of the main glacier.

The most famous of the hanging valleys is the one that ends with the waterfall known as the Grey Mare's Tail. This 61 m high waterfall is about 13 km up the valley from this point. The Tail Burn issues from Loch Skene, a fine example of a moraine-dammed loch. The loch, waterfall and some of the surrounding hills are under the care of the National Trust for Scotland.

Just 2 km farther up the valley from the waterfall is Birkhill cottage; this once served as a summer inn and the Galashiels' schoolteacher Charles Lapworth (1842–1920) stayed in it while he was studying the geology of Dob's Linn. The linn is situated about half-way between the Grey Mare's Tail and Birkhill cottage; it is found by first locating the confluence of three streams on the west side of the main road, then following the westmost stream up a narrow gully. Lapworth found many graptolite fossils in the black shales in the main cliff near the linn. These graptolites were 'colonial' organisms that lived in the sea some 400 million years ago and the fossils enabled Lapworth to date the surrounding rocks. He published his findings (*The Moffat Series*) in 1878 and later became Professor of Geology and Mineralogy at what is now the University of Birmingham. Because of the significance of the site, Dob's Linn is visited by geologists from all over the world and a plaque has been erected on Birkhill cottage as a tribute to one of Scotland's greatest geologists.

Belshaw Bridge to the Wamphray Water (5·5 km)
After following the Moffat Water for a short distance, the track swings right and runs alongside a plantation. A cattle grid is reached at a boundary wall and about 200 m to the left of the cattle grid is a little wooded hill on which are the remains of Cornal Tower. The tower was probably built in the sixteenth century and had walls about 1 m thick; unfortunately only part of the tower's north wall is left.

There is soon a view over to the west and it should be possible to see the A74, the Old Brig Inn and Beattock Hill Fort. The track soon nears the Cornal Burn which can be heard on the left. The track winds its way uphill through the forest and takes a sharp turn to the left at a waymarked junction just before crossing the Cornal Burn. There is a sign with 'warning maximum load 2t gross' just before the small bridge over the burn; a ford is provided for heavier vehicles.

About 600 m later, the house of Craigbeck Hope will be seen on the right. This will be a most welcome sight to many walkers as it offers bed and breakfast accommodation and refreshments. The track soon starts to descend and there is a sharp bend to the right before Birch Hill. On the right (i.e. to the south) is the narrow valley of the Wamphray Water, a tributary of the River Annan. It is worth looking at some of the steepest slopes above the western side of the stream – they are exceptionally steep yet, somehow or other, the foresters have managed to plant trees there.

The Wamphray Water to Craigmichan Scar (1·5 km)
Just after the track takes another bend to the right and goes over the Wamphray Water, the Way turns left at a waymarker and follows the stream through a fire-break; Birch Hill is on the left. An accommodation leaflet box is soon passed. The slopes on Croft Head (636 m) on the left soar high above the path. Their upper parts are bereft of soil and long trails of scree run down through the trees. Cross a stile over the fence on the left; keep following the stream and walk over the grassy moor towards a sheep enclosure just before Craigmichan Scar.

Frost action and running water have attacked the easily eroded rocks on the south-western flank of Capel Fell (678 m) to produce Craigmichan Scar. The Selcoth Burn tumbles over a small waterfall at the side of the scar. The slopes on either side of the burn are long and steep and are very dangerous, especially in wet conditions or if there is a covering of snow or ice.

Walkers wishing to reach low ground from here can take a path that bears left just before the sheep enclosure and heads north-west, high above the Selcoth Burn; great care should be taken on this path. The farm of Selcoth is 3 km away and is only 1 km from the A708.

Craigmichan Scar to Over Phawhope (4 km)

Craigmichan Scar to Ettrick Head (2 km)
The Way bears right immediately after the sheep enclosure and climbs well above the dangerous slopes. The Way takes the higher

of two paths that will be found and if the grass is slippery then an even higher route should be taken. Winter walkers may well be glad of an ice-axe.

The Way now descends to meet the Selcoth Burn which is crossed at a small bridge. A path then climbs uphill and past a waymarker that can be seen on the skyline. On the right, the Selcoth Burn can be seen coming down the northern flank of Loch Fell (688 m), one of the highest hills in the district.

Care should be taken on the next stretch of moorland in poor visibility. The Way heads just north of east and towards a gate and a stile on the fence that runs in a north-west to south-east direction from Capel Fell (on the left) to Wind Fell (on the right). The fence marks the boundary between Dumfries and Galloway Region and Borders Region so once over the stile the walker is in the Borders and well on the way to Cockburnspath. If there is a problem in finding the stile in bad visibility, then it will be found to the north-west (i.e. the left) of the fence's lowest point. The fence also marks an important watershed: previously, all the rivers that the Way crossed flowed towards the west coast, but now they will flow towards the east coast.

Once over the boundary fence, keep heading in the same direction towards a forest which is entered at a stile. Bear left and follow a stream down to a forest track where a right turn should be taken. The Way has now reached Ettrick Head, and the valley of the Ettrick Water (a tributary of the River Tweed) stretches away to the north-east. The high and rounded hill that is ahead and to the right of the track is Ettrick Pen (692 m).

Ettrick Forest

The name Ettrick is well known in Scottish history because of the famous hunting-grounds of Ettrick Forest. The forest covered most of Selkirkshire (which was essentially the valleys of the Ettrick Water and the Yarrow Water) and some of the land farther north. A medieval 'forest' was a hunting reserve governed by special laws;

Craigmichan Scar. The Way heads to the right of this and follows the Selcoth Burn.

it was not necessarily a tree-clad area, though of course all forests had areas of cover for game. This great forest of David I was in existence by *c.* 1136. The forest had oak, birch and hazel and it was part of the old Caledonian Forest that grew in Scotland after the end of the Ice Age.

The forest had large numbers of wild animals roaming about it and it was valued as a great hunting reserve. It was also a hiding-place for thieves and the Scottish kings made sport out of chasing both the animals and the thieves. An old account relates that in 1528 James V 'made proclamation to all lords, barons, gentlemen, landward-men, and freeholders, that they should compear [appear] at Edinburgh, with a month's victuals, to pass with the King where he pleased, to danton [daunt] the thieves of Tiviotdale, Annandale, Liddisdale, and other parts of the country; and also warned all gentlemen that had good dogs to bring them, that he might hunt in the said country as he pleased'. The call was duly answered by the astonishing total of 12,000 men!

James later introduced 10,000 sheep into the forest, replacing an equal number of bucks that had lived there. The number of trees was further reduced and the hills began to take on the rather bare appearance they have today. It is worth remembering that the district has a man-made landscape – flocks of sheep are as unnatural here as the serried ranks of conifers that have recently been planted on the hillsides.

Ettrick Head to Over Phawhope (2 km)
Follow the track downhill. Forestry covers many of the hillsides but there is still a broad grassy expanse on either side of the Ettrick Water. Some circular sheep enclosures are seen by the stream. The buildings at Over Phawhope and Potburn can be seen farther down the valley.

The track bends to the left when the Entertrona Burn is met and the Over Phawhope Bothy is then on the left. There is a Way

Over Phawhope Bothy. The Way follows a track down the Ettrick Valley to the bothy before it crosses the Ettrick Water by means of the bridge seen on the right.

notice-board on its wall and a notice on the door carries the words:
'With the owners' permission this bothy is maintained by the
Mountain Bothies Association.' It is quite a roomy building that
could accommodate about ten people and it is a fine place to have a
lunch break – especially if it's raining! The outbuilding beside the
bothy has an interesting entrance to it at one end – but for sheep
only!

Over Phawhope to Scabcleuch (9·5 km)

Continue on the track after the bothy, pass a notice with 'Potburn
South' on it and then cross a wooden bridge over the Ettrick Water.
A plank at the end of the bridge has 'Constructed by 1TP 66 SQN
RE' written on it; this refers to the Royal Engineers from Dover
who built it. The track passes through the farm of Potburn. This
very isolated farm is far from the amenities of the Border towns and
as it is not connected to the public electricity supply it has to
produce its own electricity by using a generator. A sign with
'Potburn Mid' on it is passed on the left just before crossing the
Longhope Burn. The track then ascends to a gate and a parking
area at the start of the narrow single-track public road.

   From the parking place there is now 8 km of metalled road to the
farm of Scabcleuch; this is downhill and gives a fast walk. Sheep
farming is important in the valley and the farms are generally bigger
and more prosperous the farther down the valley they are. The
numerous sheep enclosures on either side of the valley date back to
well before the conifers were planted. The modern forestry
plantations have taken over great stretches of the hillsides and they
are criss-crossed by wide fire-breaks and unsightly access tracks. A
sign with 'Potburn North' is passed beside the bridge over the East
Grain. Broadgairhill farm is passed on the left 1·5 km later. There is
a nice little rocky gorge and a stand of Scots pines just after the
entrance to Nether Phawhope.

   At the next farm, Over Kirkhope, the Kirkhope Burn has
brought down a lot of gravel and boulders from the hills and there
are some Scots pines near the bridge. There was once an old village,

a chapel and a graveyard a few hundred metres upstream of the bridge, but only a few mounds remain to mark the site. Just before the bridge over the burn, there is a small milestone on the left. There is no inscription on it, but it is placed 22 miles from Selkirk. There is a bench-mark on the left wall of the bridge.

Shorthope is passed on the right and a little after Brockhoperig a wooden shed beside the road houses equipment used for measuring the flow of water in the river. The next farm (Cossarshill) has a small campsite and a small stock of provisions for sale.

The Way leaves the road (and goes left) when the farm of Scabcleuch is met.

The Ettrick Valley

The road continues down the very pleasant and sparsely populated Ettrick Valley to Selkirk.

Just 2 km down the road is Ettrickhill where there is a tall sandstone monument to James Hogg (see p. 215) bearing the inscription: 'Erected on the site of the cottage in which James Hogg . . . was born.' Ettrick Church is nearby; it has a square tower with the words 'Erected AD 1824' on it. At the eastern end of the church is a staircase leading to the 'laird's gallery' inside the church where the local landowner had his personal seat high above the rest of the congregation. James Hogg is buried just a few metres south of the church-tower and next to his headstone is one inscribed: 'Here lyeth William Laidlaw the far-famed Will o' Phaup who for feats of frolic, agility and strength had no equal in his day.' Will, who was James Hogg's grandfather, was the last man in Ettrick to speak to fairies. The grave of Tibbie (Isabella) Shiels (see p. 212) and her husband Robert Richardson is beside a tree to the west of the church-tower.

Accommodation can be found after the B709 is met at Ettrick, 5 km down the road from Scabcleuch. Angecroft Caravan Park is then 1 km away (B709 to Langholm), while on the B709 to Selkirk are Honey Cottage Caravan Park (3 km away) and Tushielaw Inn (4·5 km away); both the caravan parks take tents.

Scabcleuch to St Mary's Loch (7·5 km)

Scabcleuch to Riskinhope Hope (4 km)

Opposite Scabcleuch farm there is a tall waymarker at a stile and beside them is a signpost with 'Public footpath to St Mary's Loch' on it. This was erected by the Scottish Rights of Way Society (SRWS), a body founded in 1845 to fight for the preservation of rights of way in Scotland. Cross the stile and head up to the top of the field where another stile can be seen. Bear to the right and follow the Scabcleuch Burn upstream. This pleasant walk over grassy moorland has Scabcleuch Hill (405 m) on the left and Craig Hill (487 m) on the right; cairns can be seen on Craig Hill.

Great care must be taken from now until the abandoned farm of Riskinhope Hope is met, especially in poor visibility. Keep near the burn when it is running in a deep gully and do not stray on to any paths going away to the left. At the head of the burn, the Way heads northwards to cross a fence at a stile beside a gate; on the left is Peniestone Knowe (551 m). This fence is a very important landmark in poor visibility; it runs between Peniestone Knowe and Rig Head and there are two stiles over it. One stile has a SRWS signpost on it (to Riskinhope and Ettrick Kirk), but the Way's stile is to the west (i.e. the left) of this.

Bear left after the stile and follow an indistinct path. This becomes more distinct as it runs below Peniestone Knowe and it passes a tall pole (which can be seen from the stile) which carries SRWS signs to Riskinhope, Scabcleuch and Ettrick Kirk. It should be noted that Riskinhope (or Riskenhope) is beside Loch of the Lowes; it is not on the Way and it should not be confused with Riskinhope Hope which the Way will soon pass. Riskinhope Hope was built after Riskinhope and was given its unusual name to avoid confusion between the two houses.

The path runs high above the broad valley of the Whithope Burn and meets a marked junction of paths about 800 m after the stile. There are two signs here, one with 'Southern Upland Way' on it, the other with 'Loch of the Lowes'. The path on the left can be taken to gain low ground quickly as it reaches Riskinhope at the Loch of the Lowes after about 2 km. The loch is just beside the

A708 (Moffat–Selkirk) and Riskinhope is 2 km from Tibbie Shiels Inn.

The Way now heads for Riskinhope Hope. The farmhouse is north-east of the junction of paths, so bear right, descend, and pass to the right of a circular sheep enclosure. The indistinct path now makes its way downhill, gradually getting nearer the Whithope Burn. A small isolated stand of trees will be seen to the north-east. Riskinhope Hope is beside this and the path heads to the right of the trees. Pass to the right of the farmhouse; it is in a dangerous condition and cannot be relied on for shelter.

Riskinhope Hope to St Mary's Loch (3·5 km)

Follow the Whithope Burn and cross it at a wooden bridge beside which is a little cairn on which is written: 'Built by Burma TP J.L.R. [Junior Leaders Regiment] RE Oct 83'; these engineers came from Dover. The word '*ubique*' ('everywhere') is also on the cairn and it is part of the Royal Engineers' motto: '*Ubique quo fas et gloria ducunt*' ('Everywhere where duty and glory lead').

Climb the east side of Earl's Hill and the edge of a forest will be seen on the right. The path meets the forest and crosses a stile beside a gate. To the right of the stile is a signpost (pointing back the way) with 'To Riskinhope Hope only' on it. Now follow a fire-break and after less than 50 m there is a notice on a tree on the right with 'Captain's Road' on it; this refers to the route that is now joined. The Captain's Road is an old route from Tibbie Shiels Inn to Hopehouse (which is beside the Ettrick Water).

The Way continues downhill on the Captain's Road, crosses a stream (the Moory Sike) and bears left to meet a forest track. Beside the track is a sign (pointing back the way) with 'Public footpath to Hopehouse by the Captain's Road' written on it. The Way turns left at the track and follows it down to Tibbie Shiels Inn at St Mary's Loch.

The track drops steeply, with rounded hills and sheep moors on either side. Broad Law (840 m) is the prominent hill to the north-west. A well-built circular sheep enclosure is passed on the right. Beside the track there are numerous outcrops of shale and a number of these show vertical 'bedding'. The layers of sediment were originally laid down horizontally on the sea floor but were subsequently folded so much that they now lie at an angle of ninety degrees to their original orientation. The rock is easily fractured and it breaks up into the sharp angular fragments that have been used to surface much of the track.

The Way crosses the Thirlestone Burn by a bridge that is described as dangerous on signs found before and after it, but which poses no danger to the walker. The valley on the left now has the Crosscleuch Burn running down it and well-built sheep enclosures can be seen beside the banks of this burn.

The view over to St Mary's Loch opens up and Tibbie Shiels Inn can be seen at the southern end of the loch. To its left (and on the other side of the lochside road) is the statue of James Hogg; this stands at the left-hand edge of a plantation.

After passing the farm of Crosscleuch, the Way passes a sign similar to the one seen at the start of the track and then leaves the track to turn right at Tibbie Shiels Inn. A Way notice-board stands at the entrance to the inn's car-park and this marks the end of this section. There is a small campsite at the inn.

The main road (the A708) is only 250 m farther down the track from the inn. The Glen Café is near the junction; it is open from April to October and it stocks a small range of foodstuffs. Beside the café are public toilets (open all year) and a public telephone box. There are no shops nearby.

Tibbie Shiels Inn
Tibbie Shiels Inn dates back to the early nineteenth century when Isabella Richardson (whose maiden name was Shiels) took guests into her home. She started the inn after her husband (who was a mole-catcher) died in 1824, leaving her with six children to bring up. Tibbie died in 1898, aged ninety-five.

Her first paying guest was Robert Chalmers who was doing research in the area for his book *The Picture of Scotland.* Her splendid hospitality and his recommendations made the inn a gathering place for numerous men of letters, the best-known being Sir Walter Scott, James Hogg (see p. 215) and John Wilson. John Wilson (1785–1854) is probably better known as Christopher

North, the pen name he used for many articles in the Edinburgh monthly, *Blackwood's Magazine*. As well as being a literary figure, Wilson was Professor of Moral Philosophy at Edinburgh University.

A plaque to the left of the inn's main door commemorates the official opening of the Southern Upland Way on 27 April 1984, and on it are some lines from 'A Boy's Song' by James Hogg:

> Where the pools are bright and deep,
> Where the grey trout lies asleep,
> Up the river and o'er the lea,
> That's the way for Billy and me.

St Mary's Loch

St Mary's Loch is one of the largest lochs in southern Scotland and it is popular in summer with walkers, picnickers, fishermen, windsurfers and boating enthusiasts. The loch lies in a deep sheltered hollow and the surrounding grassy hillsides are bare, except for a few lone trees and some new conifer plantations. It was undoubtably much more richly (and naturally) wooded in the hunting days of the great Ettrick Forest, but by Sir Walter Scott's time it must have lost most of its trees judging by his description of it in *Marmion*:

> Far in the mirror, bright and blue,
> Each hill's huge outline you may view,
> Shaggy with heath, but lonely, bare,
> Nor tree, nor bush, nor brake is there,
> Save where, of land, yon slender line,
> Bears thwart the lake the scattered pine.
> Nor thicket, dell, nor copse you spy
> Where living thing concealed might lie.
> ('brake' = 'bracken')

The loch's deep rock basin was carved out of the mountainous landscape by the valley glaciers that flowed down the valleys of the

Yarrow Water and the Megget Water. These 'over-deepened' the valley, leaving the present loch's bottom well below the level of its outlet, the Yarrow Water. St Mary's Loch used to be joined to the rather smaller Loch of the Lowes, which is to the south, but debris carried down by the Crosscleuch Burn and the Ox Cleugh has built up a gravelly delta that now separates the lochs, though a small stream still carries water between them.

There are quite a number of other deltas around St Mary's Loch including those produced by streams such as the March Sike, Bowerhope Burn, Thorny Cleugh, Kirkstead Burn and the biggest one, the Megget Water. The Megget Water has carried down so much debris from its valley that it has built a submarine ridge that divides the loch into two basins. Most of the river's water is now impounded in a reservoir (see p. 221) and this has slowed down its work of further dividing the loch into two smaller lochs.

The Rodono Country Hotel is the handsome building that stands in a prominent position above the loch's western shore. It was built as a mansion in 1866 and its name comes from Rodonna, an ancient barony that included the Megget Water. This was granted to Melrose Abbey by King Alexander II (1198–1249) in 1236.

James Hogg

James Hogg's statue stands just west of the junction of the lochside road and the road from Tibbie Shiels Inn. James Hogg (1770–1835) is one of the best-known Border characters and he was affectionately known as the Ettrick Shepherd. His family had been shepherds for centuries and at one time he worked on the farm at Blackhouse (see p. 226).

He was first published in 1794 with 'The Mistakes of a Night' in *The Scots Magazine* and his meeting with Walter Scott in 1802 led to the publication of some poems in *The Mountain Bard*. He also put his practical knowledge to good use in *The Shepherd's Guide, being a practical treatise on the diseases of sheep*. His new literary income allowed him to start a farm in Dumfriesshire but this unfortunately

St Mary's Loch and Tibbie Shiels Inn. The inn stands behind the sailing-club's clubhouse.

proved a financial failure. Hogg then moved to Edinburgh where he spent a great deal of time writing. *The Queen's Wake* (1813) was the breakthrough he needed and it established his reputation as a poet. He moved to the farm of Altrieve in Yarrow (see p. 223) in 1817 and married in 1820. His last years saw the publication of such diverse material as poems, historical works and articles in *Blackwood's Magazine*.

This bronze statue of Hogg was sculpted in 1860 by Andrew Currie who was also a native of Ettrick Forest, and it shows the Ettrick Shepherd sitting on a tree stump with his dog Hector at his feet. In his hand is a scroll bearing the words: 'He taught the wandering winds to sing' which is from the last line of his poem *The Queen's Wake*. The plinth carries more lines from his poems and the carvings of sheeps' heads remind the onlooker of the poet's upbringing in a shepherding family.

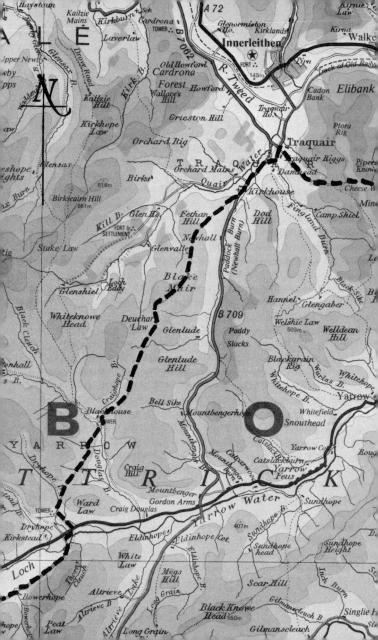

Section 9 St Mary's Loch to Traquair

Information

Start of section: At Tibbie Shiels Inn at the southern end of St Mary's Loch (NT240205).
End of section: At the village hall in Traquair (NT331345).
Distance: 19 km (12 miles).
Stages:
1. Tibbie Shiels Inn to the Yarrow Water (5 km).
2. The Yarrow Water to Blackhouse (4 km).
3. Blackhouse to Traquair (10 km).
4. Traquair.
5. Innerleithen (off the Way).
Breaks in route:
1. At the north end of St Mary's Loch (at the A708).
2. Blackhouse (to Craig Douglas and the A708).
3. Near Glenlude Hill (NT290288) (to Glenlude and the B709).
Conditions: This section gives a good walk over moorland and the views from Blake Muir are particularly fine. The first stretch from Tibbie Shiels Inn to the northern end of the loch is along a path then a track, both with good views to the other side of the loch. Thereafter there is a fairly easy moorland walk to Blackhouse Tower and then a long and steady climb up a track (then path) to reach the top of a forest (to the west of Glenlude Hill).

The next stretch of moorland down to the B709 gives superb views but great care must taken as it is very exposed and route finding may be difficult in poor visibility. The final stretch is an easy walk along a narrow (but sometimes busy) road to Traquair.
Points of interest: Views of St Mary's Loch, Dryhope Tower, Blackhouse Tower, views from Blake Muir, Traquair House, Innerleithen.
Maps:
1. Ordnance Survey no. 73.
2. Bartholomew no. 41.
Transport: There are bus services between Traquair and Peebles, and between Traquair and Selkirk. Innerleithen is on the Edinburgh–Melrose bus route (via Galashiels, Innerleithen and Peebles).

Car parking: On route: near the north end of St Mary's Loch, near Blackhouse, near Traquair Parish Church. At Traquair: at the village hall.
Accommodation: Gordon Arms Hotel (off the Way), Innerleithen (off the Way; various).
Notes: A most pleasant walk, especially on Blake Muir. There are no shops until Galashiels, but Innerleithen is only 2·5 km from Traquair.

Tibbie Shiels Inn to the Yarrow Water (5 km)

Tibbie Shiels Inn to Bowerhope (3 km)
This section starts at the Way notice-board at Tibbie Shiels Inn. Go through the car-park and cross a stile at a gate where there is a sign with 'St Mary's Loch Sailing Club members only' on it. Follow the track that runs in front of the wooden club-house and then follow the eastern edge of the loch. The path passes through March Wood at the foot of the March Sike. The Rodono Country Hotel can be seen on the opposite shore. A notice warning of the danger of fire stands at the start of a new forestry plantation and a few 'token' deciduous trees have been planted near the shore.

Much of this section's route follows an old drove-road but there are no obvious physical signs of the old route to be seen at this point. This eighteenth-century route came from Peebles where there had been common grazing rights since at least 1506. From Peebles, the cattle were driven southwards, keeping to high ground to avoid the boggy areas. The route went over Kirkhope Law and Birkscairn Hill and passed to the west of Brakehope Rig. It then followed the Douglas Burn to meet the Way at Blackhouse (see p. 226). The Way and the drove-road follow the same route from Blackhouse to Tibbie Shiels Inn. From the inn, the cattle were driven past the Loch of the Lowes, over Pikestone Rig and past Ettrick Church on their way to their southern buyers.

As the Way rounds Bowerhope Law, the valley of the Megget Water is passed on the opposite shore, and some houses and a little church are seen there. About 1·5 km to the right of the church is a prominent tree-lined gully above which is a low-walled enclosure and a few trees. This is St Mary's graveyard, the only remains of the church that has given the loch its name.

The site has a history going back many centuries and it was on record in 1292 as the church of St Mary of the Lowes. The church was destroyed in the middle of the sixteenth century but was later partially rebuilt and used for services until the middle of the seventeenth century. The old church is believed to have been situated in the north-west corner of the enclosure. On the last Sunday of each July it is the venue for the unusual ceremony of 'blanket preaching', a memorial of the Covenanting times. In those days the congregation did not have the use of a church building so the services were held outdoors and in bad weather the preacher sheltered under a wooden framework over which a blanket was draped.

Turn right when a dyke is met in order to cross it at a stile; cross two more stiles at gates. Walk to the left of a dyke and cross a stream in order to reach the shore again. Part of the grassed-over dam of the Megget Reservoir can now be seen in the Megget Valley.

The Megget Reservoir is a huge new reservoir (opened in 1983) that has been built to supply water to Edinburgh. The dam is situated 3 km from St Mary's Loch and it is possible to walk along the dam's wall. The Megget Valley was part of the hunting lands of the Ettrick Forest and two towers in the valley (Cramalt North and Cramalt South) were probably used by hunters in pursuit of game. Before the valley was flooded to form the reservoir, the remains of the north tower were removed and reconstructed near Cramalt farm which is about 1·5 km west of the dam. Just 4 km to the west of Megget Reservoir is Talla Reservoir which has supplied water to Edinburgh since 1905.

The well-sheltered farm of Bowerhope is now passed. St Mary's graveyard is just across the loch.

Bowerhope to the Yarrow Water (2 km)
Cross a stile at a gate and join the track that runs along the lochside. Dryhope Tower can now be seen 2 km away to the north-east. The

Way will follow the track that is seen behind the tower then pass to the right of the prominent cairn on the skyline.

The gravelly area at the northern end of the loch has been greatly altered during the construction of the sluices that now regulate the water-level and unfortunately the reinforced embankments at the loch's outlet have been left as ugly scars. A fish ladder has been installed beside the sluices. The Yarrow Water begins here and it is one of the Borders' best-known rivers; it flows for some 30 km from St Mary's Loch to its confluence with the River Tweed. Although the Way does not meet the Yarrow again, the river is seen when the Way is heading towards the Three Brethren (see p. 242).

William Wordsworth (1770–1850) wrote about Yarrow Water three times. In 'Yarrow Unvisited' (1803) he dismissed it unseen with the words:

> What's Yarrow but a river bare,
> That glides the dark hills under?
> There are a thousand such elsewhere
> As worthy of your wonder.

His first visit to Yarrow changed his view and in 'Yarrow Visited' (1814) he wrote:

> But that I know, where'er I go,
> Thy genuine image, Yarrow!
> Will dwell with me – to heighten joy,
> And cheer my mind in sorrow.

In 'Yarrow Revisited' (1831) he showed that he had been convinced of its charm:

> Flow on for ever, Yarrow Stream!
>   Fulfil thy pensive duty,
> Well pleased that future Bards should chant
>   For simple hearts thy beauty.

The Yarrow Water to Blackhouse (4 km)

The Yarrow Water to Dryhope Tower (1·5 km)
The Way crosses the Yarrow Water and turns right immediately
after the bridge. Cross a stile and then follow the river-bank
to another stile. Now bear left to yet another stile beside the
main road – the A708 which runs between Moffat and Selkirk.
Broadmeadows Youth Hostel is at Yarrowford, 17 km along the
Selkirk road.

The Gordon Arms Hotel is 3·5 km down the road towards Selkirk
and at the point where the A708 and the A709 cross. The hotel is
best known as the last meeting place (in autumn 1830) of Hogg and
Scott. A short distance from the hotel along the Innerleithen road
(the B709) is Mountbenger, where Hogg once farmed. This venture
was unsuccessful and he described the site as 'a gey cauld place',
'staunin' yonder on a knowe in a funnel, in the thoroughfare of a
perpetual sugh' ('sugh' = 'the moaning of the wind'). Altrieve (now
called Eldinhope), the farm where Hogg spent his last years, is also
on the A709, a short distance to the south-west of the hotel.

Cross the road and the stile that leads into a field. Follow the
dyke on the left and pass between two corrugated iron sheds farther
uphill. A little later a pile of stones can be seen to the right of the
Way. While these may have been gathered in order to clear the
field, there are numerous similar piles near Dryhope Tower and it
has been suggested that these may be associated with burials in
some long-gone society.

A stile is crossed at the top of the field and the Way meets a track
running in a north-south direction. The Way joins this and heads to
the right towards Blackhouse, but on the left is the interesting
sixteenth-century Dryhope Tower.

Dryhope Tower
This four-storey tower is in a dangerous condition and there are
some nasty-looking cracks in the top half of the building so it should
not be entered. Its lowest floor was a vaulted storehouse, the first
floor was the main hall and above that was a wooden-floored storey
which still has its vaulted roof intact. A ruinous circular staircase is

in the tower's northern corner, near the main entrance. Outside the tower are the grassed-over remains of various outbuildings.

The best known of Dryhope Tower's inhabitants was Walter Scott of Harden (Auld Wat of Harden), an infamous border reiver. Wat was married to a relative, Mary Scott, who was born in the tower in 1550 and who was known as the Flower of Yarrow because of her beauty. Their wedding contract was witnessed by five barons, none of whom could read or write his own name so a notary had to sign the contract for each and every one of them. Sir Walter Scott (the author) claimed descent from Wat and his wife through their grandson Wattie Wudspurs. In 1592, Auld Wat was implicated in the Raid of Falkland, the attempt by the fifth Earl of Bothwell to kidnap the King, James VI (I of Great Britain). James escaped to St Andrews and ordered that, as punishment for Auld Wat's involvement, Dryhope Tower be demolished; it was later rebuilt, probably in 1613.

In 1784, one very unexpected visitor to Dryhope was the Italian balloonist Vincenzo Lunardi. He had earlier made an ascent in a hydrogen-filled balloon from the Strand in London in front of a crowd of 20,000 people. Spurred on by the tremendous interest shown in this new science of 'aerostation', as ballooning was then called, he made several flights in Scotland and his first ascent from Edinburgh was watched by 80,000 people. In Craig-Brown's nineteenth-century history of the area, the event is described as follows: 'In 1784, Lunardi, voyaging in his balloon from Glasgow, mistook St Mary's for an arm of the sea, and made an unsuccessful attempt to land at Dryhope, losing an anchor, a flag and a quantity of rope. The flag was cut up into four excellent handkerchiefs.'

Dryhope Tower to Blackhouse (2·5 km)
From Dryhope Tower the Way ascends the track, passes another pile of stones and follows Dryhope Burn. The track heads towards a cairn on the south-eastern side of South Hawkshaw Rig and after about 500 m the Way turns right at a grassy track. This runs

Dryhope Tower. St Mary's Loch can be seen to the left of the picture.

between the cairn on the left and a circular sheep enclosure and a gully on the right. The track climbs up to the left and splits; the Way takes the left fork and runs downhill through a gully to a waymarker.

The Douglas Burn can now be seen 1 km to the east. This is quite a powerful burn (a tributary of the Yarrow Water) and the size of its valley gives some indication of how impressive a river it once was. Gravel barriers have been built beside the burn to prevent it cutting farther into its steep banks and on its east bank is the track that connects the farm of Blackhouse to the A708.

Ignore the path going to the right after the waymarker; head north-east and descend to a waymarker at a large grassy patch. Turn right and walk round the eastern flank of South Hawkshaw Rig. A circular sheep enclosure is passed on the right and a line of silver birches can be seen ahead. These are beside the burn in Hawkshaw Cleuch, the gully which runs between South Hawkshaw Rig and North Hawkshaw Rig.

The path widens and the Way bears left soon after the sheep enclosure, so head uphill, gradually nearing the burn. Turn right at a hollow above the bank and descend to a wooden bridge that takes the Way over the burn. Climb over a stile and follow the fence on the right.

Gradually move away from the fence after passing a waymarker and join a track which runs downhill towards the Douglas Burn. The burn is crossed by a wooden bridge that was erected in 1987. Bear right after the bridge and head for the Blackhouse track. The A708 is 3 km away to the right, but the Way goes left at the track and passes to the right of a cottage, Blackhouse Tower and Blackhouse farmhouse.

Blackhouse

Blackhouse Tower was built in the late sixteenth century. This roofless ruin had two storeys: the lower one was a storehouse and the upper one had a wooden floor, a vaulted ceiling and a fireplace.

Blackhouse. Blackhouse Tower can be seen to the left of the farm buildings. The Way follows the stream up on to the moors.

A circular tower with a wide spiral staircase stands just inside the main tower's entrance.

The area was held by the Douglases for a long time and the most famous member of the family was Sir James Douglas (the 'Black Douglas', 1286–1330). He was a strong supporter of King Robert the Bruce in the War of Independence against the English and it is said that he fought in seventy battles and was victorious in fifty-seven of them. One of his most audacious exploits was the capture of Roxburgh Castle, in 1314, when his attacking troops were disguised as black oxen. He was knighted on the field at Bannockburn in the same year.

Because of ill health, Bruce was unable to fulfil his ambition of going on a crusade but he wished that after his death his embalmed heart should be carried to Jerusalem. Douglas attempted to carry out this wish, but while on the mission he was killed in Spain in a crusade with the Moors. The heart was never taken to Jerusalem but it was brought back to Scotland and interred at Melrose Abbey; the body of Bruce had earlier been buried in Dunfermline Abbey.

Blackhouse Tower was the scene of the ballad 'The Douglas Tragedy', which tells how Lady Margaret Douglas and her lover Lord William hurried to the tower, chased by her father and her seven brothers, who were against the match. A bloody battle ensued, resulting in all ten losing their lives. Legend had it that seven stones near the tower marked the places where each of the brothers died.

Blackhouse is also connected with James Hogg and Sir Walter Scott. Hogg worked as a shepherd at Blackhouse farm from 1790 to 1800 and shared his interest in poetry with Willie Laidlaw (1780–1850), the son of his employer. In 1802, after Hogg had left Blackhouse, Laidlaw introduced him to Scott, starting a long and important friendship. Laidlaw later worked for Scott, acting as his secretary and writing down the stories that Scott dictated.

Blackhouse to Traquair (10 km)

Blackhouse to Blake Muir (4·5 km)

Walk past the farmhouse and through the gate on to the forest track which follows the Craighope Burn uphill. The track allows height to be gained quickly and after it narrows to a path there is a view to the south-west to St Mary's Loch; the cairn on South Hawkshaw Rig can be seen to the right of the loch.

Once out of the forest, the path comes to a stile beside a gate and there is a good panoramic view over the hills from this point. Minch Moor (567 m) can be seen behind the afforested hills to the north of east; the next section passes behind Minch Moor's summit. To the left (and behind Minch Moor) are the Moorfoot Hills. The Cheviots can be glimpsed far away to the east of south. To the south-west are the Moffat Hills and to the left of them are the hills at the top of the Ettrick Valley.

On the right (i.e. to the east) is Glenlude Hill (469 m) and to its left can be seen the Glenlude Burn running down to the farm of Glenlude which is on the B709 (Gordon Arms–Innerleithen). If the weather is bad then a descent (over rough ground) can be made to the farm in order to reach low ground rather than cross the exposed moors. If this is done, then turn right after the stile, follow the dyke and then turn left at the next dyke; take care when the burn is met.

Very great care must be taken on the next stretch in poor visibility. Bear left after the stile to head towards a waymarker that can be seen on the skyline. Deuchar Law (542 m) is ahead. The Way will be crossing that hill about 1 km to the right of the summit, but well to the left of the prominent sheep enclosure that can be seen on the hill's eastern ridge.

Keep heading in the same direction (east of north). The ridge that is now being followed heads north-east and the north side of this must be gained in order not to lose too much height before meeting the Yellow Mire Burn. Cross this burn and follow it downstream for a short distance in order to get on to a wide path that heads east of north. This narrows and climbs to a waymarker on the skyline; this point is due east of the summit of Deucher Law. The three tall cairns known as the Three Brethren can be seen on a hilltop 14 km away to the east.

Blake Muir is now straight ahead. The path bears left and descends the hill; there is soon a view to the left of the well-tended fields in the valley of the Quair Water. In poor visibility take care not to stray to the right. Cross a stile beside a gate. This stile is an important point to reach in bad visibility – the fence it crosses runs downhill from the ridge on the left. A distinct path now heads uphill through the heather to cross Blake Muir.

Blake Muir to the B709 (3·5 km)

Join a grassy and very significant track that is found running in a marked depression on the left and then follow a fence on the left. There is now another good view of the valley of the Quair Water. A number of prominent hills stand behind the Quair Water, with Birkscairn Hill (661 m and with a cairn) on the left. This hill was previously mentioned as being on the route of the old drove-road. To the north-east, Innerleithen can be seen in its sheltered position on a bend in the River Tweed. The valley of the Leithen Water can be seen above Innerleithen. The track now follows the long ridge that curves round to the left, towards Fethan Hill (372 m) which is to the north.

It is soon possible to see the turreted roof of the very elaborately styled Glen House on the left. This was built in Scottish Baronial style and enlarged in 1874. It was the birthplace of Captain John Porteous, a most unpopular figure in Scottish history. In the years following the Union of the Scottish and English Parliaments (1707) there was great resentment against the taxes being raised in Scotland by the British Government. Taxes on malt had led to riots in 1725 and smuggling to avoid taxes was widespread. In 1736 two smugglers were sentenced to death in Edinburgh, but one helped the other to escape and the remaining offender (a popular fellow) was due to be hanged. Porteous was in charge of the city guard and after only a slight disturbance, the soldiers fired on the crowd which was watching the hanging – four people were killed. Porteous was tried and sentenced to death; however, he was pardoned by Queen Caroline, an act that angered the people of the capital. One night a group of men broke into the Tolbooth where Porteous was being held, took him outside and hanged him from a street signpost, an act that outraged the British Government and the Queen, but met with general approval north of the border.

Cross a stile beside a gate and follow a track across the high pastures down to a stile that is to the left of an isolated stand of conifers. The hamlet of Traquair can be seen in front. Keep on the indistinct track as it heads north and away from the trees. The Way then nears a dyke on the right and crosses it at a stile beside a gate. Follow the dyke on the left as it passes to the left of a stand of conifers. A track then takes the Way downhill to meet the B709. The track passes behind a two-storey house which stands by the roadside; a waymarker is found on the left, just beside the road.

The B709 to Traquair (2 km)
Turn left at the B709 and pass Traquair Parish Church which is on the left. This was built in 1778 and altered in 1821 and it stands on the site of earlier churches that date back to 1510. An interesting architectural feature is the outside stairway and the entrance to what was once a gallery. The middle window on the wall nearest the road has the date 1778 carved above it. This wall also carries a tablet erected to Alexander Brodie (d. 1811), inventor of 'the register stoves and fire hearths for ships' that were used by the Royal Navy. Brodie was a blacksmith who was born in Traquair and he built Innerleithen's first woollen factory (see p. 233). Numerous old memorials, many with hour-glasses and skull and crossbones on them, stand in the graveyard. Behind the church is the burial vault of the Earls of Traquair and above its entrance is the family's coat of arms, with its two bears, and the motto 'Judge nought'.

The Way continues along the road, passing the well-built farm buildings at Kirkhouse on the right. A minor road that is passed on the left goes up the valley of the Quair Water and past Glen House. The farm that can be seen just a little distance down that road, Orchard Mains, has some very fine buildings, especially its roadside barn. A Victorian letter-box with 'Letters only' and 'VR' on it can be seen on the right, opposite the road-end. Damhead farm is passed on the right then the road crosses the Fingland Burn. On the bridge is a plaque with 'Fingland Bridge 1961' inscribed on it.

The Way then meets Traquair at the junction of the B709 and the B7062. Innerleithen is 2·5 km to the north and Peebles is 12 km to the north-west. A tall red sandstone war memorial in the form of a Celtic cross stands at the junction; it has the inscription 'Lest we forget' on it. A tall waymarker just before the memorial points to the right, where a narrow road takes the Way to the village hall which is found on the left. There is a Way notice-board at the hall and this marks the end of this section.

There is a car-park beside the hall and a public telephone box at the main road junction. There are no shops or public toilets nearby.

Traquair

Traquair's history goes back to at least Roman times and remains of those far-off days have been found locally. In the twelfth century the village was similar in importance to Peebles, and in the eighteenth century its population was more than Innerleithen's. However, Traquair is now a small collection of houses and its name means 'hamlet of the Quair'. It is best known for the historic Traquair House which is nearby.

Traquair House

There was a royal hunting lodge at Traquair in the time of Alexander I and the present building dates back to 1512, making this one of the oldest inhabited houses in Scotland. Later additions in the seventeenth century were made only after the course of the River Tweed had been changed in order to safeguard the building's foundations.

The house is open to the public during the summer and there are interesting mementoes of various people associated with the house including Mary, Queen of Scots. Perhaps the best-known features of Traquair are the 'Bear Gates' which are at the end of the long grassy driveway to the house. It is said that these gates were closed in the eighteenth century by the fifth Earl of Traquair who promised that they would not be reopened until a Catholic Stuart king was on the British throne.

The entrance to Traquair House is 700 m along the B7062.

Innerleithen (off the Way)

Although Innerleithen traces its prosperity back to the opening of its first woollen mill by Alexander Brodie about 1790, its fame in the nineteenth century was due to the pen of Sir Walter Scott. In 1824 Scott's novel *St Ronan's Well* was published and it publicised the local spring, which was associated with St Ronan. James Hogg also played a part in popularising the village as he helped organise the St Ronan's Games from 1827 to 1835.

The wells can be reached by walking up Hall Street (which is opposite the road to Traquair) then turning right at St Ronan's Terrace. The buildings associated with the well, including a very attractive veranda, will be seen on the left after the road makes another turn to the right. It is the oldest spa in Scotland (the present pump-room was built in 1826) and is open daily from April to September. The house beside the wells is about 400 years old.

Robert Smail's Printing Works is at 9 High Street (i.e. on the A72). This is under the care of the National Trust for Scotland and is open to the public. The printing works was started in the 1840s and the original printing press was water-powered. Almost opposite this, on the wall of 8–10 High Street, is a granite plaque bearing the words: 'Robert Burns visited Innerleithen on 14th May 1787'. There is a small local museum in the council offices in Leithen Road which is open (infrequently) during the summer.

The village has a number of hotels, bed and breakfast establishments and shops. The signpost to the Tweedside Caravan Site (which takes tents) is found after walking north-eastwards along the High Street and crossing the Leithen Water.

Section 10 Traquair to Yair Bridge

Information

Start of section: At the village hall in Traquair (NT331345).
End of section: At the car-park at Yair Bridge over the River Tweed (NT458324).
Distance: 15 km (9½ miles).
Stages:
1. Traquair to Hare Law (5·5 km).
2. Hare Law to Three Brethren (6 km).
3. Three Brethren to Yair Bridge (3·5 km).
4. Selkirk (off the Way).

Breaks in route:
1. After Hare Law (to Yarrowford).
2. After Broomy Law (to Broadmeadows Youth Hostel and Yarrowford).

Conditions: This section gives an excellent moorland walk over the historic route on Minchmoor. The Way follows a narrow track for much of the route up to Minch Moor. Forests give some shelter until the descent from Hare Law then the route is over open moorland to Three Brethren. This is a fine walk but it could be very unpleasant in bad weather. Route finding should not be a problem. The Way enters forest soon after Three Brethren and descends on paths and tracks to Yair Bridge.

Points of interest: Fine views all the way from Minch Moor to Three Brethren, Selkirk (off the Way).

Maps:
1. Ordnance Survey no. 73.
2. Bartholomew no. 41.

Transport: There is a bus service along the A7 (see p. 245).
Car parking: On route: nowhere. At Yair Bridge: just downstream of the bridge on the southern bank of the River Tweed.
Accommodation: Walkerburn (off the Way; various), Broadmeadows Youth Hostel (off the Way), Clovenfords (off the Way; various), Selkirk (off the Way; various), Galashiels (next section; various).
Notes: This is a short section that can be combined with Section 11

for a good day's walk. Alternatively, part of it can be combined with Section 9 as Broadmeadows Youth Hostel is conveniently situated below the Way and this hostel could be a suitable finishing point to a day's walk. There are no facilities (except a public telephone box) anywhere near Yair Bridge. There are no shops until Galashiels.

Traquair to Hare Law (5·5 km)

Traquair to Minchmoor Road (0·5 km)
This section begins at Traquair's village hall. Turn left at the minor road beside the hall and follow the road until it bends to the right (to the local school). The Way takes the track that goes ahead at the bend and a signpost points the Way in the direction of Minchmoor. Appropriately, the house passed on the right is called Minch Gate.

Minchmoor Road
The Way now follows one of the Scottish Borders' oldest routes, Minchmoor, named after the local hill of Minch Moor. Various routes across the hills between Traquair and Selkirk have been used over the centuries. The oldest was probably the one that went from Traquair over the northern side of Minch Moor, then over Hare Law and Brown Knowe to the north of Broomy Law, over Peat Law and Linglie Hill and then across the Ettrick Water near Lindean; the Way follows most of this route. Alternative routes left the oldest route by following Long Philip Burn (which is south of Peat Law), or going south of Brown Knowe or going on the south side of Minch Moor.

In the thirteenth century the old road was used on the journey between Kelso Abbey and its lands at Lesmahagow, which is to the west of Lanark. In 1296 it was used by Edward I (the 'Hammer of the Scots') when he was crossing the country via Peebles. This was obviously not a road to be taken by innocent travellers on their own as it was frequented by robbers and in 1505 it was recorded that a man was given the task of keeping the road free from robbers for eight days each year at the time of the Roxburgh Fair, which was held on 5 August. In 1645 Montrose fled from the battle of

Philiphaugh on the route that follows the Long Philip Burn.

From the time of the Union of the Scottish and English Parliaments, the road was often used by drovers taking their cattle south from Peebles. After following the south bank of the Tweed they used the Minchmoor route then probably headed for the Hawick district on their journey down to England.

Minchmoor Road to the Cheese Well (2·5 km)

As the track begins the long climb up to the moorland, Innerleithen is seen over to the left. The roof (and a flagpole) of Traquair House may be seen to the west of north. The house stands near the River Tweed, which flows to the south of Lee Pen (502 m), the rather pointed hill above Innerleithen.

The Way crosses the high pastures and the walls on either side of the track indicate the substantial width of the old drove-road. The forest soon closes in on the track as the climb gets steeper but at a gap on the right it is possible to look back at the route taken by the Way at the end of Section 9. Its route can be traced as it crosses Blake Muir and passes two stands of conifers on the eastern flank of Fethan Hill.

The Way soon crosses two wide forest tracks and the steepness of the Way on this stretch must make the walker wonder how the cattle fared on such a route. The trees on the left give way to a broad expanse of heather moor and after another climb a waymarker is found at the junction of a number of routes. There is a good view from this junction: the winding valley of the Quair Water can be seen over to the west and to its left is Fethan Hill. Take the path/track that is going to the left and heading towards another plantation.

More conifers are passed on the left and as the route levels off there is a little stream to be crossed. Its water comes from the Cheese Well which is about 10 m to the right, at a grassy gap in the heather.

The name comes from the old practice of leaving cheese there as a gift to the well's guardian spirits and it is interesting to note that the practice of offering cheese to fairies is not uncommon in old Welsh tales. Two stones sit above the well. A rectangular one has

the inscription 'Cheese well' and a diamond-shaped stone has 'Cheese well' engraved on it too, as well as the date 1965 and a thistle. The history of the well is uncertain but it certainly goes back a long time as the well is marked on Joannis Blaeu's map of Scotland (1654).

The Cheese Well to Hare Law (2·5 km)
The track climbs once more and the heathery expanse on the right is topped by the summit of Minch Moor (567 m). Near this stretch's highest point (and where a dyke is met on the left) the village of Walkerburn can be seen through a gap in the trees. Walkerburn is a small village on the north bank of the River Tweed that owes its existence to the mill that was founded there in 1854 by Henry Ballantyne. The mill, now operating under the name of Clan Royal of Scotland, houses the Scottish Museum of Textiles. From a few metres above the track at this point there is a view of the red roof of the Peebles Hotel Hydro which is 13 km away to the north-west. Peebles is one of the most attractive of the Border towns – it has a broad and interesting main street and is a popular tourist centre.

As the Way begins to descend there is a glimpse of the Eildon Hills (see p. 266) to the east. Cross a track at a clearing and ascend the southern flank of Hare Law (509 m). Leave the forest at a stile beside a gate. At this point there is now a fine view over to the right. Wanders Knowe (492 m) is immediately to the right and the Yarrow Water (see p. 222) flows behind it.

Hare Law to Three Brethren (6 km)

Hare Law to Brown Knowe (1 km)
Walkers should ensure that they do not unintentionally stray down a path on the right instead of starting the ascent of Brown Knowe. The path on the right is named 'Minchmoor Road' on the Ordnance Survey map and it goes to Yarrowford.

Just before the summit of Brown Knowe is reached, the Way cuts

The Cheese Well.

through a broad earthen wall known as Wallace's Trench. This ancient earthwork runs in a north-south direction and the purpose of the broad trench and its associated embankment is uncertain. Furthermore, it must have been built well before the time of William Wallace. It was probably constructed as a barrier across a track that was a precursor to the Minchmoor Road.

There is a cairn and a junction of fences at the summit of Brown Knowe (524 m). Ahead, there is a superb view of the Eildon Hills. The cairns known as the Three Brethren are to their right, above a forest. Looking back, a cairn can be seen on top of Minch Moor. Cross the stile beside the gate and follow the fence that is on the left.

The view from Brown Knowe

As the path begins the descent of Brown Knowe there are good views of some historic places in the valley of the Yarrow Water.

Newark Castle can soon be seen about 4·5 km away to the south-east. It is sitting in a prominent position on a knoll just above the Yarrow Water. This roofless tower is five storeys high and has walls over 3 m thick. The first record of it was in 1423 when it was called the New Werk, to distinguish it from its predecessor, the Auldwark, and it was used as a royal hunting seat in Ettrick Forest. In 1645, when the Covenanters roundly defeated the government's army at nearby Philiphaugh, one hundred prisoners were summarily shot in the castle's courtyard. Five years later it was occupied by Cromwell after the Battle of Dunbar.

On the northern side of the Yarrow Water, and just opposite Newark Castle, is Foulshiels, the birthplace of Mungo Park (1771–1806), one of Scotland's best-known explorers. After qualifying as a doctor, he travelled through West Africa in 1795–6 in search of the source of the River Niger. He followed the river for about 500 km, suffering great hardship in the course of his travels, and when he arrived back home he described his adventures in *Travels in the Interior of Africa* (1799). In 1805 he started a second attempt to follow the river but many of his companions died of disease and he was drowned in 1806 while being attacked by local people.

To the south of Newark Castle are the grounds of Bowhill, though the mansion (built in various stages in the nineteenth century) cannot be seen. This notable building is famous for its collection of paintings and French furniture and it is open to the public during the summer.

Brown Knowe to Three Brethren (5 km)

As a small cairn is passed on the right, the village of Clovenfords can be seen 6 km to the north-east. Sir Walter Scott used to stay at an inn in Clovenfords before he had a home in the district and this period is commemorated by a statue of him outside the Clovenfords Hotel. In 1869 a local gardener started the Tweed Vineries and about 5,000 kg of grapes were produced each year.

Smailholm Tower can be seen 25 km away and to the left of the Eildon Hills. The tower was built early in the fifteenth century and it stands in a prominent and strong position; it is now in the care of the State and is open to the public. Sir Walter Scott's grandfather stayed at the nearby Sandyknowe farm and, as a boy, Scott was a frequent visitor to the tower. He introduced it into *The Eve of St John* and *Marmion*.

The Way descends and meets a waymarker at a dyke; an isolated line of trees stands in front. In poor weather it would be possible to follow the valley on the right to descend to Yarrowford. Cross the stile over the dyke and climb above the trees, following the dyke on the right. The Way swings left as it crosses the north side of Broomy Law (463 m).

The wooded hill on the left is Craig Hill (382 m) and the River Tweed flows behind it. Cross a stile at a fence and soon a waymarker will be found at a junction of dykes on the right; there is a good view up the Yarrow Water from here. The Way continues past the waymarker, but the dyke that runs away to the right points downhill towards the hamlet of Yarrowford. Broadmeadows Youth Hostel is only 1·5 km away from this point. This was opened in 1931 as the Scottish Youth Hostels Association's first hostel.

Keep beside the dyke, cross another stile, and walk to the right of a plantation; the dyke/fence on the right leads up to Three Brethren.

The Three Brethren

The Three Brethren are tall cairns, each about 3 m high, that dominate the summit of Three Brethren (464 m). The three fences at the summit mark the boundaries between the lands of Yair, Philiphaugh and the burgh of Selkirk, and each of the cairns stands on a different piece of land. An Ordnance Survey trig point stands beside them. The cairns are visited on horseback by people taking part in Selkirk's Common Riding festivities.

The view from the summit is outstanding, with ranges of hills stretching out in all directions. The most noticeable landmarks are the three Eildon Hills, which are directly to the east. The town of Melrose, which will be met at the end of Section 11, is to their left, and Smailholm Tower lies between the hills and the village. To the south-east lie the Cheviot Hills and Cheviot (815 m) is the prominent hill at the left of the range, about 50 km away. The two tall aerials to the south are both for television.

Looking over to the north-west, the hills that stretch back behind Walkerburn are the Moorfoot Hills, while the Lammermuir Hills are to the north-east; the Way will skirt the southern edge of these during Section 13. The two cairns on Twin Law (see p. 289) can be seen with binoculars just to the right of the aerial on Meigle Hill (423 m, 5 km to the north-east); the cairns are 30 km away. Much nearer, the small house of Calfshaw is just 3·5 km to the north of east. During the next section the Way passes to the left of the house and between the two stands of trees that are behind it.

Three Brethren to Yair Bridge (3·5 km)

A tall waymarker points downhill and in a south-easterly direction. The Way now runs between the forest on the left and the boundary fence on the right. The path heads towards Peat Law (426 m), but bears left, enters the forest and descends to a track which is crossed

The Three Brethren. This viewpoint commands a very fine view over the valley of the River Tweed. The Eildon Hills can be seen in the distance.

diagonally. After a further descent, another track is met; turn right. Follow this track until it meets a stand of beeches on the left, then bear left on a wide path. Farmland can be seen through the beeches and birches and soon the mansion of Yair is glimpsed through the trees. This was built in 1788 and shares its name with the forest to the west of it. The River Tweed flows beside Yair and beyond the river is the mansion of Fairnilee (see p. 252).

The Way bears left to join a forest walk through Lindinny Wood and a number of plaques have been erected by the Forestry Commission to explain what types of trees have been planted and how the forest is changing. The steep path descends to the A707 and Yair Bridge over the River Tweed can be seen on the left. On the right is a car-park and the Way notice-board that marks the end of this section.

On the other side of the car-park is a path that leads past an information plaque and up to a viewpoint. This gives a view of the next part of the Way and it is a fine place to stop for lunch.

Yair Bridge takes the A707 (Innerleithen–Selkirk) across the River Tweed. Clovenfords is 4·5 km to the north and Selkirk is 7 km to the south. The A7 (Edinburgh–Carlisle) is 3·5 km away and it can be reached by crossing the bridge and turning right at the B7060.

The bridge was completed in 1762 and prior to that the Edinburgh–Selkirk road crossed the river at a ford about 3 km farther upstream, just below the mouth of the Caddon Water. Yair Bridge is a handsome three-arch structure, with its lower part built of shaped sandstone blocks and its upper parts of random rubble. The bridge is narrow and has no footpath but it has refuges built over the piers. The bridge has been strengthened and repaired many times and much work was done on it in 1987–8.

There is a public telephone box near the buildings at Fairnilee farm on the northern side of Yair Bridge. There are no shops or public toilets nearby.

Yair Bridge.

The River Tweed

The River Tweed rises at Tweed's Well (9 km north of Moffat) and flows 157 km before it meets the North Sea at Berwick-upon-Tweed. The Way first met one of its many tributaries when the Ettrick Water was followed and other tributaries will be met until the Eye Water (which flows into the sea at Eyemouth) is met at Blackburn Mill, just 6 km from the east coast.

The centuries of warfare between Scotland and England meant that the lands near the river saw bloodshed on many occasions. Indeed, Berwick-upon-Tweed has changed hands no fewer than thirteen times and it has been an English possession since 1482. The last 3 km of the River Tweed are in England and the river marks the border between the two countries for the next 26 km upstream.

The river has been at the centre of Border life for centuries and in the 'reiving days' the peel towers were deliberately built on alternate sides of the river to facilitate the passing of bonfire signals up the valley when invaders were seen approaching. In the nineteenth century, railway and road engineers made more peaceable use of the river valley when they were choosing their routes. The River Tweed has a reputation as a fishing river with both salmon and sea-trout being numerous enough to attract anglers from far afield; there are many hotels near the river that are popular with the anglers.

The river has gained worldwide fame because of the high quality cloth and the woollen garments that are produced by the many mills in the district. Although the most famous type of cloth is called 'tweed', this word does not come from the name of the river: it is said to have originated in 1832 from a one-time misreading in London of the word 'tweel' which was the name given locally to one of the types of cloth.

Selkirk (off the Way)

Selkirk occupies the site of a Tironensian abbey founded *c.* 1113 by David I. The abbey was moved to Kelso in 1128. A castle was established in Selkirk and King William the Lion (1143–1214) issued many of his charters there.

As the town slowly developed, it gained a reputation for shoemaking and the name 'souters' (Scots for 'shoemakers') was given to the burgesses of the town. This trade has now died out and Selkirk's modern economic success was based on the establishment (in 1835) of woollen mills beside the Ettrick Water. These tall mills are situated on the broad haugh below the town and beside them are the newer industries that have been established more recently, including the Selkirk Glass factory which is open to the public.

Selkirk has a triangular-shaped market-place in the centre of which stands a statue of Sir Walter Scott (see p. 259). Behind this is the old court-house on whose wall is a plaque inscribed: 'In this building from 1803 to 1832 Sir Walter Scott as Sheriff of Selkirkshire administered justice.' The court-house is open during part of the summer and it has a display of mementoes associated with the town's history and with Scott.

In the western corner of the market-place stands the Part Well and behind this is a walled structure incorporating stones taken from the East Port, one of the old fortified gates that led into the burgh. Also to the west of the market-place is the Tourist Information Centre which is housed in Halliwell's House Museum. The museum has well-arranged displays explaining the history of the area, including the reconstructed interior of an old ironmonger's shop.

Kirk Wynd runs to the south-east from the market-place and along that road are the ruins of the Auld Parish Kirk. This may be the place where, in 1298, William Wallace was proclaimed Guardian of Scotland. Sir William Wallace (c. 1270–1305) was one of Scotland's best-known patriots. The details of his early years are not well documented but after he had been outlawed for killing the English Sheriff of Lanark, he gathered around him an increasing number of followers who were determined to drive the English out of Scotland. His most famous victory was at Stirling Bridge (1297) after which he became Guardian of Scotland. In 1298 he lost an important battle at Falkirk and had to flee. After spending some time in France, he came back to Scotland and was captured, taken to London and barbarously put to death.

Along the High Street from the market-place is a statue of Mungo

Park and yet farther along, and standing outside the Victoria Halls, is the statue of Fletcher. Fletcher was one of about eighty Selkirk men who supported James IV on the battlefield at Flodden (1513). After the terrible defeat at the hands of the English army led by the Earl of Surrey, Fletcher was the only one of the eighty to come home. He is depicted carrying a captured English banner which he brought back with him.

The town has many hotels (some of which are fine-looking buildings dating back to the nineteenth century), bed and breakfast establishments and numerous shops. The Victoria Park Campsite and the local swimming-pool are situated near the Ettrick Water.

Section 11 Yair Bridge to Melrose

Information

Start of section: At the car-park at Yair Bridge over the River Tweed (NT458324).

End of section: At the chain suspension bridge over the River Tweed at Melrose (NT545345).

Distance: 12 km (7½ miles).

Stages:

1. Yair Bridge to Galashiels (5 km).
2. Galashiels.
3. Galashiels to Galafoot Bridge (3 km).
4. Galafoot Bridge to Melrose (4 km).
5. Melrose.

Breaks in route:

1. Elm Road (to Galashiels).
2. Galafoot Bridge (to Galashiels).
3. Melrose Parish Church (to Melrose).

Conditions: This is one of the easiest sections of the whole Way. It is also the one with most contrasts as it crosses a nice moor but later passes Galashiels' gas-holder and sewage works!

The first stage, from Yair Bridge to Galashiels, is on a path over very pleasant open moorland. This could be unpleasant in bad weather but route finding should not be a problem. Road, track and good paths then take the Way above Galashiels and past Sir Walter Scott's home of Abbotsford to a point under Galafoot Bridge. The 'industrial scenery' comes next before a very nice walk along the south bank of the River Tweed.

Points of interest: Galashiels, Abbotsford, the River Tweed, Melrose, Melrose Abbey, the Eildon Hills.

Maps:

1. Ordnance Survey no. 73.
2. Bartholomew no. 41.

Transport: There is a bus service between Edinburgh and Melrose via Galashiels, Innerleithen and Peebles. There is also a bus service between Edinburgh and Carlisle via Galashiels, Selkirk and Hawick.

Car parking: On route: near Woodend, at Barr Road, at
Abbotsford Road, at Galafoot Bridge. At Melrose: at the
suspension bridge, near the abbey, in the market-place.
Accommodation: Galashiels (various), Melrose (various),
Gattonside (next section; various).
Notes: Galashiels is a good shopping centre and Melrose is a
pleasant town with lots to see in it. Those with enough time and
energy could also climb the Eildon Hills for a magnificent view of
the district. There are no shops until Galashiels.

Yair Bridge to Galashiels (5 km)

Yair Bridge to Calfshaw (1·5 km)
This section starts from the car-park at Yair Bridge. Cross the River
Tweed to the north bank and follow the A707 as it bends round to
the left. The mansion of Yair, which is just upstream, can be
glimpsed through the trees. The Way turns right immediately after
the buildings at Fairnilee farm – a tall waymarker and a SRWS sign
with 'Public footpath to Galashiels' on it show the route to be taken.
Walk past the farm and then through a little wood. Soon Fairnilee
House will be glimpsed about 500 m to the left. The present
building dates back to 1908 and supersedes an earlier mansion that
was sited below it. The woods around Fairnilee were established a
long time ago and they were mentioned in accounts as far back as
1649.

   Cross the road that goes to Fairnilee House and continue uphill
between two fields. The view is now beginning to open out and the
Three Brethren can be seen above the forest to the south-west.
Turn right when a conifer plantation is reached. Cross the stile at
the end of this wood and bear left on a track that crosses open
pastures above Calfshaw. Selkirk can now be seen about 5 km away
to the south.

Calfshaw to the Catrail (2 km)
The track forks near Calfshaw. Take the track on the right, cross a
little stream above the house and ascend to a gate. Cross the stile

and follow the track that runs to the left of a drystane dyke and passes between two stands of trees on Hog Hill. Follow the dyke on the right and cross one stile at the side of it. The fields on the right have been neatly divided by numerous dykes and in them are many heaps of angular stones that were gathered when the land was being improved. Head to the left of a prominent wooded hill that is in front and cross a well-constructed stone stile about 200 m to the west of the wood.

Continue heading north-eastwards and Galashiels will be seen ahead in the valley of the Gala Water. The Way passes to the left of the previously mentioned wooded hill and then crosses a stone stile. Follow the dyke on the right and walk high above the sheltered pond that is on the left. Cross two more stone stiles and enter a little beech wood. The Way follows a noticeable ridge while going through the wood; this is the ancient earthwork called the 'Catrail'.

The Catrail is a construction that has provoked debate for generations. At this point it is a definite embankment, with a trench at its side, and it runs south towards Rink Hill which is 2 km away. It has been suggested that the earthwork marked a boundary and that it ran from a fort at Torwoodlee (3·5 km to the north) to Linglie Hill (half-way between Three Brethren and Selkirk). Various writers have postulated that it went much farther, but the evidence is inconclusive. This part of the Catrail is sometimes called the 'Picts' Work Dyke'.

The Catrail to Galashiels (1·5 km)
Leave the wood at a waymarked stone stile which is to the left of a gate. Bear left, heading in the direction of a tall church steeple in Galashiels. Follow a narrow path and gradually near the dyke and the trees on the left. The wooded Gala Hill (276 m) is on the right and the farm below it is appropriately called Wood End. Descend and approach the junction of the dyke and a tall wall beside a wood. Turn left, go behind the wall and then meet a minor road where there is a waymarker and a SRWS signpost with 'Public footpath to Yair Bridge' on it pointing back the way. Turn left and head into Galashiels.

After passing some houses on the right, a sign with 'Southern

Upland Way' on it directs the walker to the right, along Barr Road. Those walkers who wish to visit Galashiels should continue going downhill on Elm Road.

Galashiels

Follow Elm Road downhill and just before Church Street is met, a plaque seen on the right bears the words: 'Sir Walter Scott of Abbotsford transacted business here with the Leith Banking Company from 1812 to 1832.' In the middle of the crossroads stands the mercat-cross, topped by three sundials and a weather-vane bearing the date 1695, the date of the cross's erection. This important site was in the middle of the old burgh and was where markets and fairs were held and where important public announcements were made. A plaque on the pedestal relates that 'near the site of this ancient cross Margaret Tudor of England was given sasine [legal possession] of her dowry of Ettrick Forest on her marriage in 1503 to James IV of Scotland which led to the historic Union of the Crowns in 1603'.

Turn left along Scott Crescent, pass Old Parish and St Paul's Church (opened in 1881) and then the historic Old Gala House will be seen on the right. A tower was built here about 1457, but the main part of the building dates from 1583. It is now used by various local clubs and societies.

Take the next turning on the right (St John Street) and follow it down to the busy Cornmill Square. The town's corn-mill stood in the square until 1912 and its culverted mill-lade runs beside an ornamental fountain that was erected in that same year. To the left of the square will be seen a bust of Sir Walter Scott (behind which are the public toilets) and to the right is a bust of Robert Burns. Also on the right are the council offices which are topped by a large clock tower; the building carries the town's coat of arms (see p. 261). In front of the building is the war memorial and Galashiels' best-known statue, The Border Reiver, which was sculpted by a local man, Thomas J. Clapperton.

To the south-east of the square is Paton Street. This leads to the

Peter Anderson of Scotland woollen mill which has a museum; conducted tours of the mill are available. Market Street, which is at the eastern end of the square, leads to the main shopping area. The Tourist Information Centre is to the north of the square, along Bank Street.

Galashiels' early importance was as a hunting seat of the Scottish kings and its name appeared in an early fourteenth-century charter; it became a burgh in 1599. Its modern growth and prosperity were based on using the Gala Water to power mills. The early mills were mentioned in a charter of 1622 but the real development of manufacturing started in the nineteenth century. The river that allowed this progress to be made also served as the common sewer at least until late in the nineteenth century when a writer observed that this fact was 'unpleasantly impressed upon the olfactory nerves'.

The town has many imposing buildings that reflect the success of the mills, and walkers will discover that this is the most industrialised town that is met on the Way. It has a good shopping centre and it offers all the facilities required by walkers. The Kilnknowe Caravan Park (which takes tents) is 2 km away – follow the A72 towards Peebles and turn right at a public telephone box when Kilnknowe Place is seen on the left.

Galashiels to Galafoot Bridge (3 km)

Galashiels to Abbotsford (2·5 km)
Barr Road is a 'no through road' that eventually ends at a gate and the start of a track. On the right are the wooded slopes of Gala Hill and to the left is a wide view over the eastern part of Galashiels. To the north is a mast on a wooded hill and to its right are the low grassy hills that the Way will cross during the next section. The Way will pass under the electricity transmission lines that can be seen on the skyline.

Soon the Eildon Hills come into full view; to their left are Melrose and the River Tweed. The track ends at a gate (one of five that are near each other) and to the left of the gate on the track is a granite tablet engraved with the words: 'Here Roger Quin author of The Borderland gazed on Scotland's Eden from the spur of Gala Hill.'

The local poet Roger Quin (1850–1925) wrote the poem 'The Borderland' as the thoughts of someone escaping busy city life to the peace of the Borders. The high point of his journey through the countryside was described thus:

> Gala Water shall not hold me –
> Tho' its mem'ries fair enfold me –
> Nor many-gabled Abbotsford, so stately and so still;
> For I'll hasten to the vision
> Of a valley fair, Elysian,
> And gaze on Scotland's Eden from the spur of Gala Hill.

Go through the gate and keep near the dyke on the left; soon Sir Walter Scott's home of Abbotsford (see later) will be seen in front of the Eildon Hills. Turn left at a track, pass to the left of the house of Brunswickhill and meet Abbotsford Road. Galashiels can be reached by turning left, but the Way turns right.

Cross the road and walk down an old minor road that has been cordoned off by a row of concrete pillars. Continue downhill and cross the A7, the busy trunk road that runs from Edinburgh to Carlisle. Walk down the minor road beside the farm of Netherbarns and cross the bridge over the route of the old Galashiels–Selkirk railway line.

This line was opened in 1856 and closed a little less than a hundred years later. It was a branch off the Edinburgh–Carlisle line which was opened on 1 June 1862 and later called the 'Waverley Line', after Sir Walter Scott's *Waverley* novels. The line was built primarily to carry sheep, wool, coal and other goods, with passenger traffic as a bonus. Once road transport developed and provided a cheaper method of carrying these goods, the lines were closed, leaving many people without public transport. The feelings

The Eildon Hills. This is the view from the side of Gala Hill; Galashiels is on the left.

of many Borderers were expressed on 4 January 1969 when the last Carlisle train left Edinburgh – at one point on the journey a bomb hoax stopped the train and when the train arrived at Hawick a coffin inscribed 'Waverley Line, Born 1849, Killed 1969, Aged 120 years' was carried along the platform.

Go left at a path when the road bends to the right, cross the minor road that runs alongside the River Tweed and walk along the woodland path that follows the river downstream. Soon Abbotsford is seen lying in a prominent position above a grassy haugh on the other side of the river.

Abbotsford and Sir Walter Scott

Sir Walter Scott bought the site on which Abbotsford stands in 1811. He later demolished the old farmhouse of Cartley Hole and started the long task of building the present large mansion in its place. Abbotsford is basically of Scottish Baronial style but it is also something of an architectural museum as it displays so many different styles and embellishments. Some of the additions include a medieval gable cross from the local Lindean Church, a sixteenth-century door from Edinburgh's Tolbooth and a seventeenth-century panel from the Guild House of the Souters of Selkirk. Other parts of the building include copies of features from a number of famous Scottish buildings such as the entrance porch at Linlithgow Palace. Scott was a romantic and his ideas about constructing Abbotsford went as far as to include medieval gargoyles!

Further purchases of land greatly extended the size of the estate. Scott was a notable example of a nineteenth-century improver and he planted the very fine woods that stand around the house. Abbotsford is open to the public during the summer and it is reached by taking the B6360 from the roundabout that is to the south-east of Galafoot Bridge (see below).

Scott was born in 1771 in Edinburgh. He followed his father into legal work but his real interest was in the romance of Border life. He could trace his father's ancestry back to Auld Wat of Harden

Abbotsford and the River Tweed.

(see p. 225) and he delighted in gathering and writing down the oral tradition of the old Border tales that had been handed down through the generations. He also studied the French romances and learned Italian in order to read Dante in the original. In 1799 he became the sheriff-depute of Selkirkshire, a job which obliged him to reside part of the year in the county.

His legal work gave him some time to devote to writing and he began to make a reputation as a poet and the *Minstrelsey of the Scottish Border* was first published in 1802. *Waverley* came out (anonymously) in 1814 and soon he was writing two to three novels a year (again anonymously) as well as poems, plays, anthologies, books on antiquities and countless other works. Some of his better-known works of this period include *Kenilworth* (1821), *Quentin Durward* (1823), *St Ronan's Well* (1824), *Redgauntlet* (1824) and *Ivanhoe* (1825). While Scott was proving himself to be a brilliant and very prolific author, his lack of control over his finances came to a head in 1825 when the collapse of a publisher landed him with a personal responsibility for the huge sum of £130,000. He threw himself into work in order to pay off his debts, turning out numerous tales, articles and complete books. Unfortunately, his health suffered because of the pace of work and he died in 1832, aged sixty-one. He was buried in Dryburgh Abbey, just 8·5 km east of Abbotsford.

Abbotsford to Galafoot Bridge (0·5 km)

The path leaves the shelter of the trees and passes under Galafoot Bridge. This tall and graceful bridge was opened in December 1975 and it carries the A6091 road that links Galashiels, Melrose and Newtown St Boswells. The road is supported on long steel girders that rest on three slim pillars.

Almost immediately before the bridge is the old Abbot's Ford, the river crossing that gave its name to Scott's house. Its name is a reminder of the route the abbots from Melrose Abbey took when driving their cattle. This is an important crossing point during the Braw Lads' Gathering, Galashiels' annual festival.

Galafoot Bridge to Melrose (4 km)

Galafoot Bridge to Melrose Bridge (2 km)
Bear right at a road junction to keep near the river; a left turn at the
junction would take the walker into Galashiels. Gala Fairydean
Football Club's ground can be seen on the left at the junction and
behind it is the Scottish College of Textiles which was founded in
1909.

To the north-west of the club's ground, and beyond the car-park,
is a little grassy area. On it is a large stone (the Raid Stane) and
below this is a plaque bearing the words 'Englishman's Syke', the
date 1337 and a motif of wild plums. This commemorates the place
where some Englishmen were killed by foresters from Galashiels in
1337. The Englishmen were on their way to Edinburgh to relieve
the (English-held) castle which was under siege and when they
stopped at this spot to eat wild plums they were set upon by the
foresters. Galashiels' coat of arms celebrates this event as it features
the date 1337, two foxes looking up at a plum tree and the motto
'soor plums'. The Raid Stane is visited by horse-riders during the
Braw Lads' Gathering.

The road passes the local gas-holder then crosses the Gala Water
just before it flows into the River Tweed. On the left side of the
bridge is a plaque with 'Gala Water Bridge 1984' on it. A large
housing scheme is then on the left – the design of the houses is in
stark contrast to the substantial stone houses in the older parts of
the town. The road runs under an electricity transmission line and a
tall waymarker on the right points the Way down a path past the
local sewage works – the walker will probably smell this place
before seeing it! This part of the Way is probably quite a shock to
walkers after all the countryside walking!

The Way crosses an old railway viaduct over the River Tweed and
follows the route of the Waverley Line. On the right is a new
housing scheme at Tweedbank. Continue going ahead on the
railway line when the metalled path bends to the right towards the
houses. About 200 m later take some steps up to the left and then
turn right at a pretty little country road.

About 1 km later the road joins an access road to an industrial estate on the right. Bear left, cross the more important road that is now met and go over the stile beside the trees that stand above the River Tweed. Just upstream is Melrose Bridge, a substantial but narrow red sandstone bridge that was rebuilt in 1762.

Melrose Bridge to Melrose (2 km)
The bank on the other side of the river has a broad haugh and it is much lower than the bank followed by the Way. The river has been meandering and the faster-flowing water on the outside of the bend of the river has eroded the bank. On the inside of the bend, the water is moving more slowly so there is a gradual accumulation of sand and gravel there.

The Way gradually descends and there is a very nice walk along the bank, with ducks and mature trees making this part of the walk relaxing and interesting. Fishermen may be seen on this stretch of the river pitting their skill (and patience) against the salmon and trout that the river is so well known for. The large building seen a field away on the right is the Waverley Castle Hotel, an early example of a nineteenth-century concrete building; it has a statue of Sir Walter Scott in front of it. Gattonside House (see p. 272) is on the other side of the river and the village of Gattonside stands behind the house. The next section of the Way follows the river in the opposite direction and its route can be seen running along the opposite river-bank.

The new Huntlyburn Hospital can now be seen some distance to the right, beyond the rugby pitches. Melrose is soon on the right, with the Eildon Hills standing high above it.

A fence bars the route beside the river as the bank is now very steep, so the Way goes through a little gate on the right. Turn left and walk along the road for a short distance before turning left again. Climb above the river on a wide path and look ahead for the pedestrian suspension bridge over the river.

The Way passes to the left of Melrose Parish Church, whose clock tower carries the date 1810. This part of the building survived a bad fire in 1908 and the rest of the church dates from after the fire. Any walker wishing to go directly into Melrose can turn right at the church – turn left when the main road is met. Beyond the church is

the ground of Melrose Rugby Football Club. This is one of
Scotland's best-known clubs and it was here that seven-a-side rugby
was played for the first time; an annual tournament draws large
crowds.

The path passes a bowling club then descends and meets the river
at an old weir. The remains of a mill-lade can be seen running away
to the right. It was built many hundreds of years ago to take water
to the abbey.

Continue along the metalled path to reach the suspension bridge
which marks the end of this section.

Melrose

The pedestrian suspension bridge to the centre of Melrose (1 km)
Those walkers who are continuing with the next section will cross
the bridge (see p. 271), but those who wish to go into Melrose after
passing the bridge should continue along the road past the farm
buildings. Take the first turning on the right and this road passes the
Melrose Motor Museum (vintage cars, motor cycles and cycles), a
woollen shop in what used to be a corn-mill, the Abbey Gardens,
Melrose Abbey (see later), Priorwood Gardens (orchard, flowers
and dried flowers) and public toilets. The road then meets the
market-place, where there is a public telephone box.

Priorwood Gardens is owned by the National Trust for Scotland
and it houses the local Tourist Information Centre.

Melrose
Melrose originated in a hamlet called Little Fordell and over the
centuries its fortunes came and went with those of the abbey. The
market-place is in the centre of the town and its focal point is the
mercat-cross (dated 1645), which is topped by the unicorn of the
Scottish arms, a mallet and a rose.

One of the nicest buildings in the market-place is Burt's Hotel, an
old coaching inn. To the left of it is the Ormiston which has a
fine clock (dated 1892) that juts out over the pavement. Beside this
building is a rather ornately decorated shop that carries the date 1863.

The three roads at the top of the square run (from north to south) to Melrose Abbey, the youth hostel (turn left after 300 m) and the old railway station. Melrose Railway Station was built in Flemish style and was opened in 1849. It was restored in 1986 and now houses a restaurant and a craft centre. The new bypass follows the route of the old railway line.

To the west of Melrose is the sixteenth-century Darnick Tower which, like many other buildings in Melrose, contains building stones taken from the abbey.

Melrose is a very attractive town with a number of shops, hotels, houses offering bed and breakfast accommodation and a youth hostel. The campsite is found by going downhill from the mercat-cross and turning left after a petrol station.

Melrose Abbey

Melrose Abbey was founded in 1136 as the Cistercians' first religious house in Scotland. David I gave them the land and various forestry and pasturage rights in the district. The monks made progress in sheep husbandry and laid the basis for what has become one of the Borders' most important industries.

Edward II sacked the abbey in 1322 and Richard II destroyed it in 1385. Around 1400 the work on rebuilding the abbey was started (in more flamboyant style than before) and this reconstruction forms the major part of the ruins that are seen today. Further raids took place in 1544 and 1545. These raids, the appointment of weak lay abbots and the Reformation all hastened the decline of this fine monument to craftsmanship. As the building deteriorated, local people took stones for their own use. However, in 1919 it became the property of the nation and the painstaking work of maintaining the fabric of the abbey is still going on.

The most prominent part of the structure is the church, with its superb south transept. To its north (i.e. towards the river) are the secular buildings and the well-preserved main drain. Beyond that is the Abbots' Hall, the Commendator's House (now a museum) and the mill-lade.

Melrose Abbey from near Melrose youth hostel.

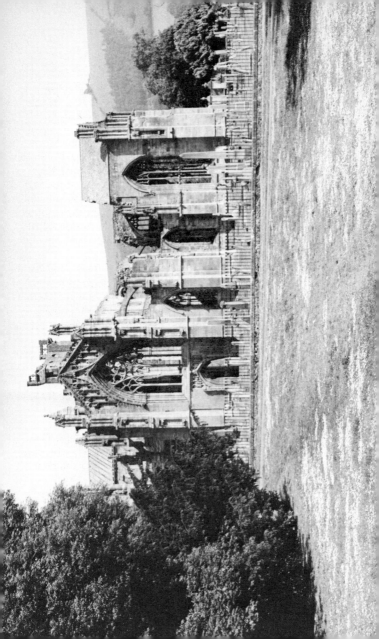

The abbey is in the care of the Scottish Development
Department; there is a charge for admission and a guidebook is
available.

Eildon Hills
The Eildon Hills are wonderfully attractive – their colour, shape
and position make them amongst Scotland's best-known landmarks.
They were originally formed from molten rock which welled up
beneath the local sandstone, pushing the sandstone upwards – no
lava ever flowed over the surface of the land. Subsequent erosion of
the overlying sandstone exposed the hard underlying rock as three
prominent hills. An alternative account of their formation is that
the thirteenth-century wizard Michael Scott chopped one hill into
three parts.

The summits provide marvellous views of the surrounding district
and the hills' strategic position attracted the Selgovae tribe who had
their capital on North Hill from approximately 50 BC to AD 80.
Significant ramparts can be seen on the hill and 296 sites of huts
have been recognised. The Mid Hill has a cairn on it which may
have contained a cist.

The Romans used the North Hill for a first-century AD signal
station. This was associated with the Roman fort of Trimontium at
Newstead, just 2 km east of Melrose.

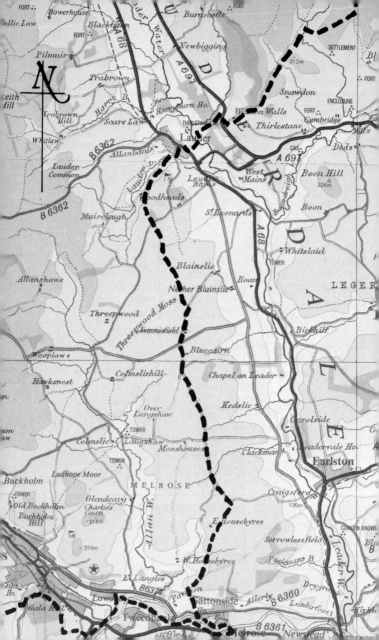

Section 12 Melrose to Lauder

Information

Start of section: At the chain suspension bridge over the River Tweed at Melrose (NT545345).
End of section: At the tolbooth in Lauder (NT531475).
Distance: 15·5 km (9½ miles).
Stages:
1. Melrose to Easter Housebyres (4 km).
2. Easter Housebyres to Fordswell (6·5 km).
3. Fordswell to Lauder (5 km).
4. Lauder.
Breaks in route:
1. At the road junction east of Mosshouses (to Earlston).
2. At the road junction after Bluecairn (to the A68).
3. At Woodheads Hill (to Lauder).
Conditions: This is a straightforward and very pleasant walk over moorland and along tracks. Paths and tracks take the Way up to near Easter Housebyres. Thereafter a path, a very straight track and then another path lead across moorland to Woodheads Hill. This stretch is quite exposed, but route finding is straightforward. The descent into Lauder is on a path and is more sheltered.
Points of interest: Views of Lammermuir Hills, Lauder.
Maps:
1. Ordnance Survey no. 73.
2. Bartholomew no. 41.
Transport: There is a bus service from Edinburgh to Jedburgh and Kelso via Lauder. There is also a bus service between Galashiels and Lauder via Melrose and Earlston.
Car parking: On route: west of Easter Housebyres, near Mosshouses, near Bluecairn, near Fordswell. At Lauder: in the market-place.
Accommodation: Gattonside (various), Earlston (off the Way; various), Lauder (various).
Notes: There are no shops until Lauder.

Melrose to Easter Housebyres (4 km)

Melrose to the B6360 at Gattonside House (1·5 km)
This section begins at the pedestrian suspension bridge over the
River Tweed. Walkers who are starting from the centre of Melrose
can reach the bridge by retracing the route described on p. 263.

A datestone above the 'entrance' to this wooden-decked bridge
carries the inscription: 'Opened 26 October 1826.' Lower down,
two metal plaques refer to the builders (Redpath, Brown of
Edinburgh) who also repaired it in 1928. The previous crossing was
a ford below the bridge and this was still used by horses after the
bridge was opened. The bridge is of light construction and it swings
about a bit as walkers cross it. Because of this, another notice warns
that 'Not more than 8 persons should be on the bridge at one time.
Passengers [!] are requested not to cross the bridge in a heavy gale.'
Yet another notice warns that a fine of £2 or imprisonment can be
the penalty for breaking any of the by-laws that govern the use of
the bridge. Stern stuff indeed.

The large house that is seen on the right, within the shelter of
some trees, is Allerly. This was built early in the nineteenth century
by Sir David Brewster (1781–1868). Brewster made many valuable
contributions in the practical study of optics, including the
development of the kaleidoscope and the improvement of the
optical equipment used in lighthouses. However, his most
important work was probably his articles in *The Edinburgh
Magazine*, *Encyclopaedia Britannica* and various scientific journals.
He played an important part in the setting up of the British
Association for the Advancement of Science (1831) and in 1855 he
wrote a biography of Sir Isaac Newton.

At the other side of the bridge is the village of Gattonside. The
area around it was granted to Melrose Abbey in 1143 by David I
and the monks took advantage of its sunny south-facing aspect and
planted their orchards there. The Hoebridge Inn can be found by
following the road into the village – it is on the right when the road
splits.

The pedestrian suspension bridge at Melrose; this takes the Way over the River Tweed.

After crossing the bridge, the Way turns left and follows the river-bank. On the other bank is the path taken by the Way at the end of the previous section. Parts of the opposite bank have collapsed, showing the very sandy material that makes up the broad haugh. Large and very beautiful trees give good shelter to the banks and there is a profusion of wild flowers here in the summer. The large mansion on the right is Gattonside House which is a home for handicapped people. This is of Georgian design and was built in the second quarter of the nineteenth century; the west wing was enlarged in 1915.

The Way now meets the B6360 at a waymarker outside the entrance to Gattonside House.

The B6360 at Gattonside House to Easter Housebyres (2·5 km)
A right turn at the B6360 leads to Gattonside, but the Way goes to the left and follows the road for about 200 m. A tall waymarker points to the right and the Way climbs a steep tree-lined track. Galashiels can be seen over to the west as the view over the Tweed Valley opens out.

The track then meets a minor road at a bend – go straight across, past the 'no through road' sign. When this road takes a bend to the left, the Way bears to the right along a track. Take the left fork when the track divides; the track on the right leads towards Earlston. The track ends at a gate and the Way now crosses high sheep pastures. The Three Brethren can be seen 11 km away and to the left of Gala Hill.

The dyke on the left is followed and the route goes under two electricity transmission lines (a rather old 33,000 volt line and then a newer 132,000 volt line which is part of the National Grid). These are the transmission lines that were seen from near Galashiels. The farm of Easter Housebyres is then passed on the left.

The River Tweed at Melrose.

Easter Housebyres to Fordswell (6·5 km)

Easter Housebyres to Mosshouses (2·5 km)
After reaching the high ground above Easter Housebyres, a very straight track can be seen in the distance heading more or less northwards. This is the next part of the Way and the track runs uphill and downhill for 3 km with only one slight change of direction.

Continue following the dyke/fence on the left and head towards Black Plantation. Pass to the left of a large pile of boulders and ascend to a stile beside some Scots pines. The Way now follows the dyke on the right, passes a pond, and joins the very straight track that was first seen from near Easter Housebyres.

As the track gains height there is a view back to the Eildon Hills and the track seems to run directly towards them. The straightness of the route and its alignment with the Roman fort at Newstead suggest that the Way might be following the line of a Roman road. During their occupation of Britain, a Roman road ran northwards from York and the part of it in this district was called Dere Street. The general line of Dere Street was from Newstead to Lauder, Soutra Hill, Dalkeith and then to the Firth of Forth at Inveresk (at Musselburgh) where a fort was established. It is still not certain exactly what line Dere Street took between Newstead and Lauder, but the Way follows one postulated route and an alternative route (which is also very straight) is about 2 km to the east of the Way.

This is a most pleasant stretch of the section, with rolling fields on either side. A minor road is crossed and Mosshouses farm is on the left. A right turn leads to Earlston, 5 km away.

Earlston is a village beside the A68 and it has some accommodation and shops. The village's recorded history goes back to a twelfth-century church but its main historical claim to fame is the old Rhymer's Tower at the western edge of the village. This has been associated with Thomas the Rhymer, a thirteenth-century poet whose talent for prophecy was a gift from the Fairy Queen with whom he stayed in Elfland for seven years.

The Roman Road north of Melrose follows a very straight route and takes the Way towards Lauder.

Mosshouses to Fordswell (4 km)

Go over the crossroads – soon Black Hill is seen on the right and Earlston lies just north of it, but out of sight. There is a good panoramic view as the track crosses Kedslie Hill (284 m) and over to the right is the agricultural land on the southern slopes of the Lammermuir Hills. These hills are the last major physical barrier to the Way as it heads towards the North Sea. The cairns on Twin Law can be seen 17 km away to the east of north.

Bluecairn farm is passed on the right and a waymarker is met at a road junction. Cross the junction, following the road sign to Blainslie and Lauder (a right turn at the junction leads to the A68, 3 km away). The Way now follows a metalled road and Jeaniefield farm is passed. Blainslie is seen rather farther away on the right and a glance at an Ordnance Survey map will show that there is not one place called Blainslie – there are five! (Nether, South, Middle, Upper and New Blainslie.) The next farm on the right is Fordswell.

Fordswell to Lauder (5 km)

Fordswell to Chester Hill (3 km)

At Fordswell the Way turns left immediately before a wood and follows a track that runs between a drystane dyke and an Ordnance Survey trig point. The trig point is a good place from which to view the route to be taken by the next section of the Way. The farm of Wanton Walls with its large sheds can be seen 5 km to the north and the Way will go past it on its route to Twin Law.

From the trig point, the Way follows the dyke on the left, goes under an electricity transmission line and then passes to the left of another wood. Once past the wood, follow the dyke on the right, crossing stiles and passing old ruined buildings *en route*. Woodheads Hill (303 m) is now climbed, with a nice wood on the right. The Galashiels–Lauder road is met just after the summit and if weather conditions are bad then it might be advisable to turn right at this junction as the road will provide a quicker and drier route to Lauder than will the Way.

Cross the road and follow the dyke on the right past another wood. The local golf course is on the right and the roof-top of Thirlestane Castle (see p. 284) can be seen beyond it. Cross a stile at a junction of dykes and climb the hill on the right. Keep to the left of the fence that runs round the edge of the golf course and follow the path as it takes a route high above Lauder Burn. The village of Lauder will soon be seen farther down the valley.

The wooded Chester Hill is passed on the right. This was the site of an ancient hill-fort which was circular in shape. There were two concentric ramparts, apparently made of stone, but unfortunately many of the stones have been taken away for other uses.

Chester Hill to Lauder (2 km)

The path splits just before a dyke on the right turns uphill – take the lower path. Low down on the opposite bank of the burn can be seen the remains of a triangular-shaped sheep enclosure. There is now a fine view up the rich agricultural valley of Lauderdale. The Way is now definitely moving into richer agricultural land and some of the farms grow cereals. Where sheep are raised, the fields can support far more animals than was the case in the hill farms that were seen farther west.

A little after the wood on Chester Hill is passed, the path divides at a waymarker. Take the left fork and head downhill towards some trees on the other side of the burn. Turn right and follow the right bank past a little bridge. Continue on the right bank until the next bridge is met; the left bank is then followed down to the Galashiels–Lauder road. The old Burn Mill is seen on the right just before the road is reached.

Turn left at the road and follow it to a sign with 'Southern Upland Way' on it pointing to the right (to a street called Factors Park). From this junction there are two alternative routes.

Those walkers wishing to visit Lauder should ignore the right turn at Factors Park and go straight ahead, past the church, to a T-junction. Look to the right at this junction and a Way notice-board will be seen on the opposite side of the road. Turn left at the T-junction and walk to the tolbooth in the market-place; this marks the end of this section.

Those walkers who do not intend to visit Lauder but who are

going straight on to the next section or to the campsite at
Thirlestane Castle (see p. 284) can take the right turn at Factors
Park and follow this down to the main road (the A68). The route for
Section 13 should now be followed.

Lauder

The village of Lauder stands above the western bank of the Leader
Water and it has a history that goes back many centuries. Its present
royal charter as a burgh dates back to 1502 but there was almost
certainly an older charter, probably dating back to William the
Lion.

The A68, which runs from Edinburgh to Darlington, goes
through the town's main feature, its very wide market-place, and
most of the town's old buildings are strung along this road. The road
through Lauder has long been an important north–south route and
hotels such as the Black Bull Hotel and the Eagle Hotel were once
important coaching inns.

The market-place is dominated by the narrow tolbooth, where
tolls were once collected. This is a plain-looking building with a
square tower, originally built in 1318 and rebuilt in 1773. The
building's upper storey was used for meetings of the local council,
while the ground floor was used as a jail up to 1840. One windowless
cell was placed under the stairs while the barred windows at ground
level show where the other cells were. Behind the tolbooth is a line
of old buildings, collectively known as Mid Row.

Lauder Old Parish Church, which the Way passes *en route* to the
tolbooth, is an interesting centrally planned structure, its design
based on a Greek cross with four arms of equal length. In the centre
are four pointed arches that carry the octagonal steeple. The
gable-end on the north side is dated 1673.

One famous (and now discredited) legend concerns James III
who, with his court and army, visited Lauder in 1482 on his way to
Berwick-upon-Tweed. James had recently surrounded himself with

Lauder market square and the tolbooth.

new courtiers such as Robert Cochrane, the Earl of Mar, and they
were at odds with more established figures like Archibald Douglas,
the Earl of Angus. It was said that Douglas organised the seizure of
seven of the King's favourites, including Cochrane, and hanged
them in front of the King from Lauder Bridge.

Although just a village, Lauder has good accommodation and a
number of shops, and it is a convenient centre from which to
explore the surrounding area. The post office and a public
telephone box are in the market-place. Public toilets are found on
the right after walking northwards past the Eagle Hotel.

The area's main tourist attraction is Thirlestane Castle (see p.
284) and there is a campsite in the castle's grounds.

Section 13 Lauder to Longformacus

Information

Start of section: At the tolbooth in Lauder (NT531475).
End of section: At Eildon Cottage in Longformacus (NT693571).
Distance: 24·5 km (15 miles).
Stages:
1. Lauder to Braidshawrig (9 km).
2. Braidshawrig to Twin Law (6 km).
3. Twin Law to Longformacus (9·5 km).
4. Longformacus.
5. Duns (off the Way).
Breaks in route:
1. Snawdon Burn (to Thirlestane and the A697).
2. Scoured Rig (to Blythe and the A697).
Conditions: This section has a superb moorland walk to Twin Law
where (in good weather) there is a marvellous view of the walker's
goal – the coast! This is certainly one of the best views of the whole
Way. However, much of the walk is over open and very exposed
ground, with little shelter, so in bad weather it can be very difficult.
However, route finding should not be a problem.
    From Lauder to Scoured Rig, the Way gradually climbs using
paths through woods and over pastures. A track then takes the Way
over exposed moorland to near Twin Law and a path completes the
walk to the summit and down to the Watch Water Reservoir. A
public road runs from the reservoir to Longformacus.
Points of interest: Thirlestane Castle, Twin Law, the view from
Twin Law, Duns (off the Way).
Maps:
1. Ordnance Survey nos. 73, 74.
2. Bartholomew no. 46.
Transport: There is a bus service between Longformacus and Duns.
Duns is connected by bus to Edinburgh, Galashiels and
Berwick-upon-Tweed.
Car parking: On route: near Wanton Walls, near Blythe (off the
Way), at the Watch Water Reservoir. At Longformacus: at the
Recreation Hall.

Accommodation: Longformacus (Eildon Cottage), Whitchester (off the Way; next section), Duns (off the Way; various).

Notes: The scarcity of accommodation at Longformacus, together with the shortness of the next section, may persuade many walkers to do Sections 13 and 14 in one (long) day. However, it is important that accommodation is booked ahead. Part of the section goes over a grouse moor where there might be shooting. There are no shops until Cockburnspath.

Lauder to Braidshawrig (9 km)

Lauder to Thirlestane Castle (0·5 km)
This section starts from the tolbooth in Lauder's market-place; walk south-east along the A68. Those walkers who take the route along Factors Park will join the A68 about 200 m south-east of the market-place.

After some late seventeenth-century cottages on the left, Factors Park will be seen on the right. The main road now runs past the grounds of Thirlestane Castle and soon the castle will be seen in the wooded parkland on the left.

Thirlestane Castle
The castle stands on the site of a fort that was rebuilt by Edward II in 1324 and occupied in 1548 by the Protector Somerset. The present building was originally commissioned by Sir John Maitland (*c.* 1545–95) at the end of the sixteenth century. Maitland of Thirlestane was James VI's Chancellor in 1587–95 and he was largely the director of royal policy until 1592.

Many alterations to the castle were carried out by the Duke of Lauderdale (1616–82). The rebuilt central six-storey tower-house and the balustraded terrace in front of the castle were built by William Bruce in 1670–6.

The Duke of Lauderdale became one of Britain's most powerful men during his time. Although he signed the Covenant he changed sides and as one of Charles II's most ardent supporters he suppressed the Covenanters and imposed the Crown's will in

Scotland. His ruthless style made him many enemies and at one point in 1679 the (English) House of Commons voted for his removal from his position of power – the Commons' move was met by its dissolution! Lauderdale retired from the affairs of State in 1680 because of ill health.

The castle houses the Border Country Life Museum and both the castle and the museum are open on most days during the summer.

Thirlestane Castle to Wanton Walls (2·5 km)

The castle's grounds are entered by taking the first turning on the left, where there is a gatehouse. The stable block, with its arched gateway, is passed on the right and the road descends to a crossroads. Left leads to the castle and the museum, right leads to Thirlestane Castle Camping and Caravan Park, but the Way goes straight ahead, along a track and across the Leader Water. This river rises in the Lammermuir Hills to the north of Lauder and flows southwards to meet the River Tweed at Leaderfoot, just 3 km east of Melrose. The Leader Water has carved its route through a narrow outcrop of Old Red Sandstone that runs from Oxton (7 km north of Lauder) down to Earlston and the rock has given this district its distinctive red sandy soil.

Turn left after crossing the river and walk upstream to the remains of an old footbridge. Turn right, pass a massive tree stump, and keep near the fence on the left. Pass to the left of a stand of conifers and turn left at a track. Keep near the fence on the left and the path now runs through a little wood and high above the Earnscleugh Water. The wood ends at a stile over a drystane dyke near Drummonds-hall (the house seen on the left); turn right at a track.

The A697 is now met and crossed and the Way goes uphill on a minor road. Looking back, there is a view to the west and south: behind Lauder can be seen the valley of the Lauder Burn and Chester Hill. The Eildon Hills are due south of this viewpoint. The minor road has a nice beech hedge on the left and it leads to the farm of Wanton Walls where a left turn is taken.

Wanton Walls to the Blythe Water (3 km)

Keep to the right of the barns; a sheep dip will be passed after the farmhouse. The Way now passes to the left of the water authority's filter station, a neat building bearing a plaque with the inscription 'B.C.C. [Berwickshire County Council] 1956' on it. Continue uphill, crossing a field and passing to the right of a water-supply installation, before reaching a stile at the edge of a wood. Ascend to a track where a right turn should be taken. Turn left after the track leaves the wood and climb over a stile into a field. Turn left again and follow the dyke.

Near the highest point of the rise, a waymarker set into a pile of stones will be seen on the right, in the middle of the field. Pass well to the left of this and head uphill towards a stile over a dyke. In poor visibility, just keep near the first dyke until this second dyke is met – then turn right to reach the stile.

There is now a fine view to the south and south-east, with the Cheviots on the south-eastern skyline. Walk directly ahead to a waymarker at a small cairn. From here, Twin Law and its two huge cairns can be seen over to the north-east. Bear to the right and descend, passing to the left of some piles of stones and old walls, and to the right of a shed (which could be a useful shelter in bad weather).

The Snawdon Burn should now be crossed; in bad weather the burn could be followed downstream to Thirlestane (2·5 km away) which is on the A697.

Turn left, cross a stile at a junction of dykes and turn right, keeping close to the dyke that is now on the right. A little later take a path on the left that runs to the left of a large pile of stones and join a track that runs above the Blythe Water.

Keep well above the terraces on the west bank and cross a fence at a stile. Now bear right and descend in order to cross the wooden bridge over the Blythe Water. The river runs past Braidshawrig farm, which will be met later on. A plaque beside the bridge commemorates its construction by the Officers' Training Corps of Edinburgh and Heriot-Watt Universities in July 1985. This is the second army bridge built here – the first was washed away in one piece (all three tons of it!) 100 m downstream in November 1984.

The landscape near the bridge is very bare and only a few trees can be seen: there is little shelter for man or beast in this lonely moorland. A vast heather moor to the north-west stretches back into the distance. Part of this is a managed grouse moor and, from 12 August to December, shooting parties may be seen and heard.

The Blythe Water to Braidshawrig (3 km)
After the bridge, follow the rough track on the left that climbs high above the river's eastern bank. When the track splits, ignore the track on the right going steeply uphill, and follow the path that leads towards a pile of stones on the right. Pass to the left of this and cross a dyke at a stile.

Head towards the fence on the right and follow it to a plantation; the farm of Blythe will be seen on the right. Cross a stile over the fence, turn left and follow the edge of the plantation for about 500 m to the summit of Scoured Rig (363 m). A track on the right comes uphill from Blythe and if weather conditions are bad then this can be used as a means of getting to lower ground. From this point there is a 5 km walk on track and road to the A697.

Cross the stile at the summit of Scoured Rig and walk through the forest on a track that goes all the way down to the farm of Braidshawrig (or Broadshawrig). This lonely farmhouse is situated in a little valley and has the streams of Easter Burn and Wester Burn on either side of it. When near the farm, look over the river to a dyke near the farm and a standing stone should be seen. This marks the spot where Charles Barclay-Maitland (1822–84), the twelfth Earl of Lauderdale, was killed by lightning while grouse shooting.

Braidshawrig to Twin Law (6 km)

The track bears right just before Easter Burn is met and the Way now climbs on to the high open moorland where both sheep and cattle graze. Some shooting butts, fashioned out of handy boulders, will be passed. Twin Law suddenly appears straight ahead. Walkers coming from the east should ignore a track (which goes to Blythe) that is passed.

A wood, a barn and a circular sheep enclosure are passed on the left – this is a fine place for lunch. The barn is well anchored to the ground by a large amount of concrete, and the need for this strong base is a testament to the high winds that sweep this moorland. The barn could be a useful shelter in bad weather. From this point it should be possible to see Rutherford's Cairn. It is about 2 m high and is well to the left of Twin Law's cairns and just below the skyline.

The track climbs and ends at a turning area near a fence; turn right and follow the fence. Watch Water Reservoir is to the north of east and Rutherford's Cairn can be seen ahead on the skyline. The Way meets a stile at a junction of fences and the fence that is now crossed marks the boundary between Ettrick and Lauderdale District and Berwickshire District. A well-defined path runs from the stile to Twin Law and on the left is the dyke that is crossed after Twin Law has been visited. If the weather is bad and Twin Law is not to be visited, then follow the dyke on the left to a stile.

Twin Law

Twin Law (447 m) gives a superb view over the surrounding countryside. To the north is the vast heather moor that blankets most of the Lammermuir Hills. Although many of the hills are over 400 m in height there are few notable summits and the range of hills is often in the form of a high undulating moorland. In contrast to the moors to the north, the view to the south is over good arable farmland, dotted with many randomly positioned stands of trees. The Eildon Hills are prominent to the west of south, with Black Hill on their left. Dirrington Great Law (398 m) and Dirrington Little Law (363 m) are the prominent hills that are to the east and are fairly near; Dirrington Great Law is the one on the left. To the north of east can be seen the Watch Water Reservoir and the Way will soon pass to the left of this. It should be possible to see the North Sea, and perhaps some ships sailing along the coast, depending on the weather conditions.

The summit is topped by the Twinlaw Cairns, two well-made

Braidshawrig, with the Lammermuir Hills behind.

barrel-shaped towers each over 3 m high that stand on separate platforms. The towers and their platforms are made from rough whinstone boulders. At each one a small stairway leads to a chair-like recess that faces the south and these will give welcome shelter to those walkers who have been enduring cold northerly winds. The eastern cairn has a small passageway beside the staircase that seems to run under the cairn. The cairns were excavated in the nineteenth century and it is said that cists were found in them. A visitors' book may be found at one of the cairns and an Ordnance Survey trig point stands between them.

The cairns are said to commemorate the deaths of twin brothers, neither of whom knew the identity of the other, who were the leaders of the Scottish army and an invading army of Saxons.

In the poem 'The Battle of Twinlaw', the scene is set by the verses:

> The Anglo-Saxons' restless band
> Had crossed the river Tweed,
> Up for the hills of Lammermuir,
> Their hosts march'd on with speed.
> Our Scottish warriors on the heath
> In close battalion stood,
> Resolved to set their country free,
> Or shed their dearest blood.

The two brothers, as the two opposing leaders, agreed to settle the encounter with a face-to-face fight to the end:

> The trumpets, raised with deafening clang,
> The fearful onset blew,
> And then the chieftains stepped forth,
> Their shining swords they drew.

The Saxons' leader fell first and, as one of his men bemoaned his death, he uttered words that told Edgar (the father of the Scottish

Twinlaw Cairns. The North Sea can be seen from this viewpoint.

chieftain) that the dead Saxon leader was his long-lost son.
However, the Scottish chieftain was already mortally wounded and

> The Scottish chief, as his father fell,
> He raised his fading eye,
> And tore the bandage of his wounds
> To let life's streams run dry.
> He kissed his sire, and his brother's wounds,
> That ghastly were and deep,
> And closed him in his folding arms,
> And fell on his long, long sleep.

It is said that upon the two brothers' deaths, hostilities were suspended and soldiers from both sides lined themselves up the hillside and passed stones up from a stream to the top of the hill so that the two cairns could be built.

The cairns certainly don't look very ancient. This is because Polish tanks knocked them down during the Second World War while on manoeuvres, but fortunately they were re-erected by a local drystane dyker.

Twin Law to Longformacus (9·5 km)

Twin Law to Watch Water Reservoir (5 km)
The Way now follows a narrow path heading in a north-easterly direction towards the reservoir. On the descent it may be possible to see the historic island of Lindisfarne, 50 km away; it should be seen to the left of Dirrington Little Law. Cross the stile over the dyke on the left then follow the fence on the right.

A notice found soon after the stile indicates that the Way is now crossing a grouse moor, so take care if there are shooting parties. The Way passes close to the butts, which all face towards the valley of the Watch Water – so you are walking across the line of fire of the butts on your right! The heather here is generally young and short and numerous patches of burnt heather will be seen on the hillsides. The old heather has been burned to hasten the young shoots which are eaten by the young grouse.

The fence is followed for the next 2 km and it passes well to the right of the prominent square-shaped Twinlaw Wood. Turn left at a track, pass the wood and descend to the Watch Water. Cross it by a little wooden bridge beside Twinlaw Ford and then look for an inscribed sandstone tablet that is to the left of the track. Below the tablet is John Dippie's Well and on the tablet are the words: 'There is no water on the Lammermuirs sweeter than at John Dippie's Well. Keeper Rawburn 1865 to 1897.' Below this is the date 1898. The farm of Rawburn will be passed later.

After passing the well, keep on the main track and follow the course of the Watch Water. The track goes past the farm of Scarlaw and a metalled road is now met which carries the Way past the Watch Water Reservoir and into Longformacus.

The grassed-over remains of a peel-tower can be seen on the right, immediately before the second cattle grid after the farm. A picnic place is passed at the start of the public road and cars can be parked here.

Watch Water Reservoir to Longformacus (4·5 km)
The Way now crosses the reservoir's spillway, climbs up to the eastern end of the dam and passes a little circular tower made of red sandstone that carries the initials B.C.C. and the date 1954. The road climbs away from the reservoir, passing shooting butts that are exceptionally close to the public road. The Way bends to the left when it meets the track to Rawburn Cottage. Rawburn farm is soon passed on the right.

Several buildings associated with the water supply are passed on the left and the main building carries the same inscription as was seen on the reservoir's tower. The Watch Water is now crossed and just beside the bridge can be seen a large steel water-pipe from the reservoir. The winding road then passes Horn House Hotel (marked 'Rathburne Hotel' on the Ordnance Survey map) on the left. This establishment now specialises in catering for the needs of people with allergies. Cross another bridge, on the downstream side of which is a plaque inscribed 'Private bridge erected by C. H. Holme of Rawburn 1900.'

The stream now joins the Dye Water and the Way follows this

river past a quarry and the local park and then meets the hamlet of Longformacus. A tall waymarker stands at the T-junction; Gifford is 21 km to the north-west and Duns is 10 km to the south-east.

On the left of the T-junction is a single-arch sandstone bridge over the Dye Water. On the bridge's northern wall is a datestone (1851) and two carved heads. On the outside wall of the downstream side there is an elaborate carving and the date 1820. Just upstream of the bridge is the water-pipe that carries water from the reservoir to the Duns area.

The road to Longformacus Parish Church is opposite the T-junction and a notice near the bridge states that the church was `originally founded in 1243. The present building was built about 1730 and renovated in 1892–3. It has a little bell-tower, a rounded apse at its eastern end and three sundials on the wall facing the graveyard. There are a number of eighteenth-century gravestones in the graveyard. The road that runs past the church leads to Longformacus House, a mansion that was originally built in 1715.

Turn right at the T-junction and pass the Recreation Hall (dated 1913 on a gable-end). A little farther on is Eildon Cottage. This is the local post office and it also offers bed and breakfast accommodation; it does not sell food. The Way reaches the end of this section at a Way notice-board that is found on the right, a short distance after Eildon Cottage.

Longformacus

Longformacus has some interesting Georgian buildings, especially those on the west side of the river, just downstream of the bridge. The third building along from the main road carries the date 1820.

Longformacus has no shops or public toilets but there is a public telephone box to the north of the bridge.

Duns (off the Way)

Duns is a small town that is the administrative centre of the
Borders. It has a large market-place in its centre, around which are
numerous shops and hotels.

Duns was created a burgh as far back as 1489 and it shares its
name with the hill of Duns Law (218 m) which is just to the north of
the town. General Leslie's Covenanting army camped there in 1639,
blocking the path of Charles I who was at Berwick-upon-Tweed.

It is possible, but not certain, that John Duns Scotus (1265–1308)
came from Duns. He was a Franciscan theologian who was well
known throughout Europe. Another local person was Jim Clark
(1936–68), world motor-racing champion in 1963 and 1965, on both
occasions driving Lotus–Ford cars. He was killed in a race at
Hockenheim in West Germany. The town's memorial to him is the
Jim Clark Room in Newtown Street and this contains many of his
racing trophies.

Just to the west of the town is Duns Castle (the grounds are not
open to the public). This incorporates an old tower built in 1320 for
Thomas Randolph, Earl of Moray.

Section 14 Longformacus to Abbey St Bathans

Information

Start of section: At Eildon Cottage in Longformacus (NT693571).
End of section: At Abbey St Bathans Parish Church (NT758622).
Distance: 11 km (7 miles).
Stages:
1. Longformacus to Whitchester Lodge (6 km).
2. Whitchester Lodge to Abbey St Bathans (5 km).
3. Abbey St Bathans.
Break in route: Whitchester Lodge (to Preston and Duns).
Conditions: This is one of the easiest sections of the whole Way.
After a short walk along a road, paths take the Way over pleasant
moorland to the track through Lodge Wood. In bad visibility, care
should be taken with route finding before Owl Wood. Another path
after Whitchester Lodge leads to a forest track that follows the
Whiteadder Water to Abbey St Bathans; trees restrict the views.
Points of interest: Abbey St Bathans.
Maps:
1. Ordnance Survey no. 67.
2. Bartholomew no. 46.
Transport: There is a bus service between Abbey St Bathans and
Duns. Duns is connected by bus to Edinburgh, Galashiels and
Berwick-upon-Tweed.
Car parking: On route: near Whitchester Lodge. At Abbey St
Bathans: near the church, at the trout farm.
Accommodation: Whitchester (off the Way), Abbey St Bathans
Youth Hostel, Moorhouse (off the Way), Grantshouse (off the
Way; next section; various).
Notes: Walkers who wish to do Sections 13 and 14 together can
quicken their progress in this section by bypassing the climb over
the moor (see p. 298). It is strongly advised that accommodation is
booked ahead. There are no shops until Cockburnspath.

Longformacus to Whitchester Lodge (6 km)

Longformacus to Owl Wood (3·5 km)

This section starts at the Way notice-board at the southern end of Longformacus. The Way goes a short distance along the Duns road and turns left at a tall waymarker along the signposted minor road to Whitchester and Ellemford.

The parish church and Longformacus House can be seen on the left. Caldra farm is passed on the right and the road descends to cross the route of a gas pipeline. Cross the Blacksmill Burn just before a small wood; a water pipeline also crosses the burn at this point. Continue on the road until a tall waymarker is found on the left, opposite the end of the field on the right.

If time is short, the weather bad or accommodation being sought at Whitchester, then continue on the road and Whitchester is met after 3 km. Whitchester is advertised as a 'Christian Guest House and Conference Centre' and it offers bed and breakfast accommodation. The road continues past Whitchester and then meets the B6355. Turn right and the Way will then be rejoined at a tall waymarker on the left after 700 m.

Go over the stile on the right and walk between a fence and a little burn; follow the fence up to the beginning of the grassy moor. The view is certainly worth the effort of the steep ascent. Dirrington Great Law is to the south-west and is the district's most prominent hill. Longformacus House can be seen in the middle distance to the west. Twin Law's cairns are on the skyline between these two directions. To the north and north-west is the farmland on the southern slopes of the Lammermuir Hills. The land encountered in this district is much lower, more sheltered and far more productive than the heather moorlands that can be seen stretching back into the distance.

The next part of the Way needs care in route finding, especially in poor visibility as there are numerous paths and tracks on this moor. Continue uphill over the rough grass and head just south of east, gradually nearing the electricity transmission line on the left. Follow the path as it goes under the transmission line and head north of east, towards the left-hand side of a small L-shaped stand of

conifers; a barn can be seen in front of the trees. Cross the Sel Burn
and pass to the left of the wood. The late nineteenth-century
mansion of Whitchester can be seen to the north, to the left of the
large plantation of Owl Wood.

Head towards Owl Wood, taking care when crossing a boggy
patch of ground, and walk to the right of this plantation and the row
of beech trees beside it.

Owl Wood to Whitchester Lodge (2·5 km)
Ascend the hill and cross a couple of stiles at a junction of fences.
Now walk on the left side of a fence beside another row of beeches.
Cross a stile over this fence at a gate and follow a track. Bear left
after another gate and join a track going downhill.

The track makes its way through Lodge Wood and then meets the
B6355 where there is a tall waymarker; to the south-east are Preston
(6 km) and Duns (10 km). There is a public telephone box at
Ellemford Bridge, 1 km north-westwards along the road.

Turn left at the B6355 and head downhill to Whitchester Lodge.

Whitchester Lodge to Abbey St Bathans (5 km)

Whitchester Lodge to Robber's Cleugh (1·5 km)
The wrought-iron gates outside the lodge have 'SL' and '1897' as
part of their elaborate design. To the right of the gates is a small
door above which is a coat of arms depicting a sword and a quill and
bearing the inscription '*Marte et ingenio*' ('By war and wit'). The
lodge itself has an inscribed tablet on which is the date 1897 and the
initials 'AS' and 'IFL' (for Andrew Smith and his wife Ida Frances
Landale). Andrew Smith bought Whitchester in the 1870s and
constructed the lodge and other estate buildings.

Continue along the road for about 100 m to a stile and a tall
waymarker on the right. The Way now climbs up a track, and over
to the left can be seen the farm of Rigfoot. Shelter belts of trees are
scattered about the hillsides. The track narrows to a path and there
is a view up the Whiteadder Water, the river that will be followed to
the end of the section. It rises about 15 km to the north-west and

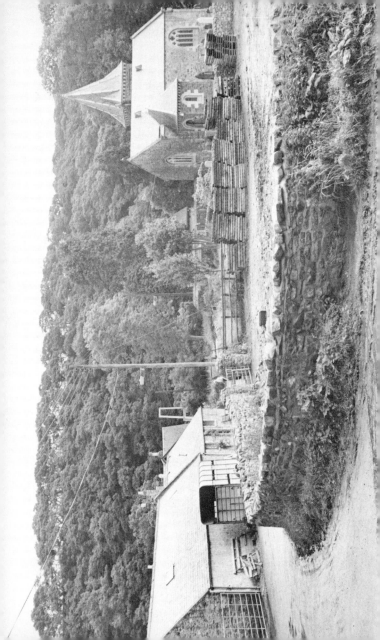

meets the River Tweed after it has entered England.

The path nears a fence on the right in order to avoid a gully. Bear to the right after the gully, keeping in sight of the fence. Aim for the right-hand corner of the plantation that is on the left in order to reach the top of a very steep gully called Robber's Cleugh. Descend the gully and cross a stile to enter the forest at a track. Turn right and follow the track all the way to Abbey St Bathans.

Robber's Cleugh to Abbey St Bathans (3·5 km)
The track makes its way through Roughside Wood as it rounds Abbey Hill (Outer) and there are occasional glimpses of the river. At the end of the forest there is a view down the river and in the distance can be seen a line of pylons on the skyline; the Way goes under their transmission line in the next section. Another track coming up from the left joins the Way. Soon Burnside farm is seen high above the opposite bank. While rounding Abbey Hill (Inner) , the track leaves the riverside and another track joins the Way from the right.

The track now makes its way downhill to Abbey St Bathans. Abbey House is passed on the left just before the public road is met at a crossroads. There is a public telephone box on the right. Left at the crossroads leads to Cockburnspath and right leads to Preston and Duns.

Cross the public road and the end of the section is marked by the Way notice-board on the wall of the Rest House (Abbey St Bathans Youth Hostel). This is directly opposite the gate to the parish church.

Abbey St Bathans

Abbey St Bathans is an exceptionally peaceful place and in 1925 James Logan Mack wrote that 'Abbey has so far been spared by fortune, the indignity of infestment by chars-a-banc [tourist coaches] and their concomitant hordes. The roads which lead to it

Abbey St Bathans. The church is on the right and the Rest House (the youth hostel) is on the left.

are narrow, and such vehicles are alike a curse to the artistic sense, and a danger to all and sundry who encounter them in such regions.'

The area around Abbey St Bathans has been inhabited for a great length of time. A Bronze Age fort sits atop Cockburn Law (325 m) which is just 2·5 km south of the church and below the fort are the important remains of Edin's Hall, an Iron Age broch. Brochs were defensive structures made of unmortared boulders that were about 7 m high and they had thick walls in which there were passageways and staircases. The broch is 2·5 km from the parish church and it can be found by following the west bank of the Whiteadder Water downstream.

A Cistercian nunnery was established at Abbey St Bathans some time before 1296 and it was probably dedicated to St Baithen, a cousin of Columba and successor to him at the monastery on the island of Iona. Contrary to what the place-name suggests, there has never been an abbey in the district! The priory was burned down in 1545 by the Earl of Hertford, during the time that was known, rather euphemistically, as the 'rough wooing'. This was when Henry VIII was trying to 'persuade' the Scots that their Queen (Mary, Queen of Scots (1552–87)) should be married to his son Prince Edward (later King Edward VI).

The little parish church stands on the site of the nunnery. It is an eighteenth-century building, though its east wall with its round-headed windows dates back to the late fourteenth century. At the back of the church there is a little tower topped by a steeple and a weathercock and above its door is a coat of arms with three bulls' heads on it. The bulls' heads (for Turnbull) are associated with John Turnbull (1820–91) who added the tower and porch to the church.

The gravestones near the church are interesting, with engravings of everyday items such as scissors and crooks that give clues to the occupations of those buried there. Just inside the church's entrance is an old sandstone gravestone dated 1705. This commemorates the death of a minister, George Home, and also Jean Hamilton, 'spows to the seid Mr George Home' who died in 1719. The stone records that Jean Hamilton 'mortified a 1000 Merks for maintaining a school master in this place' (1 merk = ⅔ of a Scots pound). Inside the church is an effigy of a prioress that is set into a recess under a window in the east wall; this dates back to the fifteenth or early sixteenth century.

From the church there is a good view south-eastwards to Abbey St Bathan's House; this was extended by John Turnbull.

The nearby farms are part of the estate of Abbey St Bathans. Most of the local estate buildings were constructed in the nineteenth century and have similarities in design and decoration. The Rest House is run on similar lines to a Scottish youth hostel (it is not actually owned by the SYHA) and it is small (only twelve beds), so it is advisable to book ahead.

There are no shops or public toilets near the end of the section.

The estate's trout farm is reached by walking 600 m south-east along the main road, past Abbey St Bathan's House. Beside the trout farm (where fish are on sale) there is a tea-room, toilets and the remains of an old water-powered saw-mill.

Nearby, a bridge crosses the river to a pottery and a picnic area. After this bridge a path can be followed up the north-eastern bank to another bridge which is just beside the hostel. The track that runs past the pottery leads up to a public road and to Moorhouse (which offers bed and breakfast).

Section 15 Abbey St Bathans to Cockburnspath

Information

Start of section: At Abbey St Bathans Parish Church (NT758622).
End of section: At the mercat-cross in Cockburnspath (NT774711).
Distance: 16·5 km (10 miles).
Stages:
1. Abbey St Bathans to Whiteburn (3 km).
2. Whiteburn to the A1 (5·5 km).
3. The A1 to Pease Bay (4·5 km).
4. Pease Bay to Cockburnspath (3·5 km).
5. Cockburnspath.
Breaks in route:
1. Whiteburn (to Abbey St Bathans).
2. At the public road after Whiteburn (to Cockburnspath).
3. At the A1 at Bowshiel Wood (to Cockburnspath or Grantshouse).
4. At Pease Bridge (to Cockburnspath).
5. At Old Linhead (to Cockburnspath).
Conditions: This is a straightforward end to the Way and the coastal views are good. The Way follows paths and farm tracks from Abbey St Bathans to the public road after Whiteburn. The route is fairly exposed but route finding should not be a problem. A good track and then a road lead down to the A1; this stretch is fast. Narrow tracks then take the Way to the A1107 and a path goes to Pease Bay.
   The coastal walk is on paths. This can be a fine walk but it must be treated with great caution in misty, wet or windy weather and in bad weather the coastal walk should be avoided.
Points of interest: The view from above Pease Dean, Cove Harbour, Cockburnspath.
Maps:
1. Ordnance Survey no. 67.
2. Bartholomew no. 46.
Transport: See p. 55 for bus services to Cockburnspath.
Car parking: On route: near Whiteburn, near the A1, at Pease Bay, at Cove. At Cockburnspath: in the market-place.

Accommodation: Grantshouse (off the Way; various),
Cockburnspath (various), Chesterfield Caravan Park, Coldingham
(off the Way; various), Dunbar (off the Way, various).
Notes: An interesting and straightforward end to the Way. There
are no shops until Cockburnspath.

Abbey St Bathans to Whiteburn (3 km)

Abbey St Bathans to the Whare Burn (1 km)
This section starts at the Way notice-board at the Rest House
opposite the parish church. Walk northwards to the Whiteadder
Water and cross it by the sturdy suspension bridge that was built
in 1987 by a team of Gurkhas; a plaque commemorates its
construction. If the bridge seems to be rather 'over-designed' for
the size of the river then it should be noted that in a great flood in
1948 the parish church was marooned on an island! The subsequent
building of the Whiteadder Reservoir (through which the river
flows) should stop the river from rising too far in the future.

Turn left and walk through the riverside wood, a very ancient oak
wood which has been left relatively undisturbed over the centuries.
The path climbs to a point just above the confluence of the
Whiteadder Water and the Monynut Water. Turn right after leaving
the wood and join a track that comes from the farm of Shannobank.

Keep to the left of the dyke that is met and follow the route of an
old drove-road. Pass to the right of a long shed and keep near the
fence on the right in order to find the path that leads down to the
wooden bridge over the Whare Burn. This burn rises about 5 km
away in the Lammermuir Hills and meets the Whiteadder Water
near the Abbey St Bathans trout farm.

The Whare Burn to Whiteburn (2 km)
Turn left after the bridge and follow the burn upstream. Bear right
at a small stream and a track; on the left is a ford over the Whare
Burn. Cross the small stream and follow it uphill to a stile on a
dyke. Bear to the left, climb on to Blakestone Moor and pass to the
right of the nearest pylon on the electrical transmission line. This is

an important line on the National Grid and it operates at 400,000 volts.

Bear left, towards a tall cairn in the field which was built by a previous farmer, John Cockburn, to celebrate his family's hundred years' association with the farm of Whiteburn. It is constructed from local sedimentary rocks, but a few white quartz rocks have also been used. It is topped by a red cockerel holding a mill-rind (originally used to support the upper millstone of a corn-mill).

Walk towards the farm buildings that are on the left and a track will be picked up that leads to two gates at the corner of the field. Cross a stile at the gate on the right, walk beside a little wood and join the farm road that runs past a barn. The Way now meets a public road opposite the farm of Whiteburn. The road can be used to get to lower ground if the weather is bad as the road on the left leads to Abbey St Bathans (4 km away). There is a public telephone box to the right of the junction.

Whiteburn to the A1 (5·5 km)

Cross the road to Whiteburn and go through a gate on the left near the public road. Follow the fence on the right in order to go round a small plantation of young trees and rejoin the farm road; turn left. When the road/track turns to the left, go straight ahead and over a stile into a field. There are now two alternative routes to the next public road. The fence on the right has a stile over it so that the walker can walk along the edge of the field that is not cultivated. Follow the appropriate side of the fence and the next public road will be found after about 700 m.

Turn left at the road and follow it for about 300 m. A beech hedge is passed and the Way turns right at a track just after a little wood. If the weather is bad, then it is possible to continue on the road to reach Cockburnspath, 7 km away (Chesterfield Caravan Park is passed *en route*). The track crosses the Eye Water, passes to the right of the farm of Blackburn Mill, then turns right after going alongside an attractive beech hedge. The surface now becomes a metalled road and the Way passes a row of houses at Blackburn farm. The farm is large and it has many well-built buildings and stone walls.

About 1 km after the farm, the road takes a sharp bend to the left and finishes the descent to the A1 road and the east-coast railway line at Penmanshiel. Bowshiel farm, with its tall grain silos and brick chimney, is seen on the left. The wood on the left just before the A1 is met is Bowshiel Wood and beside it runs Pease Burn. The Way will be following the burn to Pease Bay, which is still 4 km away. A road sign with 'Blackburn 1' on it stands at the junction of the minor road and the A1.

The A1 is the east coast's main road and it runs from Edinburgh to London via Newcastle, Doncaster and Leicester. Although many stretches of the A1 are of a very high standard, numerous other parts are narrow and overcrowded. At this point it is not even a dual carriageway.

Cockburnspath is 5 km to the north and Grantshouse is 2 km south of this point; Grantshouse has two hotels and a shop. A café is situated about half-way along the road to Grantshouse.

The east-coast railway line

The railway line was built in the mid-1840s by the North British Railway. The line ran from Edinburgh to Berwick-upon-Tweed and in 1850 it was linked with the route to London when the Royal Border Bridge was opened at Berwick-upon-Tweed. The trains could then operate one of the fastest services in the world, and in 1853 the Flying Scotsman took about eight hours to go from Edinburgh to London. Today the diesel-powered locomotives that operate the route take about four and a half hours to complete the same distance and the planned electrically powered trains will do the journey in four hours.

The construction of the line in the Cockburnspath–Penmanshiel area was plagued by many problems – both engineering and social. A six-span stone bridge had to be built north of Cockburnspath over the Dunglass Burn and a 250 m long tunnel had to be built here at Penmanshiel. To compound the difficulties, the construction sites were often waterlogged. The labourers were a mixture of Irish Catholics and Scottish Protestants; sectarianism often resulted in trouble and there was a serious riot in October 1844. The simmering animosity was made worse by the fact that the contractor paid the labourers in tokens exchangeable only in his shop, and by his selling them whisky, which gave him a substantial profit. Pay-day was often feared by the local people and on one occasion the company's directors (unsuccessfully) called upon the Lord Advocate for military protection for the local people.

The railway line can be seen running below a new and very high cliff. The line follows a new route that had to be built after a tragic accident that happened on 17 March 1979. Up until that time, the line ran through the Penmanshiel Tunnel, but this was not wide enough to take the rolling stock that was to operate a new intercontinental freight service. The roof collapsed during the enlargement of the tunnel and two men were trapped while thirteen were fortunate enough to escape. Special equipment was brought in for a rescue attempt, but the collapse was too complete and the men's bodies were left entombed. A small memorial has been built to the two men (Gordon Turnbull and Peter Fowler) and it can be seen on a platform that has been built on the hillside, above the tunnel where they died.

The east-coast line was put out of action until the new cutting was made and new track laid. The A1's route also had to be changed as a result of the railway line being moved farther west and the road's old route will be walked on once the A1 is crossed.

The A1 to Pease Bay (4·5 km)

The A1 to Pease Dean (1·5 km)
Turn left at the A1 and cross it as soon as possible, taking great care as this is an extremely busy road. Follow the old route of the A1 northwards and cross the Pease Burn. Bear right at a junction and cross a bridge over the railway line. A mass of dog roses may be seen near the railway line during the summer. Cross the Pease Burn once more and turn left at a forest track at a notice with 'Penmanshiel' (the name of the forest) on it.

Bear left when the track divides and pass to the left of Penmanshiel Cottage. After ascending quite a steep incline, the

Way turns sharp right on to another track and doubles back for a
while. Take the left fork when the track splits and head north-west
again. If the weather is bad then continue on the lower route (i.e.
omit the zigzag) – the Way will be met less than 2 km later.

The Way climbs high above the valley of Pease Dean but the
noise of the traffic on the A1 is never lost. The valley was an
important barrier to north-south travel for a long time and its steep
sides forced the North British Railway to take its present route
rather than the straighter coastal route via Coldingham.

The view from above Pease Dean
The view to the west is generally over farmland, but the main
landmarks are towards the north-west.

About 8 km to the north-west is the new Torness nuclear power
station and its tall, massive buildings are a blot on this pleasant
countryside. This very controversial power station has two
advanced gas-cooled reactors (AGRs) and has a generating capacity
of 1,400 MW, one hundred times the output of Earlstoun Power
Station (see p. 129). The Fife coast lies behind Torness.

Just to the left of Torness is the Barns Ness lighthouse and to its
left is the huge cement works near Dunbar; this building is another
dreadful eyesore.The cement works has been built on a large
outcrop of limestone that has been used for a long time, and at
Catcraig (to the west of the lighthouse) there is a preserved limekiln
and a geology nature trail.

The town of Dunbar can be seen behind the cement works.
Dunbar has had a long and turbulent history and its now ruinous
castle was an important stronghold on the east-coast route between
Scotland and England. The town is now a popular holiday centre.

Between the lighthouse and the cement works is the island of
Bass Rock; it is about 26 km away. It is 95 m high and is a volcanic
'plug' composed of trachyte. The island has a remarkable history
dating back to when St Baldred had a cell on it in the early seventh
century. It was sold to the Government in 1671 and was used as a
jail for the Covenanters' leaders, including Alexander Peden. In
1691 the garrison was surprised by some Jacobites and it was held by
them in the name of James VII of Scotland (II of Great Britain).

With aid from the French, they held out for nearly three years. Its modern use is rather more peaceful as it has a lighthouse. The island is probably best known as a gannetry as many thousands of gannets breed here. Indeed, the colony is so important that the birds' scientific name *Sula bassana* comes from the island.

Directly to the west is Ewieside Hill. On the northern end of its summit are the remains of a large fort, some 90 m in diameter and with three concentric ramparts. To the north of west is a television relay transmitter. Cockburnspath can be seen to the north-west, just behind some trees. Cove farm and the hamlet of Cove can be seen by the coast.

Pease Dean to the A1107 (2 km)

Soon there is a glimpse of Pease Bay and its caravan site. The Way now joins up with the lower route mentioned earlier. Go over a stile at a gate and continue through the pleasant Aikieside Wood; this belonged to Coldingham Priory in the reign of David I. Oak was traditionally the most important tree in the wood, but many were felled during the First World War and were later replaced by firs and larches. The trees were of great use to King Robert the Bruce when he stopped here in 1317 to cut timber to build catapults for the siege of Berwick-upon-Tweed. When he was here a messenger brought a Papal Bull from Pope John XXII suggesting a truce, but Bruce refused to accept the Bull as it was not addressed to the King of Scotland.

The track meets the A1107, which runs from the A1 to the fishing port of Eyemouth; Cockburnspath is 3 km to the left. On the left is the very impressive Pease Bridge that spans Pease Dean. The bridge, which is 38 m high, was built in 1786 by Thomas Henderson and was then said to be the highest bridge in the world. The sandstone structure has four arches and to lighten the load on the piers, the spandrels (the parts between the tops of the arches) are pierced. The bridge was built on the site of the traditional east-coast route which then crossed the valley by a series of zigzags. Oliver Cromwell was here in 1650 and was impressed by the road's strategic importance.

Walkers with an interest in geology and with some time to spare

may wish to take a detour to one of Scotland's most important geological sites – Siccar Point. This is 2·5 km away and is found by turning right at the A1107 and following the signs to Old Cambus Quarry. The Point is reached by heading north-eastwards and then down a very steep grassy slope (which could be dangerous when wet or windy).

Siccar Point was 'discovered' by James Hutton about 1790 and there he found a series of steeply inclined beds of greywacke and shale overlaid by gently inclined beds of Old Red Sandstone. This 'unconformity' helped him understand the way in which sediments became solid rock over long periods of time and he embodied his ideas in *The Theory of the Earth* (1795) which argued against the 'Catastrophists' who held that all geological formations owed their origin to the Biblical Flood.

The A1107 to Pease Bay (1 km)
Cross the A1107 and climb down a few steps at the start of the path that winds its way through the woods. The path may be overgrown and the vegetation may obscure steps; it can also be muddy and rather slippery so care should be taken. In wet weather it may be preferable to continue on the A1107, then taking the next two left turns. Following this route, the Way will be rejoined at a stile after the Pease Burn is crossed at a wooden footbridge.

When the path meets level ground near Pease Burn, turn right to walk along a wider path. A waymarker takes the Way to the left when the path splits. The burn is now crossed and it should be followed downstream to a stile beside a minor road and opposite the Pease Bay Caravan Site.

This is a wide bay and is almost entirely filled by the massive caravan site (which does not take tents); the site has a shop. The local rocks are formed from the warm-coloured Old Red Sandstone and the prominent outcrop on the west side of the bay is appropriately named Red Rock. The bay has a pleasant sandy beach.

Pease Bay. The coastal walk after Pease Bay looks over to the headlands farther south.

Pease Bay to Cockburnspath (3·5 km)

Pease Bay Caravan Site to the west side of Pease Bay (1·5 km)
Turn left at the road and climb the hill, passing a waterfall that can
be seen (or just heard) in the wooded gully on the right. The
remains of St Helen's Church can be seen high above the eastern
end of the caravan site. This simple Norman church in the old parish
of Aldcambus was originally built in the twelfth century but the
western gable is a fourteenth- or fifteenth-century construction.
In 1100 the Manor of Aldcambus was granted by Edgar Atheling
(*c.* 1050–*c.* 1125) to the monks of Durham.

Turn right immediately before the first houses on the right at Old
Linhead. If the weather is bad then the cliff-top walk should be
omitted. In that case, continue along the road and rejoin the Way at
the little cottages near Cove farm (see p. 316).

The old cottage beside the road has a pantiled roof, a traditional
east-coast roof covering. Do not follow the track that goes round
behind the cottage, but keep to the side of the cottage and take the
path that is found on the right. This leads down to a gully and the
little waterfall on the Cockburnspath Burn at an exposure of Old
Red Sandstone. Cross the stream and ascend to meet a fence beside
a field. Keep near the fence as the cliff-top path can be narrow and
slippery in places.

Three headlands can be seen to the east. The first (at the eastern
side of Pease Bay) shows the bright red colour of the Old Red
Sandstone; the second headland is at Siccar Point, though the
famous geological exposure cannot be seen; the third headland is
Fast Castle Head and the top of the tower of Fast Castle can be
seen.

The castle, now a ruin, was held in the early fifteenth century by
an English garrison under Thomas Holden who used it as a base for
raids against the surrounding countryside. In 1580 it came into the
hands of John Logan, described by Sir Walter Scott as 'one of the
darkest characters of that age'. Logan became involved in the
'Gowrie conspiracy' in which King James VI (I of Great Britain)
was to be kidnapped at the home of the Earl of Gowrie and taken to

Fast Castle. Logan's involvement in the failed conspiracy only came
to light nine years after his death. Nevertheless, his bones were
taken into court and were condemned for high treason. It is
believed that Sir Walter Scott used the castle as the site of Edgar
Ravenswood's Wolf's Crag in *The Bride of Lammermoor*.

   The path passes above the western end of Pease Bay and
sea-birds may be seen in the ledges here. The village of
Cockburnspath can now be seen over to the west.

The west side of Pease Bay to Cove (1 km)

The overgrown concrete remains of old military installations can be
seen after the path takes a left turn. There is soon a view of Cove
Harbour and the interesting rock formations around it. At the back
of the harbour is the opening of the tunnel that runs through the
cliff (see later). Eider ducks, cormorants and other sea-birds may be
spotted. Pass to the right of a gate and follow the seaward side of
the fence. If conditions are bad then the track at the gate leads past
Cove farm; turn left after passing the farmhouse (see p. 316).

   The path runs above the harbour and towards the houses at Cove.
To the north is the fine cliff that runs between Cove and Reed
Point; this is the nesting place of many sea-birds. The Isle of May
can be seen 30 km away to the west of north. This is 46 m high and
has a lighthouse on it. The first lighthouse was built in 1635 when a
tower 12 m high had a coal fire burning on it all the time. The island
has the ruins of a thirteenth-century chapel which was dedicated to
St Adrian.

   The cliff-top walk ends at a stile just before the houses at Cove.
The Way goes left here, but many walkers will want to see Cove
Harbour. This is reached by turning right and walking past the
houses towards a minor road and a car-park. Turn right at a flight of
wooden steps that leads to the old road down to the harbour.

Cove Harbour

Near the end of the old road is a fenced-off mine shaft which
connects with another shaft deep inside the hillside. The entrance to
the tunnel that was seen earlier on is met just before the harbour is

reached. This was built in 1752–3 and it leads to the back of the harbour. It was once connected to four cellars that were probably used for curing and barrelling fish.

Once through the tunnel, look to the left where a landslip in the nearby cliff has covered the entrance to a cave that may have been used for smuggling. At the back of the harbour is a house which was once used for curing herring and which until fairly recently was used by salmon-fishers. Wooden shutters protect the windows from North Sea gales. Two small buildings can be seen on the other side of the harbour. These were once fishermen's cottages but they are now used as storehouses.

In 1795 sixteen fishermen regularly worked from the harbour and they fished for crabs, lobsters, whitefish, cod and herring. A 1793 report stated that it was not uncommon to see a hundred herring boats at Cove, but today there are only two lobster boats and a few pleasure craft.

Harbour walls were constructed on a number of occasions and traces of them can still be seen beyond the present west harbour wall. The present harbour walls date from 1831 when the harbour was used for fishing and general cargo. The arrival of the railway harmed the cargo business, but it was a sudden storm on 14 October 1881 that put paid to Cove's fishing. Four boats were lost and eleven out of the twenty-one local fishermen perished in less than one hour on that fateful day.

There are a number of interesting rock formations near the west harbour wall and the prominent pinnacles and ridges are called 'the Goats'.

Cove to Cockburnspath (1 km)
Cross the stile that is near the houses at Cove and walk between two fields to reach the buildings at Cove farm. Cross a track and head downhill, passing between the farm and a cottage. Turn left at the minor road that runs up from Pease Bay then sharp right to pass in front of some cottages. Walk along a track, beside which is a

Cove Harbour. The tunnel through the cliff can be seen on the extreme left.

hawthorn hedge, and under the main railway line. Soon Cockburnspath is in front – a welcome sight for the weary walker. The Cockburnspath Hotel is directly ahead and around it are a number of buildings with pantiled roofs.

The A1 is met again and there is a sign with 'Southern Upland Way' on it on the house on the right. Turn left and walk along to the granite memorial that was erected to local men who died during the First World War; the memorial is topped by a Celtic cross. Cross the road, passing to the right of the hotel and another sign with 'Southern Upland Way' on it. The police station, a public telephone box, public toilets and a general store are passed on the opposite side of the road. The road leads into the market-place and the official end of the walk, the mercat-cross, provides a most welcome seat.

Congratulations!

Cockburnspath

The village appears in written documents as Colbrandespade *c.* 1130; Kolbrand is a Norse personal name. Other early references date from 1128 when David I mentioned 'the tithes [levies of ten per cent] of all whales and sea beasts which shall pertain to me from the river Avin to Colbrandpaith' and from Bower who stated that the Scottish lands after the battle of Neville Cross (1346) stretched 'from Cockburnspath to Soutre to Carlops and Crosscryne'.

The village's proximity to the main east-coast route meant that local people were often caught up in the wars between Scotland and England and so the district has had a very unsettled history. In 1612 the village became a burgh of barony, thus giving the people certain trading and legal rights, and later the village became a stopping point for the coaches that plied the east-coast route. The layout of the present-day village owes much to this time.

The village developed around the market-place, which is dominated by the old mercat-cross. The cross has an ornate, but

Cockburnspath market square. The Way ends at the mercat-cross.

weathered, head. The east and west faces have thistles carved on them, while the north and south faces have roses. A notice on the pedestal explains its history: 'This cross was erected in 1503 by King James IV of Scotland in celebration of his marriage to Princess Margaret Tudor, to whom he presented the Lands of Cockburnspath as a dowry.'

Cockburnspath Parish Church (St Helen's) is to the south of the market-place. A church stood on this site in the fourteenth century and it may have suceeded an earlier building. The present structure is T-shaped and there are various indications of old windows in the present outer wall. The most interesting part of the church is the tower in the middle of the west gable. This contains a stone spiral staircase leading to a gallery and a bell-tower. The gable-end dates from the fourteenth century, while the tower is late sixteenth- or early seventeenth-century. There is an unusual sundial at the south-west corner of the building, just above the gutter. The face of the dial is on the underside of a stone ring and the hours are carved on this. To the left of this ring is a shaped projection which may have been the gnomon of another sundial that was once on the gable-end. A small tomb-house is at the south end of the church; it bears the date 1614 but it may have been built earlier than that.

Cockburnspath is a quiet little village that has many attractive-looking cottages, a number of which have pantiled roofs. The last Way notice-board is just off the market-place. It is one street east of the entrance to the church and is opposite the post office. There is a general store in the market-place. Chesterfield Caravan Park (which takes tents) is 2 km south of the village.

Bibliography

ANDERSON, SEMENS HOUSTON, *The Southern Upland Way: Report of a Survey of Walkers in the Summer of 1984*, Glasgow, 1985.

ANDREW, KEN, *The Southern Upland Way: Eastern Section*, HMSO, Edinburgh, 1984.

ANDREW, KEN, *The Southern Upland Way: Western Section*, HMSO, Edinburgh, 1984.

ANDREW, K. M. and THRIPPLETON, A. A., *The Southern Uplands*, The Scottish Mountaineering Trust, Edinburgh, 1976.

BALDWIN, JOHN, R., *Exploring Scotland's Heritage: Lothian and the Borders*, HMSO, Edinburgh, 1985.

British Association for the Advancement of Science, *Scientific Survey of South-eastern Scotland*, Edinburgh, 1951.

BROWN, JOHN, *John Leech and Other Papers*, David Douglas, Edinburgh, 1882.

BULLOCH, J. P. B. and URQUHART, J. M., eds, *The Third Statistical Account of Scotland: The County of Peebles and the County of Selkirk*, Collins, Glasgow, 1964.

CLAVERING, MOLLY, *From the Border Hills*, Thomas Nelson & Sons, Edinburgh, 1954.

COCHRANE, PETER, *Abbey St Bathans*.

CUNNINGHAM, R. R., *Portpatrick Through the Ages*, Portpatrick, 1985.

DICK, C. H., *Highways and Byways in Galloway and Carrick*, Macmillan & Co., London, 1927.

Dumfriesshire and Galloway Natural History Society, *Transactions, Third Series, Vol. 54, 1979*.

EDLIN, HERBERT, L., ed., *Galloway Forest Park*, HMSO, Edinburgh, 1974.

FEACHEM, RICHARD, *Guide to Prehistoric Scotland*, Batsford, London, 1977.

GREIG, D. C., *British Regional Geology: The South of Scotland*, HMSO, Edinburgh, 1971.

HALDANE, A. R. B., *The Drove Roads of Scotland*, Edinburgh University Press, 1971.

HARPER, MALCOLM McL., *Rambles in Galloway*, Thomas Fraser, Dalbeattie, 1896.

HOUSTON, GEORGE, ed., *The Third Statistical Account of Scotland: The County of Dumfries*, Collins, Glasgow, 1962.

LAIRD, JOHN and RAMSAY, D.G., eds, *The Third Statistical Account of Scotland: The Stewartry of Kirkcudbright and the County of Wigtown*, Collins, Glasgow, 1965.

LANG, THEO, ed., *The Queen's Scotland: Glasgow, Kyle and Galloway*, Hodder & Stoughton, London, 1953.

LANG, THEO, ed., *The Queen's Scotland: The Border Counties*, Hodder & Stoughton, London, 1957.

LINDSAY, MAURICE, *The Lowlands of Scotland*, Robert Hale, London, 1956.

MACK, JAMES LOGAN, *Abbey St Bathans*, John Wilson, 1925.

MACLEOD, INNES, *Discovering Galloway*, John Donald Publishers, Edinburgh, 1986.

MARGERY, IVAN D., *Roman Roads in Britain*, John Baker, 1967.

Meteorological Office, *Scotland's Climate – Some Facts and Figures*, Edinburgh, 1979.

MURRAY, J. and PULLAR, L., *Bathymetric Survey of the Scottish Freshwater Lochs (Vols 1 and 2)*, Edinburgh, 1910.

PRICE, R. J., *Scotland's Environment during the Last 30,000 Years*, Scottish Academic Press, Edinburgh, 1983.

QUIN, ROGER, *The Borderland*, A. Walker & Son, Galashiels.

RANKIN, ERIC, *Cockburnspath*, T. & T. Clark, Edinburgh, 1981.

Royal Commission on the Ancient and Historical Monuments and Constructions of Scotland, The, *County of Berwick*, Edinburgh, 1915.

Royal Commission on the Ancient and Historical Monuments and Constructions of Scotland, The, *County of Dumfries*, Edinburgh, 1920.

Royal Commission on the Ancient and Historical Monuments and Constructions of Scotland, The, *County of the Stewarty of Kirkcudbright*, Edinburgh, 1914.

Royal Commission on the Ancient and Historical Monuments and Constructions of Scotland, The, *County of Wigton*, Edinburgh, 1912.

Royal Commission on the Ancient and Historical Monuments of Scotland, The, *Roxburghshire (Vol. 2)*, Edinburgh, 1956.

Royal Commission on the Ancient and Historical Monuments of Scotland, The, *Selkirkshire*, Edinburgh, 1957.

Society of Antiquaries of Scotland, The, *Ancient Border Highways*, Proceedings, Vol. 58, 1924.

STELL, GEOFFREY, *Exploring Scotland's Heritage: Dumfries and Galloway*, HMSO, Edinburgh, 1986.

TABRAHAM, C. J., *Melrose Abbey*, HMSO, Edinburgh, 1981.

Wanlockhead Museum Trust, The, *Mining History Trail*, Wanlockhead, 1979.

Wanlockhead Museum Trust, The, *All About Wanlockhead*, Wanlockhead, 1983.

WHITTOW, J. B., *Geology and Scenery in Scotland*, Penguin Books, Harmondsworth, 1979.

Index